Gathering Ecologies
Thinking Beyond Interactivity

Immediations
Series Editor: SenseLab

> "Philosophy begins in wonder. And, at the end, when philosophic thought has done its best, the wonder remains"
> – A.N. Whitehead

The aim of the Immediations book series is to prolong the wonder sustaining philosophic thought into transdisciplinary encounters. Its premise is that concepts are for the enacting: they must be experienced. Thought is lived, else it expires. It is most intensely lived at the crossroads of practices, and in the in-between of individuals and their singular endeavors: enlivened in the weave of a relational fabric. Co-composition.

> "The smile spreads over the face, as the face fits itself onto the smile"
> – A. N. Whitehead

Which practices enter into co-composition will be left an open question, to be answered by the Series authors. Art practice, aesthetic theory, political theory, movement practice, media theory, maker culture, science studies, architecture, philosophy ... the range is free. We invite you to roam it.

Gathering Ecologies
Thinking Beyond Interactivity

Andrew Goodman

OPEN HUMANITIES PRESS
London 2018

First edition published by Open Humanities Press 2018
Copyright © 2018 Andrew Goodman

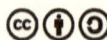

This is an open access book, licensed under Creative Commons By Attribution Share Alike license. Under this license, authors allow anyone to download, reuse, reprint, modify, distribute, and/or copy their work so long as the authors and source are cited and resulting derivative works are licensed under the same or similar license. No permission is required from the authors or the publisher. Statutory fair use and other rights are in no way affected by the above. Read more about the license at creativecommons.org/licenses/by-sa/4.0

Cover Art, figures, and other media included with this book may be under different copyright restrictions.

Cover Illustration © 2018 Leslie Plumb
Cover Design by Leslie Plumb

Typeset in Open Sans, an open font.

Print ISBN 978-1-78542-052-8
PDF ISBN 1-78542-053-5

Freely available online at:
http://openhumanitiespress.org/books/titles/gathering-ecologies

OPEN HUMANITIES PRESS

Open Humanities Press is an international, scholar-led open access publishing collective whose mission is to make leading works of contemporary critical thought freely available worldwide. More at http://openhumanitiespress.org

Contents

Acknowledgements   9

Introduction: Thinking beyond interactivity   11

1. Interactivity and relation: The myth(s) of interactivity   30
2. Thinking action and event   54
3. Once more with feeling: Whitehead's concept of feeling and a trans-human ethics   74
4. Thinking parasitic action   98
5. Walking with the world: towards a minor approach to performative art practice   110
6. Entertaining the environment   134
7. The noise in the noise: micro-perception as affective disruption to listening and the body   154
8. A thousand tiny interfacings: fertile acts of resistance   176
9. Sacrificial RAM: locating feeling and the virtual in software   198

Conclusion	232
Notes	240
Bibliography	300
Index	330

For three teachers who encouraged me to write:

Max Balchin

Karen Ward

Edward Colless

Acknowledgements

Thanks must go to the many people who have contributed their knowledge, support and enthusiasm to the making of this book. First and foremost my thanks go to all the members of the Senselab with whom I have had the pleasure of collaborating and learning from, and without whom I could not have thought through these ideas. Amongst many, many Senselab members who deserve thanks, this includes Erin Manning, for her unending enthusiasm and warmth and for sharing art making and writing with me, Nathaniel Stern for various collaborations and his unbounded energy, Alanna Thain for her writing on my work and key conversations, Sam Spurr for artistic collaborations, Anna Munster for her valuable feedback, support and many helpful suggestions, and Andrew Murphie and Lone Bertelsen for their support, suggestions and feedback, and for sympathetic reading of papers in progress. Thanks also to a several people who contributed to the editing of earlier versions of various chapters: Din Heagney for his sterling efforts editing chapters and controlling footnotes, and Trinh Vu and Leonie Cooper for their many constructive suggestions. Thanks to a number of people who have contributed to my own artistic processes during this time through support, collaboration and feedback, including Oliver Cloke, Tony Falla, Samantha Bews, Luhsun Tan, Andrea Ekersley, Kent Wilson, Jude Anderson and Caroline Kennedy-McCracken. Thanks must also go to the anonymous reviewers of the manuscript for their careful reading and efforts to improve the writing style and content of the book.

Finally, thanks and love to my daughter Lucy for her humour and patience throughout the long process.

Earlier versions of some chapters have appeared in print before. Sections of Chapter One and Chapter Two appeared as "Rethinking Interactivity." *ACMC Interactive Conference Proceedings*, Victoria, 2012. Edited by Matthew Hitchcock, Australasian Computer Music Association. A version of Chapter Five appears as: "Walking with the World: Towards an Ecological Approach to Performative Art Practice". *Walking and the Aesthetics of Modernity: Pedestrian Mobility in Literature and the Arts*, edited by François Specq and Klaus Benesch. New York: Palgrave MacMillian, 2016. An earlier version of Chapter Six appears as: "Entertaining the Environment: Towards an Ethics of Art Events." AJE: Australasian Journal of Ecocriticism and Cultural Ecology, vol. 3, 2013/2014. A conference paper version of Chapter Eight appeared as "A Thousand Tiny Interfac(ing)s." *Proceedings of the 19th International Symposium on Electronic Art, ISEA2013, Sydney*. Edited by K Cleland, L Fisher and R Harley, 2013.

Introduction:
Thinking beyond interactivity

Imagine you are out walking in the street. To go for a walk is to create, through the endless flow of interaction, bodily and spatially. With each step – and within each step – perceptual, sensorial and social possibilities are opened up, assemblages of forces gathered, altered and reconnected, complexities multiplied, memories activated. The moment is saturated with affectual relations and intensities (Lorrainne 2005, 73–4). With the fall of the same step, previous possibilities perish, simultaneously propelling the endless opening of fresh possibilities of connection (Manning 2009, 38–9).

Try to map all the relations that go to make up one instant, one occasion: within your body, between body and world, mind and body, object and object – all the various 'machinic' combinations producing experience. You will have to consider subatomic, atomic and molecular forces with their general disregard for what we view as discreet bodies. You will want to account for the way the texture and gradient of the terrain shapes movement, rhythm and posture; how sensory perception, vision, hearing and touch and so on begin to ready the body for the next step; how the force of physical habits and body memory shape patterns of movement in the moment. Also present will be all the events of relation that have gone into making each tree, stone, person and sound you are interacting with, affecting your body more or less forcefully. Then there are the mental forces – 'inextricably intertwined' with the physical (Whitehead 1978, 325) – memories, anticipations, evaluations, random associations made and forgotten, affects that will subtly or bluntly alter you, the myriad mental processes that sit behind conscious perception, yet nevertheless shape and reshape your body. Beyond that instant, in the next occasion, the concrescence of all these forces creates anew this simple act of walking the street. It is a constant, complexly enmeshed act of creativity: when we look honestly, all things, as Whitehead says, are vectors of relations (1978, 309).

Such an everyday act is saturated with complexity and invention, and is rich with potential. But now imagine you are in a gallery, in some interactive installation. Things happen as you move around – sounds, lights or video. Perhaps triggered by your presence, the work pretty much does its own thing and its actions seem somewhat random, or perhaps it continues to develop as you engage, with a concentration on a demonstration of how your actions affect its workings. Either way, this type of work often lacks the complex, intertwined-ness of body and work, the perceptual nuance, the fluidity, the surprising originality of connection and thickness of experience of a simple walk outside.

In general in this book my intention is to focus on a productive move towards exploring positive developments in the field, and so the critique of the poor state of interactive art is painted with broad strokes. I will, however, begin with a brief description of a here-unnamed work I encountered early in the process of writing that contrasts with this imagined walk and illustrates some of the problematic areas that concern me. This particular work formed part of a large exhibition of a broad range of interactive works. Inside the gallery were various pieces that responded to touch, movement or other interactions with the audience, with shifts in sound or video projections and so on. These included a couch that purred as you stroked it, a series of pot plants that made sounds as the audience moved amongst them, and a digital 'mirror' that reflected a greatly aged version of the participant's face. All were at least mildly amusing works, if a little one dimensional in their aesthetics and outcomes, with very direct and limited links between the actions of the viewer and the changes in the works these gestures triggered.

The particular work that affected me most negatively was situated in a bare shipping container outside the main gallery. It was set up as a very small rave club that would respond to audience members' dance moves to produce sound. It was silent and empty, other than a large speaker system, when I entered the space as the exhibition opened on a chilly 10-degree morning. The young invigilator then approached and enthusiastically encouraged me to begin dancing in order to trigger sounds. As I hesitated she became more forceful in her pleas for participation. I hovered near the door, unwilling to make a fool of myself in the service of as yet unheard music. Eventually the invigilator gave up in disgust and began to throw herself around the room as the very loud beats began, still pleading with me to join in. Needless to say I beat a hasty retreat, having not only not participated but having been made to feel guilty for my lack of enthusiasm and willingness to sacrifice dignity for the sake of this artist's work. The sense of obligation and potential humiliation of the experience was certainly powerful compared to the mild amusement of the works inside the gallery, however it was mostly a feeling of distaste for the genre that was evoked for me. It was closer to the uncomfortable duty of a work presentation than the more open-ended exploration and play that one might wish from an art-experience, whether as a solitary pleasure to be enjoyed in one's own time, or as a collective investigation with a feeling of relational connection and trust.

My concern with this work is not only that the interactive component (movement triggering sound, with the sound's volume and speed relating in some way to the size and speed of the gestures) was somewhat limited in its aesthetic imagination, with little variation in reaction from participant to participant or over time within one interaction (although

I think this is a valid criticism of the work). The distributed agency frequently attributed to interactivity is often lacking in these linear, prescribed constructions of relation. At best, as Brian Massumi argues, the interactive experience might seek to expand awareness of the processes of perception and relation (2011, 45), yet too often remains programmatic and replays the same standardised reactions, lacking in subtle and surprising combinations of associations, sensations, affects and prehensions. This is not to suggest that the role of interactive art is to mimic life, but rather that many such works display a paucity of life's rich, heightened experience of connection and potential.

My larger critique, however, is an ethical one, deeply concerned with the politics of an enforcement of power relations that instrumentalise bodies and seek control rather than explore the possible expansion of expressive capacities. While there was certainly a series of relations established between the viewer or participant and the artwork in this example, these were highly problematic. The piece demanded 'work' from the participant, prescribing the types of relations and interactions that would be recognised by the technology and requiring a high level of energy from this viewer in order to produce itself (replicating the neoliberal dynamics of society that require the constant donation of immaterial labour). The participant was clearly in the service of the artist, not collaborating in any meaningful way. 'Choice' here became limited to opting in or out, with little possibility of nuanced and singular participation. Like many interactive art experiences, this event did not work to enhance my 'life-world' through any exploration of further potential combinations of bodies and artwork components, but instead replicated the dominant power relationships of society through obligation, control of gestures and the limitation of expression.

The limitations of this work made me wonder: what would happen if we were to radically shift our notions of what interactivity is or might be? What would happen to 'interactivity' if we expanded the concept of it greatly and explored its essentially environmental or ecological potential? What would happen if we stopped limiting interactive potentials to human subjects, or to these subjects in conversation with an artwork across the abstracted and artificial divide of the 'interface'? What if we shifted scales – and worked across scales – and thought also the potential for interactive or *relational* development between, for example, an algorithm and a sensor, a sound vibration and a foot, an affect and a perception and so on?

In highlighting this example I don't mean to suggest that interactive art should be 'nice', or that it should promote a bland positivity. Certainly there must be a place to explore tricky, slippery or challenging relations and propositions in art. However, there is a difference between the relational entanglement created by a work such as this example that offers only a heightened precarity to the individual ego in the face of obligation, and one based on a collective 'positive' extension of potential. The relationality that the neoliberal world already offers us is one of shared ecological, social, economic and psychic precarity that certainly creates a connectivity between people, but this is chiefly one of a shared vulnerability not an enjoyment of collective potential. Nor would it be enough for such a work to merely deterritorialise and delocalise or create and capitalise on speculative movement or reconfigurations of these already toxic connections (Guattari 2008, 33). Capitalism already operates successfully in this field of speculative and preemptive control, and, as I argue in Chapter One, the politics of relation in interactive work too often homogenise and constrict experience and orient the participant towards these dominant power structures. Nor can we truly imagine a work that would help us to 'escape' from such networks. Rather, to remain ethical, relational works need to pay attention to and care for what else might be going on: for the differential seeds or 'isolated and repressed singularities' (Guattari 2008, 34) that might suggest transversal movements and other, hidden potentials.

Such potentials, rather than re-individualising and controlling yet another aspect of living, might, as I advocate throughout this book, instead be situated in an emphasis on Whiteheadian 'novelty' that is enjoyed at an ecological level and not on a level of individualised or subjective human enjoyment.

Terms such as positivity, collective enjoyment, novelty and connection may well raise alarm bells. They will remind some readers of exactly the empty promises of consumerist entertainment already on offer, and the bland, identity-based and resolutely neoliberal iterations of relational aesthetics available for consumption at any major gallery. Here perhaps the concept of affirmation better describes the particular direction I am seeking to head towards in this discussion. Affirmation is *speculative*, seeking not to confirm the already-prescribed and thought relational possibilities, but to experiment freely and immanently (Manning 2016b, 201). Affirmation seeks to potentialise, thus it moves towards an increase in intensity or differentiation in the event (novelty) rather than homogenisation. To be clear, affirmation is of the event, not pitched at the level of an individual, subjective positive or negative emotional response. The event enjoys its expressions of novelty, which involve both the explorations of new conjunctions and disjunctions. An affirmative interactive practice might seek to expand and explore how components of an event can interact. This does not necessarily imply a concern for any individual component; rather it might seek to affirm ongoing ecological differentiation.

Affirmation pitches discussions at a very different level to that of criticism. In the context of this book, it will become apparent to the reader that the works are not 'critiqued' in the negative sense of this term. That is, they are not there to be evaluated against some predetermined criteria of the new face of interactivity that the book might, from the outside, be mistakenly seen to be proposing. Their role is not to have the opinions or judgments of the author bestowed upon them, but, as Brian Massumi has written of this affirmative and 'immanent' style of critique, to perform a 'dynamic evaluation that is lived out in situation' (2010, 338).[1] This is 'eventful' and seeks to engage with and acknowledge the singularities of a particular situation rather than resort to generalisations. Rather than leading to a shoring up of established positions, immanent critique might instead 'foster unforeseeable differentiations' (Massumi 2010, 338). In the context of the various discussions of artworks within this book, their inclusion implies neither any attempt to 'assess' or qualify the art, nor a ringing endorsement for all aspects of each work. Nor does it imply any assumption that these works form a 'canon' of important, new or ideal interactive models. Rather, they are there because there are some aspects of them that might productively help both the author and reader to think through the various concepts in their particular intersection with a singular art event, and potentially to lead such thinking into both unexpected and ever more diverse readings of the conceptual material at hand. Such thinking happens in the middle of the majoritarian events and theories, as minor undercurrents or dérives. It suggests a particular attention to what else might be happening: to transversal events that begin to split, fracture or unsettle expected outcomes or thoughts. In line with this, the aspects of the artworks that are examined are often incidental to their main focus. For example, in Chapter Five I discuss aspects of Nathaniel Stern's *Compressionism*, focusing on the particular and awkward assemblages and rhythms of bodies, spaces and technical objects, rather than on the undoubtedly beautiful photographic outcomes of these performances. Similarly, in discussing Rafael Lozano-Hemmer's *Re:Positioning Fear: Relational Architecture 3* in Chapter Eight I focus on an accidental incidence of disruption to the original work that overlaid the existing event with new tonalities and intentions.

Affirmation is performative or processual, and thus in this book the interrogation of the concept of relation is performed through the lens of what is broadly termed 'process' philosophy.

Process is a creative event of formation of an entity through the 'transformation of the potential into the actual' (Guattari and Rolnik 2005, 311). Whitehead terms the placement of process as primary within thinking a shift from the 'material' to the 'organic'.[2] Process philosophy's focus is ontogenetic, concentrating on how events (which here includes objects, relations and forces) come into being, rather than with the states they pass through (Massumi et al 2009, 37). Philosophically, this entails a shift from a hylomorphic view of the world as composed of discrete objects and subjects enduring in relative stability over time and which then interact with each other, to a view of the world as an ongoing, continually unfolding series of events of relation. This is an expanded notion of relation as emerging within an art event, concerned not with its demonstration or metaphoric representations, but with the power of conjunctive and disjunctive relational forces to creatively differentiate. That is, with the capacities of entities to affect and be affected in order to advance events. Thus it replaces ideas of transcendence – where development is focused on the achievement of an ideal, pre-described form – and focuses instead on the drive towards novelty and further differentiation.[3] As Whitehead puts it, this is a novelty conditioned by its relationship to past events – 'an urge towards the future based on an appetite in the present' (1978, 21).[4]

In this approach, all relations need to be considered for their role in forming events, and thus William James' 'radical empiricism' forms an important base here, in asserting that *only* that which is experienced and *all* that is experienced must be admitted into its construction of the world (2010, 18). In this expanded model, thoughts and concepts are events in and of themselves, rather than projections or representations, and are as much a part of this enaction as objects. As such a process philosophy approach not only eradicates ideas of preformed or ideal subjects, it also, as Whitehead notes, 'abolishes the detached mind' (1978, 56). Relations that connect experiences, as James states, 'must also be admitted' as real and a place 'found' for them in the system (2010, 18).

As Massumi notes, an implication of this system is that most of these relations exist only as potential, and therefore the virtual must also be considered as 'real' (2008, 39–40), with both actualised and potential relations being crucial to an understanding of the ability of relations to develop openly. Thus, expanded empiricism provides, as will be argued in the first chapters of this book, a path to 'thinking beyond' the purely mechanical and overt interactive elements between stable objects, and into a richer and more complex series of formative forces operating within a field; while still grounding thinking in lived experienced and avoiding the traps of transcendence and representation.

With this position of the primacy of forces, an expanded and open definition of what constitutes a body is possible. The body referred to here is not limited to the subject, or to a fixed or post-individuated stable entity, but is itself 'a process of intersecting forces (affects) and spatio-temporal variables (connections)' (Braidotti 2002, 21). That is, bodies not only have capacities to interact with external forces and entities, but also are in themselves formed from the ongoing meeting and conversation of forces, and are therefore 'continuous' with the external world (Whitehead 1968, 21), as they also have 'internal resonances' and plays of forces (Simondon 1992, 305). Bodies are creative systems or emergent ecologies themselves, always more than any stable subjectivity, which might be better seen as a partial resolution in ongoing individuation that has always the potential for further movement. Rather than define a body by its representational qualities, the term body is here defined, as Massumi has described it, by 'what capacities it carries from step to step' (c2001, 4): in other words, by its performativity and its abilities to interact within an ecology of which it is an active participant (Grosz 1994, 194).

Within this process-orientated view, not only bodies but also other entities – including inanimate objects – can also be defined by their abilities to interact with their environment, and they too can be thought of as complex negotiations of relational forces or events in themselves (Whitehead 1978, 73, 41). If entities all have their own capacities to affect and be affected by other forces and entities (Whitehead 1978, 856, 230), they are therefore always capable of further changes, of influencing and being influenced. This gives an opportunity to consider the interactive potential of not only human bodies, but also the affective capacities of all components of an art event's ecology. This thinking has the potential to greatly expand interactivity within a system, and suggests an obligation to begin to think about how non-human components of a system have capacities to interact with each other. In other words, it implies the necessity to consider a larger ecology at work, rather than focus purely on artwork-participant relations while assuming that other relational forces and objects will remain fixed or are less important to the developing relational meshwork.

Here we might, for example, begin to consider the emergent relations (and collective becomings) of and between a speaker vibration, a floor and a diffracted sound wave as examined in Chapter Seven. Or we might pay attention to the relations between movement, shadows, a light sensor and an electrical current, and so on, whilst at the same time thinking about their connections to various bodily assemblages – sense organs, surfaces, forces of movement. This, I argue, has scope to expand notions of interactivity through thinking the potential of much more complexly intermeshed and collectively emergent tensions within an art event, activated through acts of prehension and transduction across its many registers. At the same time, the implications of these ideas potentially move the discussion on interactivity beyond 'new media' artworks.[5] As will become apparent both from the choice of works and the aspects of these works discussed, interactive potential should not be limited to works obviously mechanically interactive in their enaction, nor to work necessarily involving 'technologies' in the most obvious sense of the term. This positions the actual artworks discussed and the implications of the discussion within a wider framework and history of relational and participatory artwork.[6]

Through these discussions on an expanded and heterogeneous relationality I develop a concept of emergent self-organisation in interactivity, which I term a 'gathering' ecology. This broadened concept of interactivity emphasises an event's ability to move towards the generation of its own outcomes out of emerging difference within relations. This self-motivated or ecological gathering is always on the level of the virtual – a gathering of potential – as much as it is an actual entanglement of relations. While in general, process philosophy is always concerned with the becoming of events, this extends becoming in the sense that it concerns not simply the idea of the becoming of an event within a field, or even that the field is co-emergent with the event. Here the very rules and potentials governing these acts of organisation are emerging or gathering as one, although this is a fragmentary, heterogeneous whole. In this sense I argue that there is a shared immanence running through an entire ecology, and autonomy of any component entity is always emergent not only with other entities that parasite it, but with the subjective forces of the ecology with which it nests.

In developing this concept I utilise several related or overlapping concepts that argue for the primary role of intensive differentiation in the becoming of events. In Chapter Three this entails a close examination of Whitehead's concept of 'feeling', a complex and abstracted ontology of relation that is for him at the basis of all becoming.[7] Here, in order to become, an emergent entity selects 'datum' from other actualised entities and from the virtual plane, intensively valuating and patterning these feelings as 'one complex feeling' (Whitehead 1978, 22) that constitutes its very 'concrescence', or event of becoming. In rethinking interactivity the particular usefulness of this system, which I outline in much more detail in the chapter, is that in this act of feeling an entity has autonomy from what has come before, in that it selects and incorporates only some of the possible information from the actualised world and some of the potentials. It therefor self-generates novelty in the world, but is at the same time always relational. There are many similarities between this Whiteheadian concept and Gilbert Simondon's system of individuation, and in the later chapters of this book this connection is explored through the idea of transduction in relation to micro-perception and sound, interfacing and generative software programming. Transduction, as 'the foundation of individuation' is for Simondon a process whereby an entity (again, in the broadest sense) generates itself through an intensive gathering of incompatible external forces into an intensive communication 'without loss, without reduction, in newly discovered structures' (2009, 12). Feeling and transduction, which cut across forces and forms to generate new intensive and extensive relations, are at the core of the thinking my exploration of the capacity of differential operations within an art event to be activators of co-causal relation within interactivity.

In thinking difference, particularly from the pragmatic perspective of the construction and interrogation of interactive artworks, the third key philosophical tool, which is examined in Chapter Four and put to use throughout the book, is Michel Serres' concept of the parasite. This he defines as the essential noise in any system of relations.[8] The parasitic disruption to relation that produces new relational connections from within an existing system is proposed as a mechanism for intensively generating change while also drawing elements into more complex interdependence. The parasite, which Serres argues is always present within relations (2007, 79) (and which both Whitehead and Simondon also argue to be constitutive of becoming in the form of the held and productive intensive differentials of an entity), problematises simple connections with its ever-present potential to further differentiate. It transforms stable systems into evolving systems of co-causality.[9] Again, all these concepts are affirmative in their focus on the processes of speculative advance towards future novelty. They are speculative in that the outcomes are not prescribed, and positive in that such advance does not erase difference but intensifies it. Thus difference here is not oppositional or negative, but a dynamic creative force for both extensive exchange and intensive development, binding heterogeneous elements into the production of the event (Deleuze 1994, 57).

While a discussion that takes process-based ideas of the emergent and intertwined nature of all events is necessarily one about relation, enthusiasm for the 'relational' must be tempered by a closer consideration of the nature of these relations. As I argue in Chapter One, the politics of relation in interactive work too often homogenise and constrict experience and curtail open experimentation. To remain ethical, relational works need to instead concentrate on enabling expressive capacities,[10] and to position heterogeneous elements in dynamic or productively noisy relation. Here within the writing I identify and emphasise the imperative to give particular attention to how the various components of an art event begin to gather and intertwine in each other's and a collective creative advance. Amongst this search for an ethical 'equality' of interactive potentiality, we must consider the 'technical equality' that Simondon calls for, which implies 'equal technical participation, even as it assumes difference' (Combes 2013, 92).[11] In this sense the 'health' of the whole ecology – in sustaining and extending its expressive capacities – is always a premium consideration in an ethical interaction. It is a question of how ecologies as sets of 'complex dynamics of relations in a given situation' (Bertelsen 2012, 41) begin to form through interactions – not only between participant and work, but between all material, conceptual and affectual components.

This interest in the ethics of emergence must also, it seems to me, be extended to include the emergence of thought and concepts, and in this the book adopts a particular methodology that could also be termed transversal. If the task of this discussion is to utilise an affirmative experimentation across conceptual and practical registers to examine the creative role of differentiation within interactive art events, then here this entails a methodology of multiple readings, multiple configurations of concepts, and multiple propositional relational encounters. This is proposed as a potential politics: an ethics addressing immanent construction. This is an ontogenetic approach to the text, practicing a tactical and parasitic method of research that could be described as a 'meta-modeling' or 'study'.

Stefano Harney and Fred Moten have proposed the term 'study' as a type of collective learning without end that is resistant to the academic disciplining through policy, reward and identity (2013, 67–8). Study is the experience itself – something already going on – sometimes underneath or inside or in spite of the structuring of knowledge and thinking that it destabalises. Study does not 'call to order' along the lines of an established hierarchy or knowledge (Harney and Moten 2013, 125–6). In this it suggests that we must be careful about not only the content of what is studied, but the methodologies employed, recognising that they are not simply organisational, but can, as Manning states, have a deleterious disciplinary affect on thought in constraining it to the already-known (2016b, 34). Rather, Manning says, study and associated becoming-methodologies such as research-creation might allow us to think beyond the known and to instead *experience* the act of knowledge becoming out of the unknown (Manning 2016b, 30–1). Just as process philosophy asks us to think objects and subjects as experiences or events, study asks us to consider the larger generation of the conditions of knowledge's emergence. Study, in this sense is not a usual kind of methodology – rather it might be thought of as a becoming-methodology immanent with the problem that we wish to think: a tactical approach.

A tactic is open-ended and opportunistic. It reuses elements of a system (as both feeling and the parasite move towards novelty but are formed from a reconfiguration of already present relation), 'without taking over [the system in] its entirety' (de Certeau 1988, xix). The tactic therefore destabilises from within as a minor movement, without necessarily imposing new order. It remains essentially *per*-formed. A tactic (such as an immanent critique) is always singular, forming in relation to the specific set of conditions within which it arises, and must be reinvented for each new set of events. Various tactics also fold into and complicate one other, so that the range and exact terrain of their productive operation can never be fully defined. In this regard, tactics must be reinvented through practice, avoiding the rigidity of sets of rules or manifestos, being co-composed with events in which they seek to intervene. In Chapter Two, the concept of the tactic is utilised to think the re-invigoration of interactive systems from within, through concepts of molecularisation and drift. In Chapter Four the parasite as a tactic is proposed as molecularising in its production of difference or movement (Guattari and Rolnik 2005, 311) within a dominant form of interactivity.

A 'tactical' approach is clearly in line with a process philosophical view of the world, centered on propositions, the gathering of forces and the immanent nature of events, rather than outcomes and closure. A methodology consistent with this impetus within a process-philosophy stream must also address a tactical *use* of process philosophy. That is, concepts must be reinvented and investigated for and within each singular occasion, not relied on as established truths. A concept itself always individuates with and within a field, and if it has a distinct 'consistency' that 'renders its components inseparable *within itself*', then this is at best a 'fragmentary whole' (Deleuze and Guattari 1994, 19, 16, emphasis in the original). Here, as Serres states, rather than assuming the possibility of a 'universal method', one should instead seek to compose 'an appropriate method from the very problem one has undertaken to resolve' (Serres and Latour 2011, 91). Within this style of inquiry the invention of knowledge is, as Simondon notes, 'neither inductive or deductive, but *transductive*', corresponding to a discovery of the dimensions or field of inquiry in conjunction with the specific question (2009, 11, emphasis added).[12]

Thus a tactical approach avoids the use of models, but rather immanently and speculatively models the problem at hand. For Guattari models are problematic in that they are 'reductions of a diagrammatic space made of intersections and disjunctions' (Parisi 2013, 4). As Manning and Massumi argue, models are 'prescriptive templates' that limit and control the discourse on actual events, which have potential beyond their iterations (2010, 28). In a related discussion, Janell Watson outlines two essentially negative ways that modelling circumvents discourse. Firstly, she criticizes the way models encourage the tendency to analyze actual events only in relation to a perceived 'norm' rather than thinking outside the restrictions of such 'dominant social order[s]' (Watson 2008, 1). Secondly, by prescribing processes, models necessarily curtail possible outcomes – that is, they reduce the freedom of the virtual to a limited set of possible outcomes (Watson 2008, 2).

In this book I have a desire to open up space for multiple potential analyses, and Guattari's concept of metamodelling, which bypasses 'the imperative of representation' (Parisi 2013, 4), is thus proposed as a suitable methodology for creating a 'becoming' model of inquiry. Metamodelling, Guattari states, is 'to render palpable lines of formation, starting from no one model in particular, actively taking into account the plurality of models vying for fulfillment' (cited in Manning and Massumi 2010, 25).[13] Metamodelling, as Guattari says, places the emphasis on the way ideas interact or have the potential to interact to produce new associations (1995a, 59). To establish a model for the analysis of interactive art risks the exclusion of elements that do not fit, such as aesthetic qualities, an under-discussed area of much interactive art criticism. Fixed models might also imply the creation of a 'check-list' of necessary elements that an artwork must contain to be called interactive; the bracketing into stabilized categories of problems and solutions; and the uncritical promotion of potentially insidious social norms.

In contrast, the process of metamodelling abandons attempts at establishing set models, accepting potential in all possible models – providing, Guattari states, they 'abandon all universalizing pretensions' (cited in Watson 2008, 3). Rather than creating a 'didactic program', metamodelling involves a disentangling of oneself from systems of modelling that 'pollute our ways of thinking', creating instead a contingent critical 'bricolage' of possible approaches to be utilised for the particular analysis at hand (Watson 2008, 3).

In this sense, metamodelling clearly experiments with a re-energising and reconnecting of existing elements (whether conceptual or physical). Metamodels are resolutely singular – that is, they allow the possibility of constructing a usable model for any given situation by 'taking bits and pieces of other models in an attempt to solve a specific, singular problem' (Watson 2008, 8). This requires embracing increasing complexity and contingency. It demands a preparedness to act contingently and cobble together usable discourses as necessary, and it also requires one to allow this assemblage to perish after the event,[14] starting afresh each time. Thus, in relation to interactivity, this methodology enables the taking of any productive path of critique necessary to accommodate new input (and the jumping from path to path), rather than setting up fixed criteria for interactivity and either ignoring contradictory information, or dismissing artworks for not living up to established definitions. I want to suggest, as Manning and Massumi do, that this freedom to adapt and change direction – to critique *immanently* and speculate affirmatively – be viewed as a positive move, which might 'energize new models of activity...[and] offer a potential to escape or overspill readymade channelings into the dominant system' (2010, 7).[15]

Metamodelling might be seen as being both speculative and pragmatic, in that it refuses methods or models imposed from without and instead encourages 'a rigor of experimentation' (Manning 2016b, 38). It might also be transversal, seeking to invent new associations and collective potentials. A particular methodology of use here is that of a 'research-creation' framework, which seeks to create resonating lines of inquiry through writing on concepts and artistic experimentation. At its best,[16] research-creation might, as Manning writes, exhibit a 'transversality', proposing 'new forms of knowledge, many of which are not intelligible within current understandings of what knowledge might look like', therefore staging 'an encounter for disparate practices, giving them a conduit for collective expression' (2016b, 27). Research-creation is of particular interest here as the writing of this book (perhaps inevitably given my own practice as an artist working within participation and interactivity) has been centrally informed by this history of my continued practical wrestling with the problems of how to turn a general *idea* of a relational work into an *actual* work that engages with technologies and bodies in more expansive and ecological ways. At many points these struggles with various artworks threw up possibilities that shifted or troubled my theoretical ideas and which suggested new possibilities for philosophical enquiry. To give one simple example out of many, Chapter Nine, while always informed by reading and writing on the subject of generative algorithms, could not have been conceived of or written in its current propositional form without my deep engagement with the practical task of trying to write a software patch that in some way enacted the concepts proposed. The concepts at this early stage were 'extra-linguistic' (Manning 2016b, 27), tenuously co-emergent with some confluence of code, software, hands, instinct, sounds, maths and the enabling constraints of the sensors and shapes of the artwork as it began to take form. In parallel, and at many other times, reading and writing on the subject opened the beginnings of practical experiments. This is particularly true of the concept of the parasite, and my ongoing attempts within artworks to create parasitic (and therefore conjunctive and disjunctive) relations of connections between various components of such works.

In this way while the book is a 'study' of the problem of interactivity, it also seeks to work beyond being something to be studied, and instead to become 'the occasion for study' (Harney and Moten 2013, 109). This a transversal approach that is an ongoing, open and collective activity. This collectivity of study might be more than a collection of subjects, and rather might include collective, diverse activities of 'thinking through' such as parallel making and writing (research-creation), a continued problematisation and multiplicitous approach to the questions (a metamodelling), and the continued intensive movement of these questions (a tactical molecularisation). Here, in 'the crafting of problems greater than their solutions' (Manning 2016b, 10) this study seeks not to conclude to a single point, but rather to build 'machines' to explore the potentials of parasitic actions and feeling, and to push the limits of interactivity, attempting to allow such speculative thinking and immanent connection of ideas on the part of the reader as well as the author. This is a mode of study in which we might find, as we read, that we (collectively) have already been in the middle of. This study, as Harney and Moten argue, is a place where 'the incessant and irreversible intellectuality of these activities is already present', and where the recognition and participation in this multi-leveled approach might allow one 'to access a whole, varied, alternative history of thought' (2013, 110) about interactivity.

1

Interactivity and relation: The myth(s) of interactivity

> 'Interactivity is a very dubious idea.'
> *Woody Vasulka*

In this chapter I want to chart some of the criticism surrounding the term 'interactivity', and the move towards the concept of 'relational' art. The intention of this critique is to move towards more of a productive engagement with the expanded potential of interactive art rather than to dwell on its past crimes. This problematic history has led many writers and artists to move away from the term interactivity and towards one of relationality to distinguish themselves from the narrow scope of these works.

One of the first difficulties we encounter in discussing interactivity might be that the term itself has no readily agreed upon definition. While some authors use it derogatively to condemn programmatic, simple to-and-fro exchanges of an object-orientated communicational model (Massumi 2002, xv)[17], others use the same term to imply a much wider range of participatory experiences that might be broadly termed relational. In *Towards an Aesthetic of the Interactive*, Alan Peacock defines interactivity as 'experiences that include a feedback loop and mutually (self-) modifying sequences and choices within the sequences that form a particular from many possibilities'

(2010, 1). Simon Penny also argues for the necessity of feedback loops and demonstrably developmental aspects in design, stating that 'the fundamental requirement of an interactive system is that it correlates in a meaningful way data gathered about its environment (usually a user's behavior) with output'. Without this, he says, there is no perception of interaction (Penny 2011, 80). These definitions, while somewhat limited compared to the more complex and subtle combinations of forces available for consideration within a relational model, do capture a popular idea of interactive art. Here interactivity is conceived of as modification over time of the work itself, and possibly the behavior of the participant, in a way that is perceptible and comprehensible to the participant.[18]

As Nathaniel Stern points out, these definitions of interactivity tend to concentrate on explanation of the fact that 'a given piece is interactive and how it is interactive, but not on how we interact' (2009, 240)[19]. That is, Brian Massumi says, there is a concentration on function, rather than quality, that limits the debate (cited in Lozano-Hemmer 2000, 201). This is tied to a focus on the representation of interactivity that fixes relation to preconceived models rather than allowing the immanent production of new ways of experiencing (Murphie 1996, 4–5).

Many writers and artists therefore prefer to move from the term interactivity to one of relationality to escape such narrow definitions. In this light Erin Manning proposes that the relational is 'active with the tendencies of interaction, but not limited to them' (2013, 29). Others have attempted a reconditioning of the term, and continue to use interactivity while implying a much wider range of qualitative potentials, believing, as Kelli Fuery states, that a prescriptive view 'must be resisted, and it can be resisted...if we view interactivity as an unstable and uncertain process' (2009, 45).[20] Limited and functionally based discussions of interactivity do, however, still contain some pertinent critique, even if in some cases they fail to grasp the potential of a wider reaching and more qualitatively based discussion.

Proponents of interactivity have promoted the existence of some qualitative – and indeed moral – judgment of difference between 'interactive' and 'non-interactive' forms. Simone Osthoff argues, for example, that Lygia Clark's work utilises the viewer's own energy, synthesising mind and body to explore the sensorial, and thus replaces the object with the experience. This experience, Osthoff argues, essentially differentiates the interactive experience from the type of engagement that painting and sculpture allow (279–80). Perhaps here there is an implication of an essential moral superiority in interactive artwork, echoed by Victor Stoichita's statement that in Rafael Lozano-Hemmer's work we 'are no longer before the (interactive) work, we are in the work' (Lozano-Hemmer 2007, 129). Similarly, both Pierre Levy's assertion that interactivity 'actualizes the decline of totalization' (2001, 131), and Roy Ascott's claim of 'moving beyond the object' from observed effect to participation, consider participatory art to be somehow in opposition to more 'traditional' forms that might distance one from the process (2003, 237, 328).

What then are our expectations of the functioning of interactive art? That it expands the range of art experiences available to the audience, offering levels of 'free choice' and embodied experience seemingly unavailable in more traditional art forms? That it will be participatory on some level unavailable in the supposedly more passive enjoyment of traditional forms; or that it will be experiential rather than representational?

The question of (free) choice is, as Alan Peacock argues, one on which the success and failure of interactivity commonly balances, stating that 'decision making of some kind is a necessary condition of the interactive' (2010, 3).[21] But are there levels of experience in which there is really open-ended decision-making or 'free will' in generative or interactive art? Can interactivity really offer more choice than, for example, a painting? Can it offer as many options to the viewer, either in the way they assimilate content or in the choices of level of involvement in the work? An exhibition of paintings might offer the viewer relatively free reign in their manner of experiencing the space: the choice to skim over some works, view them in any order, dip in and out of concentration and so on – all fairly banal choices that one would take for granted. Interactive works on the other hand, as Massumi cautions, often dictate prescribed and limited actions in order to achieve results, creating 'a kind of tyranny to interaction' (2008, 1, 3). Such interactive works can then enclose us, as Louise Poissant says, 'into a schema of manipulation rather than propos[ing] a real space for dialogue' (2007, 245)[22]. In these situations, Mona Sarkis argues, the participant in interactive art remains a passive 'user', assembling the artist's vision without any real free choice (1993, 13). Thus she claims the interactive possibilities of technologies promoted by their producers are often 'adopted in a careless and uncritical manner by...artists and philosophers' (Sarkis 1993 13).

It should therefore not be taken for granted that participation in interactive art events necessarily grants freedom from the normative viewer–artwork paradigm. Rather, participation potentially co-opts art practice into the construction of mutable, exploitable bodies (Stern 2012, 26–7). As Manning pointedly states:

> To be forced to play is like being forced to touch. Not only does it potentially do violence to the complex relational field in co-composition, it also presupposes an already homogenous arena of engagement (2013a, 129).

These contentious elements of interactivity and control might be broadly thought of as three problematic and overlapping 'social-assemblages': productivity, linearity, and histories of control and power embedded in the technologies. Behind these assemblages lies the issue of the naturalisation of a representationalist or essentialist modelling of experience.[23] Critiques of these aspects of interactivity link it to bio-politics, consumable entertainment, demonstrability and its didactic applications. Here interactivity, in failing to escape such discourses might become the 'dubious idea' of Woody Vasulka's comment.

Productivity and exchange

The productive structuring of interactive art experiences is situated within the history of the commercialisation of its aesthetics and technologies. While we might commonly think that artists repurpose commercial technologies into more artistic production, Penny argues that there is an historical dialogue between the two that is largely ignored. The 'techno-formalist' concerns (Penny 2009, 4) at the center of 1990s' media art explorations laid much of the groundwork for gaming interfaces, for immersive training systems utilised by the militarily and commercial sectors (such as flight simulators), and for social media platforms on the internet (Penny 2009, 21). These non-art world technical advances – combined with new media works themselves – were, according to Penny, 'informed by the previous thirty years of "art and technology", installation art, performance art and video art' (2009, 11). He proposes that not only do artists recommission technologies of control, but that many of these more prescriptive and troubling applications have arisen, if inadvertently, out of artistic experiments in manipulation.[24]

The concentration on technical advance, alongside the necessary collaboration with companies and research laboratories invested in the commercial applications of such advances has lead, as Penny points out, to the adoption of a certain philosophical stance that has leant itself to the development of interactive systems based on the dynamics of consumerist exchange.[25]

These applications promoted certain Platonic ideas about the division of mind and body, naturalising '"objective external real", "sense-data" and "representation"', and the thinking of participants as 'users' or consumers (Penny 2009, 22). Here, Penny argues, the concentration on a distancing vision, produces a 'scopophilic obsession with the eye and vision...[producing] a technology of the phallic gaze, the conquering eye, in which the holistic nature of embodied being [is] elided' (Penny 2009, 22). As such, certain power structures have become a largely unquestioned norm of interactivity: stable systems of objects and bodies exchanging via an interface; users responding to already-formed sets of information; systems that draw attention to their mechanics through reward for behavior; and a focus on representations and exchanges of content within predefined parameters rather than co-emergence (Manning 2009, 63). This might be a focus on 'being – as a generalized ontological equivalent' rather than 'manner of being' (Guattari 1995a, 109). Such a conception of interaction, Stengers argues, implies 'terms that make a difference for one another, but a difference that does not modify their identity' (2011, 514),[26] and thus, in this context, an interactivity that fails to challenge the roles of consumer and consumable object that might perhaps begin to be questioned by more open-ended relational works.[27]

Participatory works sometimes claim to escape this paradigm through a certain freedom from representational content[28] – aiming for visceral experience over narrative, contemplation or reflection. While in one sense it is true that a painting's content is constructed by the artist prior to the encounter with a viewer, even in the most didactic, narrative-driven image, there presents the possibility, one could argue an inevitability, for a freedom of association, for the viewer to link elements to memories. For example, a viewer might make personal and cultural associations, such as colours reminiscent of a flag, facial features associated with a friend, lighting effects that trigger memories of a half-forgotten film, muscle memory or a prehension of movement made conscious through an association with a figure's awkward pose. This association is not simply a reliving of old memories, but an actualisation of potential that creates new thought in the event of artwork and viewer, matter and memory. These subtle connections are exactly the kind of 'interaction' that fits with Manovich's argument that the notion of interactivity must become inclusive of notions of psychological processes, and mental as well as physical or temporal connections (2001, 56–7).

Many artworks might therefore be read in this psychological sense as loosely 'generative' – not 'mechanically' as in some participatory works,[29] but in that the event or experience still emerges from the combination of viewer and work that in its singularity inevitably begins to escape the confines of the artist's control. Interactivity, however, can often struggle to allow such excessive layering and complicating of dialogues. Productive interaction is often lacking the multitude of potential connections and struggles to become excessive, to outstrip function and destabilise orderly systems of exchange.[30]

The 'tyranny' of interactivity is that it is based not just on required participation, but also on the reduction of such participation to the parameters of linear, programmatic and productive exchanges. The 'connection' promised through interactive participation can often remain at a level of relation that stays safely within systems of information exchange, harnessing participation into the circulation of flows of desire within capitalism (Massumi 1992, 200–1). Here the dynamics of interactivity can be seen to contribute to the construction of exploitable bodies within such a paradigm (Stern 2012, 26–7). There is a danger here that these problematic dynamics might work not only to construct the body as a kind of databank of new information to be fed into the workings of the system, but that as such systems become 'naturalised'. That is, productive and limited exchange becomes the anticipated relationship with a work to which participants then moderate their actions and expectations. As discussed below, this relationship becomes an internalised response to the environment and bodies are problematically performed as data or 'immaterial labour' to be exploited (Foucault 2010, 206–13).

It is perhaps then no wonder that interactive technologies form the basis of much entertainment industry spectacle, and interactive systems and displays sit so comfortably in didactic museum displays. Ironically, the very participation that in art is intended to free the viewer from constraints instead operates very effectively to contain, direct and lecture them.[31] As Massumi argues, to utilise such technologies in a becoming and emergent fashion, they need to be freed from 'exchange-value', to move beyond 'prodding a participant to gain a response', and take on a more speculative nature that allows an excess to emerge (2008, 9)[32]. The artist involved in developing interactive systems might be charged here with an obligation to think beyond these co-optable dynamics of relation that so easily lend themselves to dominant power structures, and develop more complex ecologies of relation that begin to resist or at least question productivity and spectacle.

Linearity: riding the interactive train

Interaction can become trivial, as Roy Ascott suggests (2003, 378), in a closed, linear system with finite data – a flicking of an 'on' switch with the viewer's presence, or a prompting of a software program to jump to the next prearranged scene, as in a video game. Preprogrammed events here lack emergent qualities that might help shape the actualized events through the immanent creation of further potential (Manning 2009, 74). The lack of physical or psychological tension created by such experiences is often in hollow contrast to everyday lived experience, as the excess of the virtual is replaced by the probable, while open-endedness is replaced by specific purposes.

What space for contemplation does the interactive installation allow? Perhaps the curse of interactive art is that often the viewer must either abandon midway through boredom, endure to a set endpoint, or at least move through in a set direction. That is, the experience remains essentially linear, 'prepackaged and predigested', as de Mèredieu states (2003, 213)[33]. Levy argues that 'cyber art' systems of interactivity operate against the totalising forms of traditional media, allowing new and greater potentials for coproduction (2001, 115–6, passim). Similarly, Ascott claims that interactivity offers empowerment and greater participation in the workings of the art event (2003, 284). Here the experience can be rather like the participation in riding a train: certainly we are bodily involved in the machinations of travel, but with limited entrance and exit points and heading inexorably in a prescribed direction. It is a kind of roller-coaster experience that contains a certain level of visceral thrill and manipulation without allowing any greater level of co-authorship of the experience (Poissant 2007, 245). The risk is that our movements loose their incipient qualities, and the many and varied levels of potential participation are instead reduced to a role of merely 'performing the software' (Manning 2009, 63).

Interactivity here becomes 'Pavlovian', as both Penny and Lozano-Hemmer have noted: a 'trivial' modality based on an action and reward system (Penny 2011, 78; Lozano-Hemmer, Boucher and Harrop 150).[34] As de Mèredieu comments, the predetermined nature of such interactive systems 'confines the spectator's actions and reactions to a well mapped art path', and the ubiquity of such forms as 'an art trapped in prefabricated "networks" [running] the risk of being transformed into a kind of global, collective "art in kit form"' (2003, 230–1). While some artists may argue that interactive works have moved beyond this paradigm,[35] many would argue that this issue is still pressing today as much work continues to focus on the performance of its mechanisms rather than an investigation of a 'becoming' of such mechanisms (Fuery 2009, 43–4)[36].

While these issues with escaping linearity arise partially from the use of technologies created for specific, productive purposes, it would be wrong to simply attribute this, as Wood does, to any inherent or inescapable properties of such technologies (2007, 16). Rather, we might see this issue as arising more specifically out of the technologies being primarily harnessed to represent relation within the interactive encounter (in itself a 'productive' use). This tends to promote the demonstration of interaction over experiential emergence (Murphie 1996, 5) and to instrumentalise the user to represent the potentials of the technologies (Penny 2011, 73, 87).

This is not to say that the comprehension of relational factors in itself denies a rich involvement in immediate sensorial experience,[37] but that the desire to clearly demonstrate to the participant that they are indeed interacting with and causing change or growth in the artwork can prevent the riskier task of enabling the performative exploration of emergent relation. Such relations may or may not reach a level of perceptible representation, and may indeed remain at the level of the virtual. In the sacrifice of the uncertainty of emergent relation for demonstrable connection, what is lost is the 'elasticity' of the larger potentiality of the event. Relations are then often made rigid and linear to ensure the pay-off of a quick and simple explicated exchange for the participant. This focus on demonstration imposes 'self-completing lines through representations that trace existing conditions and attempt to repeat them', as Andrew Murphie argues of representation and virtual reality (1996, 6),[38] through its need, even anxiety, to facilitate the *perception* of an interactive experience. As artist David Rokeby notes, the

> 'Simplified representations [of interactivity] replace the relationships to which they initially referred. This substitution turns the interesting ambiguities of control and subjectivity in interactive art into serious issues of control, manipulation and deception' (NDb).[39]

This serves to bring, once again, the modality of interactivity back to the language of gaming, where 'unprescripted' potential is replaced by variations of the possible (Massumi 2002, 9).[40] Exploration of 'becoming' in any larger sense, which is essentially non-linear, is replaced by the rehearsal of the already formulated and comprehended (Braidotti 2002, 118).

Histories and networks of control

It is certainly true, as Manning warns, that the sensory technologies at the base of many interactive works have 'problematic pasts, both as displacers of the corporeal body and in assemblages of control' (2007, 118). As I have argued above, Penny presents a potentially even more troubling history where artists must share some of the burden for the ways their technological experiments have been put to use. Mark Dery optimistically advocates that the repurposing of such oppressive technologies within artworks is a potentially political act that displaces the power dynamics by making art with such tools of control (1996, 14). More pessimistically systems in which an artist employs these tools to control the interactions between bodies and artwork could be thought to mirror the political utilisation of surveillance by governments to create systems of control. Therefore in such systems the work could still be said to celebrate the power of the technology.[41] Indeed, Penny argues, while these technologies are deployed in novel ways, they retain many of their original functions, including the potential for control inherent in the representation of relation (whether body–technology, body–body, or body–subject) (2003, 268)[42].

Such representational modes of production can be linked to the reinforcement of the status quo – static systems of discrete subjects incapable of escaping a pre-constructed mode of being.

There is no doubt that these technologies have at least the potential to reproduce such power relations, and it is disingenuous for artists to simply assume that art can avoid such pitfalls without a close examination of whether there has been a true shift in the dynamics.[43] However any argument that such technologies necessarily have only the capability to produce these power relationships seems flawed. Despite the undoubted links between surveillance and interactivity, this would tend toward a 'technological determinism', as Murphie and Potts argue, framing understanding of technologies as objects capable of independently creating certain relations of power within society, rather than considering them for their functions within certain contexts (2003, 13, 32).

Whether inherent or not, surveillance might be thought to 'capture' the body, both in the flattening of the experience of a body to a fixed identity or subjectivity, and the fixing of it within a readable space.[44] The reduction of the potential of a body in some virtual reality (VR) immersions to a representation divorced from the complexity of embodied sensory immersion in the world leads, Dery argues, to a 'static body' locked into 'observation mode' (1996 234–5). This is, Penny states, a 'thinning out' experience in an action of 'standardization, reductivism, efficiency [and] instrumentality' (2013, 7–8). Although these critiques are both specifically aimed at virtual reality, while interactive art events utilise the same structures to fix or interpret bodies,[45] they will remain subject to the danger of falling into similar power relationships, despite their claims to a greater level of embodied participation than other forms of art. Such representational use of bodies denies their ever-individuating nature, and can contribute to disengagement with the corporeal – the separation of images from body that is part of the operation of surveillance.[46] These are not inherent properties of the components of the art assemblage, but arise because the components combine to produce similar problematic network-control paradigms. It is through the performance and repetition of these 'specific bodily acts that bodies are reworked and that power takes hold of the body' (Barad 2007, 63).

Matteo Pasquinelli's analysis delves further into the problematic and essentially neoliberal aspects of network culture and the digital. He interrogates the 'post-Fordist' move to immaterial labour and charts ways in which, far from escaping capitalist systems of exchange, creative commons and immaterial property always have material property implications that both remain exploitative of labour and absorb innovative and 'revolutionary tendencies' (2008, 87–9, 23–4).[47] Pasquinelli argues that far from freeing bodies, the rise of the digital has lead to a new sphere of exploitation as digital machines parasitize the labour of living bodies: a new dynamic model of 'cognitive capitalism' applicable across dimensions or modes (2008, 97).[48] What happens, we might wish to ask here, when an interactive work demands the labour of the viewer for its operations? How might the enthusiastic turn in major art events and galleries towards relational aesthetics be at the very least inadvertently creating exploitative relations that, rather than questioning power, work to enhance its operations on highly personal levels, both physically and cognitively. Are there other ways in which a participant might be engaged that do not reinforce existing (or indeed invent new) methods of inequality?

Certainly as a beginning point, where any technologies of control (including capitalist exchanges) are concerned, we need to interrogate, interrupt or shift the kinds of power dynamics that are enacted and the networks that are constructed. Within this we need to question the ways that such technologies encourage the replacement of embodied experience with representational models, and the imposition of normative subject–object relations. Here it is not enough to simply claim that the end product differs from the original design aims of those technologies. More detailed and critical examination, particularly of the larger structures and systems within which such technologies are operating, is required.

It is important that artists investigate ways to escape the mechanics of the production of exchange, subjectivity and networks of control, in order to allow a rethinking not just of the component parts or productions of these machines, but also of the ways in which these parts form problematic relations. This is an interactivity that moves beyond the performance of a mechanism, as Fuery suggests, becoming itself immanently interactive as a technique for the processes of individuation (2009 43–4).[49] As Deleuze notes, it is never enough to trace a line away from something, but rather lines of flight need to continue to be generated for the work to remain performative (Deleuze and Parnet 1987, 29).

Art as event: a relational model

The arguments above begin to suggest some of the problematic ethics of interactivity that are present not just in individual explorations of the genre, but whenever the underlying structuring of the production of the experience is unquestioned. Rather than dwell on these points at length or critique individual works, the purpose here is to propose potential tactics for the thinking beyond those kinds of relations identified in the previous section. Here, more than a critique of specific iterations of the modality, I would suggest that the issues raised are the inevitable outcome of an essentialist system of interactions, which attempts to stratify the reality of co-emergent change (Massumi 2002, 207).

Thus it is not enough to simply demand more from the interactive artist and critic: more complexity, more imagination, more inventive solutions, citing that it is a relatively 'young' art form and arguing for its inherent qualities. More imaginative creativity will always have its place, but the issue underlying the limitation of interactive artworks lies primarily, I would argue, in a philosophically limited conception of an object, a subject, and a work of art. It is this thinking that underlies the narrowness of both the invention and critique of interactive art – a narrowness in the selection of evidence as Whitehead might argue, which, in its attempts to reduce the field of discussion to a manageable stability, succeeds only in denying the actual nature of the event.[50]

What happens to interactivity when rethought through the prism of a process philosophy? As Barad states, a 'dynamic conception of matter is an unsettling of nature's presumed fixity and hence an opening up of the possibilities for change' (2007, 63). If we encourage an ecological approach that emphasises co-emergence and inter-dependence, could we rediscover a fluidity and layered inventiveness and begin to both think and construct interactive art differently?

From material to organic thinking

Massumi argues that interactivity describes a simple back and forth between two elements that remain discrete (in Lozano-Hemmer 2005, 201),[51] reflecting a material view of the world in which the viewer is a stable subject and the artwork is a stable object. Seen through process philosophy, however, the scenario is very different as these stable and persistent subjects and objects are replaced by entities that are themselves processes (Whitehead 1978, 41, 309).[52] For Whitehead these actualised entities are atomic. That is, they do not change in themselves; rather they exist only in the instance of their becoming, perishing in actualisation to be replaced by new actualisations, an endless advance towards intensity and invention. Viewed in this way, 'objects' are 'cuts' in processes of concrescence of complex events of relation, while 'subjects' (or 'superjects' in Whitehead's preferred term) arise out of experience, rather than interacting with the world in a transcendent manner (Whitehead 1978, 155).

This can be related to Simondon's concept of individuation – an ongoing process of development of an entity that always 'contains latent potentials'. Individualisation is here thought of as a 'cut' in this ongoing process (Simondon 1992, 300). Individuation is not, however, a single process of development, but rather 'overlapping phasings happening in non-linear time'. A 'dephasing' or cut occurs when events 'tune toward…a discrete iteration, a remarkable point' that is a 'shift in level from individuation to individual' (Manning 2013a, 17–18).

Such concepts can begin to challenge how we think of, make and experience interactive art. They imply the need to view art objects, events and subjects as produced through, and as a result of, the complex play of forces. This does not deny that objects, bodies and subjects exist prior to the art event, but that further potential can be activated through the event relational engagement. Here relationality immerses entities in a field that might be quite distinct from the back and forth conversational model of the interactive paradigm (Manning 2013a, 130). The processual is crucial in this expansion of interactivity, in that it opens the forming relations and the entities they initiate to a multiplicity of becoming that necessarily outstrips any unity of subjectivity.[53] It brings into play the ongoing, overlapping individuations – states of constant generation rather than progression to one particular endpoint. These processes of individuation are, as Massumi says, forward looking and rich with potential (cited in Manning 2013a, xi).

Manning poses a question about life in general that applies here to participatory art: 'what if, instead of placing self-self interaction at the centre of development, we were to posit relation as the key to experience?' (2013a, 2). As in life in general, the artwork here *is* the encounter: art as an event of relations. This notion of relationality, as Massumi says, addresses objects and bodies from the point of view of their ability to change and respond – 'a coming together in a fusional event...a telescoping into a potential becoming' (in Lozano-Hemmer 2005, 4).

The relational is an immediate 'emergent process', where something new occurs out of the relations (Manning and Massumi 2011, 8; Couze 2010, 139). Thus when Lozano-Hemmer insists that his work is not interactive but 'relational' he means that the focus is not on the fixed or mechanical elements of interaction, but on the potential for establishing relations that always have an immanent, virtual quality to them (Gorschluter 2009, 103).[54] This approach allows him 'to think of the computer and technology as potential language with which you can make relationships emerge, as opposed to preconceiving the outcome' (Lozano-Hemmer, Boucher and Harrop 2012, 152).

A number of artists have attempted to move beyond the potentially limiting paradigm of interactivity by adopting a relational approach. As noted in the introduction, there is a 'prehistory' to the discussion of a relational model, notably in philosophical writings and texts produced by artists Roy Ascott and Lygia Clark, and scientist-artist Gordon Pask that emerged in the earliest days of discussion on 'interactivity'.[55] As Ascott states: 'now that we see that the world is all about process, constant change, we are less surprised to discover that our art is all about process too' (2003, 157). His concept of 'telematic art' (Ascott 2003, 231) proposes a move away from the object to the examination of process – an art that explores an 'interconnectedness' of interweaving fields and forces, able to evolve in an unpredicted, heterogeneous manner – an art that is a state of 'perpetual play' (158–9, 11).

Gordon Pask's work, according to Usman Haque, shows an interest in unspecified goals that moves it beyond the realm of much contemporary interactive art (2007, 58)[56]. Haque argues that Pask's artworks and his elaborate 'conversation model' of interaction demonstrate an interest in an active, shared field and 'mutually constructive' relationships (2007, 55).[57] In his own dense and complex writing Pask emphasises the importance of creating work where both technical systems and human participants might cooperatively adjust their relational capacities in an emergent ecology (1961b, 230–4; 1961a, 102).[58]

Clark's writing provides a more lucid understanding of the scope of a process-based view of the world, and the relational potential of an art practice. Clark writes of her work as non-object based – 'an experience that does not leave a trace' but is an act that 'contains...its own becoming' (cited in Suchan 2008, 6).[59] She writes of dissolution of the space between subject and object, a 'vibrating body' affected by worldly forces (cited in Martin, Ruiz and Rolnik 2000, 73, 104), and 'relational objects' designed to instigate affectual connections that might 'launch the spectator into unforeseeable becomings' (Clark cited in Suchan 2008, 12, 10). Here Clark calls for art to evolve beyond 'the simple manipulation and participation of the spectator' and for it to engage in 'the process of bringing the participant's freedom of action to light' (Clark cited in Suchan 2008, 12, 10).

A relational approach is explicitly adopted, at least theoretically,[60] by a number of more contemporary artists. In the field of architecture Greg Lynn could be cited, particularly his calls for a practice based on theories of complexity that engage with multiplicities to escape both identity and contradiction (1998, 161). One might also cite the more far-reaching explorations of emergent body-space by Arakawa and Gins discussed later in this book,[61] and Penny writes as a new media artist about the shift towards an enactive, performative approach to participation (2011, 83). This 'performative ontology' Penny says, expands interactivity towards that of 'machine ecology' (2011, 94–5, 100). Similarly, Nathaniel Stern describes the body and world as 'implicit in one another', a 'per-formed' rather than 'pre-formed' relationship – a body which is emergent 'through its active relations to other matter-and-matters in progress' (2011, 233; 2012, 34). As such, for Stern the creation of relation is 'continuous; it is embodiment's...always ongoing formation', and he compares this to the 'more finite' possibilities of interactivity that are responsive but restrictive (2012, 8). Likewise, Rokeby argues for a complex interactivity that resonates between participant and artwork (cited in Penny 2011, 84).

Participation, Manning states in summing up 'relational' art, differs from the programmatically interactive in its tending towards the virtual and gathering of forces from the field. Manning writes that it is not about 'the plan of the movement or the partitioning of the individual bodies in space. It is the relational force that persists from the collective movement's incipient cueings and alignings, the incipient priming gathered as a force field not of the bodies per se, but of the active intervals their relational movement creates, intervals that in turn propose multiplicities in the moving' (2013b 342).

While it is not the purpose of this discussion to provide such a critique, these concepts of the relational in art should be noted as easily distinguishable from the 'relational' as conceived in 'relational aesthetics', which, as Stern remarks, considers and limits itself only to relations between already constituted subjects (2012, 48). The *embodied* relational approach referred to here, while it still considers the social as a force contributing to the individuations of the body and subject, must also consider a much broader spectrum of relational possibilities. Similarly, an embodied model of relation is in marked contrast to artists such as Stelarc, for instance, who invests in the transcendence of the body through the bio-technological melding. Stelarc, Dery argues, upholds a Cartesian distinction between body and mind, reducing bodies to the position of machinic commodity and making them the ideal subject for power (1996, 232, 164, 154–235).[62]

A relational model(ing)

The operational politics of the relational are, on the other hand, improvisational, fluid and emergent, as Manning states (2009, 41),[63] a 'becoming' connectivity that moves with and is attentive to the force of the field with which one co-emerges (2013a, 212–3). The event of the connections and their co-emergence with bodies is co-causal.[64] This describes the way relations develop between the body and the work as a 'mutual incipiency' that is a process of change and response (Massumi in Lozano-Hemmer 2005, 201). This may be considered as self-evident information, for if, as process philosophy proposes, all things are events of relation, are not all artworks thus composed, regardless of the artist's intentions? The way many interactive works operate, however, is to attempt to stabilise such unfoldings, erase the connections to the virtual – the future potential for 'immergence'[65] – and establish enduring actualised connections and representations of connections.

The shift in emphasis to the relational concerns affording an emergent or potential event that may occur or is occurring. A work might still be thought of as existing beforehand, as an object or proposition for an event, but it exists *as* an event only in a temporal relationship – or rather as a nexus of relationships – with the viewer, enfolded and unfolded through interaction, and each nexus of relations creates a singular event.

As a 'proposition' the potential event of art-objects/spaces and bodies can move beyond obstacles that 'delimit the event according to pre-constituted interiorities' to act instead as 'propositions for an ecology of participation' (Manning 2013a, 114, 185). Embodied enaction of an event is always directed towards the 'next' – further potential differentiations – the continuing evolution of the event (Varela, Thompson and Rosch 1992, 205), and therefore open always to the pull of the virtual. Such events create body-artwork assemblages – contingent networks of interconnections with multiple, unplanned, potentially contradictory variables of relation.[66]

The participant's concentration shifts to the buildup of energy and rhythm between and within body and work; how the event moves beyond a mapping of simple cause and effect and into something that enables its own generative tendencies (Massumi 2008, 13). Such complex multiple actions and potential relations might catalyse a singular experience, moving beyond what can be articulated. Thus what is felt or perceived here in the moment might be intensities of pure sensation, a building of energies expressed through ever reconfiguring combinations of movement, sound, image, posture, and so on – while also including potentially contradictory affectual relations that push and pull at the body.

A relational art event might begin to concentrate on enabling the conditions for new connections to arise, a richer palette that might include slippery, hard to define, conjunctive and disjunctive forces: affects, inarticulate sensations, micro-perceptions, and emotional tonalities. Such fuzzy and inarticulate forces, which can never be fully compressed into productive perception, might move the work further away from any prescribed outcomes, outstripping functionality as an inarticulate remainder affecting the body beyond cognition. This philosophical stance of relationality, O'Sullivan states, points (perhaps optimistically) away from 'consumption' and towards an 'art practice as a process...always producing' (2006, 24).

Interactivity and relation   51

Bridge: Into the midst: immersion immersive

While in theory it is easy to agree on a general shift to relational modelling, it remains problematic for the practising artist engaged with an interactive or 'relational' art to structure fluidity and maximise open-ended potentiality in more practical terms. This is particularly true when working with interactive technologies designed with other outcomes in mind. An example of some of the practical issues involved in attempting this shift to the relational can be seen in *Into the Midst*, a five-day, collaborative research-creation workshop and public presentation in the *SATosphere* – the Society for Art and Technology's interactive and immersive projection dome in Montreal, Canada.[67]

The project sought to explore alternative potentials of a space constructed with seemingly rigid divisions between the artists' technical and spatial control of events and the viewers' lack of control of the space.[68] Key to the usual operation of the dome was that the scale of the space and the configuration of the seating constrained its use to an undoubtedly spectacular, but somewhat passive, viewing space. The design encouraged all viewers to recline while focusing their attention on relating to the surround sound and giant images that wrapped around and cocooned them.

The *Into the Midst* artists hoped to activate more varied experiences within the space, with general tactics including encouraging attention to the edges of the space, the projection of images and sounds that disrupted the smooth illusion of immersion, and creating opportunities for participants to directly relate to one another beyond simply sharing the viewing of the projections.[69] Thus the series of interventions that were employed within the space were designed to disrupt the habitual configurations of relation between audience members, artists and audience, and the audience and the spatial dynamics of the dome. In these aims the artists in the project sought not to

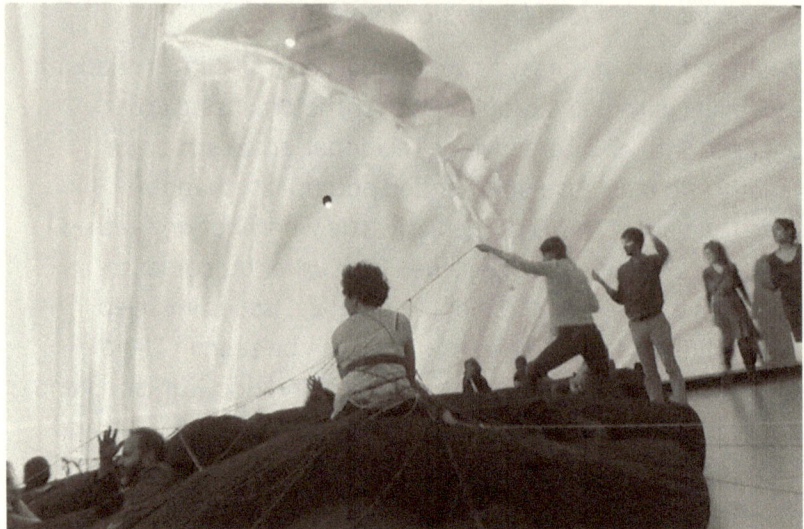

Figure 1.1 Senselab collaborative project, *Into the Midst: Immersion* Immersive (performance documentation), Society for Art and Technology, Montreal, 2012. Photo: Hannah Buck

simply ignore or diffuse the various technical mechanisms built into the space to provide spectacle, but to reuse them in a more speculative and unconventional manner (see Figure 1.1).

However despite the concerted efforts to extend the potential of the dome's mechanisms in its public presentation, the normative paradigm of the dome as a space for relatively passive consumption of immersive imagery continued to overwhelm the efforts of the artists. The event too easily became an extension to, rather than an interruption of, the 'entertainment' space and habits that such places tend to encourage.

The lure of the projected imagery continued to centralise the viewers' focus. The design of the space seemed to suggest that it primarily concerned itself with a relationship between a relatively passive subject and events predicated on 'out of body' experiences (such as spectacles of virtual travel reminiscent of nineteenth-century panoramas), rather than with any embodied potential that might be exploited within such a large area. The (deliberately) ephemeral interventions failed to sufficiently disrupt these dynamics to allow new configurations to arise and disturb the stratification. The lack of differentiation in the layout and clear divide between projection space and viewing space were all elements that contributed towards this rigid structuring.[70]

My own participation in this project crystallised some of the key issues around the difficulties in moving the interactive experience beyond habitual divisions of artwork and subject, and in enabling relations to operate outside the (again habitual) paradigm of the passive consummation of the demonstration of the spectacular.

It proved extremely difficult to utilise the technologies built into the space without creating a work that ended up principally demonstrating the undoubtedly impressive capacities of the technology. Potentially disruptive transversal relations that might have interrupted the centralised focus were too easily overwhelmed by the force of attraction of the overhead light show and the 36-speaker surround-sound system, and those viewers who attended the public showing found themselves, for the most part, adopting this passive position within the space, despite the various activities designed to disrupt this action. Even the artists involved found it difficult to not succumb to the lure of the projected spectacle above, despite our shared interest in moving beyond this experience.

Technologies of interaction demonstrated in this project that they have the potential to control and limit relation when not carefully constructed to operate otherwise, and that habits of operating within a known paradigm can be hard to shift, even for those with such intent. Here it became evident that the construction of relation in and of itself can still easily conform to dominant and perhaps constrictive paradigms, and that any ethical platform of emergent relation must find new ways to interrupt the habitual means of engagement. Participants' bodies similarly needed to be addressed in individual ways, and encouraged to engage on multiple levels, rather than as a generalised ideal. The kind of dominant relation between fully-formed subject and work that the SAT's dome space assumes as primary also needs to be put into question by relations that allow movement of differing kinds and scales of connection and *disconnection* to emerge.

For me, this project highlighted that, as Penny notes, there is, at times for all of us, a considerable gap between the theory and practice and between broad intention and outcomes (2011, 72).[71] While the relational model previously outlined is the one pursued within this research, much of this theory on broader philosophical level only begins, at best, to address the more practical concerns of how to enact such systems within a participatory framework. How to structure a work to allow for multiple, surprising outcomes, and how to create organic movement – the complex flow of prehension, synthesis and perishing, pursued endlessly by further such creation – remains a question. These issues are at the heart of this research, and the next chapter begins to address these more forward-looking and practical concerns in detail: considering the question of 'how to' think beyond interactivity and constructing some of the potential tools that might be required to realise such an aim.

Here chaos in itself does not seem to be an answer, and nor is mimicry of the everyday. Rather, it is that particular 'thickness of experience' – the surprise of unusual connection and revelation that the art event can offer – which needs to be retained without losing the kind of underlying complexity and entanglement gained from everyday experiential involvement in the environment.

2

Thinking action and event

Introduction

> The creation of a chaosmos is what interactive art
> and art with new technologies should head towards,
> as only then can outcomes be protected from chaos
> without turning interaction into a choice of alternative
> stratified options.
>
> *Andrew Murphie*

A reimagining of interactivity along relational lines introduces the possibility of a 'minor' interactivity. This involves a continued activation or problematisation of the major form, in order to avoid a return to any oppressive stasis. Here the concept of the assemblage and the notion of art as an event and as a machine are introduced to enable a closer investigation of something at the heart of this research: the creative power of noise or interference in relation and its role in increasing the self-organising capacities of the interactive event.

This rethinking must also involve more practical tools that allow an interrogation of singular instances of relation. It must be remembered that 'relation' in itself is not an answer, since, as I have argued, much interactive work is relationally oppressive in working to fix and contain relational difference and generation along programmatic lines. As Claire Bishop points out in her critique of current trends in socially relational art, relational works are quite capable of enforcing the status quo through blind promotion of social inclusiveness in the works while 'the structural inequalities of society remain uninterrogated' (2009, 241). It is important therefore to think of relational propositions that might allow a certain freedom to reinvent or mobilise existing relation – to produce potential movement.

Minor interactions

As Simon O'Sullivan argues, 'minor' and 'major' are not polar opposites. Rather, the minor can be thought of as a reactivation of the components of a system from within (2006, 71), allowing the system to become something other than its major or established form. The 'becoming-minor', for Gilles Deleuze and Félix Guattari, is therefore a tactic with which to pervert or trouble the structure of an oppressive system in order to explore ways to allow the oppressed qualities of the major to oppose its oppressive qualities (1986, 10)[72]. The minor, as O'Sullivan says, breaks with the habitual formations, and challenges dominant regimes of the form to allow further movement or open change in the system (2006, 69). In this sense, 'becoming' is always minoritorian, as Erin Manning states (2015, 3), in that it is about the activation, movement or further individuation beyond a stable form.

Using the concept of the minor suggests a thinking of the relational potential of interactivity that, rather than being oppositional or reactive to the critiqued dominant paradigm, seeks to explore the further potential of the components of the systems, utilizing the same elements but with a different structural logic. That is, if the major or normative form of interactive artworks tends towards control and signification of subjects and objects, subordinating the wider relational potential, then the becoming-minor of interactivity might be a turn towards the relational that encourages these controlled forces or qualities to flourish. Here the expressive, expansive pull of relations might be utilised to problematise the major structure.[73]

This might re-energise interactivity's potential, giving rise to an uncertainty within what was fixed in order (Murphie 1997, 68), and allowing new productive capacities to be explored. It is not about the production of a new stabilised 'form' of interactivity but the production of the conditions that enable continued agitation of the elements (an 'expressive machine') (Deleuze and Guattari 1986, 28). Thus the minor here does not designate specific productive outcomes, but rather the 'revolutionary conditions' in which continued exploration might be produced. It is, as Massumi states, directional in that it moves away from stasis, but not 'directed-to' any particular endpoint (1992, 103, 18). Potentially, this disturbs any stabilisation and instead emphasises the productive nature of disorganisation itself. It allows for consideration of the particulars of an event, and the relations and entities co-composed with it, rather than following any established path (Murphie 1997, 72–3). In this, it has specific disruptive implications for fixed or linear interactivity. The move to the relational here is a tactic with which to reactivate and charge (interactive) structures with new potential.[74]

Molecularisation and the assemblage

The concept of molecularisation is closely linked to the minor, as an opening up of stratified relation. The 'becoming-molecular' of a system is the decentering of a formally stabilised whole into parts. This both decentres the system and allows new communications or exchange between components (Deleuze and Guattari 1986, 50, 41): a hyper-differentiation that encourages new potentials, intensities and complexities to arise.[75] In a 'molar' configuration, as Brian Massumi says, a set of entities are molded to a prescribed set of connections, becoming a 'disciplined' or 'dominated' group of individuals that have a fixed identity imposed upon them. As Massumi notes, the molecular still exists within this molar regime, but it is controlled and free relational movement is contained (1992, 55). A molecular configuration of the same entities allows local activations: transient and improvised connections to take place (and perish).[76] Thus, becoming-minor is also always becoming-molecular (Deleuze and Guattari 1987, 272), an increase in movement or intensity within a stratified system.

Within the paradigm of interactive art, the 'molar' perspective might be seen, firstly, as the discrete body of the viewer taken as a whole, and the artwork similarly viewed as one idea or fixed assemblage of components. Secondly, it might be the fixed relations between work and viewer that prescribe the types of relations and outcomes possible between them. Thirdly, the molar position might also prescribe the event overall according to a preconceived notion of interactivity. A molecular approach to the same art event would open up the potential of new ways of relating inside these 'wholes', filling the systems with fluctuations, uncertainties and tentativeness that are its opening up to new singular expressions (Guattari and Rolnik 2005, 162).[77] Here the site(s) of interaction might become mobile and multiple, delimiting the resultant events of interaction. Pragmatically, any such artwork will be composed of both molar and molecular components or tendencies, and the aim might be to encourage an increase in potential for internal movement and change.[78]

In this sense, as Deleuze and Guattari state, molecularisation tends towards the creation of 'machinic' assemblages (1986, 37) – collections of entities functioning immanently and pragmatically, rather than being 'subordinate to the laws of resemblance' (Massumi 1992, 192). Assemblages do not create fixed bonds between components; rather the entities are linked through shared collective potentials (Guattari 1995a, 35). An assemblage is 'ad-hoc' in that it is composed of available material, and it is dynamic – as all its relations remain active – a 'volatile mix' of forces, part and materials (Bennett 2010, 24–5). Assemblages maintain the individual qualities of components and the differences between them – rather than repressing these for the sake of the whole – while at the same time collectively and potentially producing or becoming something else. The assemblage is an organisation of relations, though not reducible to this, and is also multiplicitous: it has an internal dynamism that always keeps its relational fields open to potential recombination (Buchanan 120, 129). In this one might say, as Bennett does, that the individual components and the assemblage together exhibit 'agency' (2005, 31–2), and components are 'molecularised' in an assemblage in that they are able to individually modulate their relations while maintaining collective coherence.

Importantly for this argument, assemblages are able to operate without resolving or erasing internal tensions. In fact, such internal differences might be seen to drive both creative organisation and production of the assemblage. These tensions saturate the assemblage with intensive potential for derivation from any realised or emergent form, as they relate 'difference to difference' and maintain an adaptive potential: 'a capacity to further differentiate differences' (DeLanda 2005, 23–4).

Here relation can be considered to exist not only between stable objects and subjects, but also within and across such idealised forms, initiating and potentialising them. Now the room for continued movement within the seemingly continuous whole begins to become apparent – the infinite gaps and discontinuities that can be activated to drive change within the event.

Within an art-event-as-assemblage, such internal modulation provides an open-endedness that enriches, rather than destroys, the now mobile whole. What also becomes apparent is that the privileging of viewer-work relations is no longer necessary. Instead, any discussion of relation can – indeed must – consider all relations as being equally open to change. This includes relations between various body organs, between these organs and technical entities, and between and within technical entities themselves. This decentering of the human in favour of a wider approach to relation is essential in order to more fully consider the forming of the larger ecology of the art event. It acknowledges the dynamic role that all the elements bring to bear on the playing-out of relational forces across the various scales and assemblages in which the interactive event is activated.

Differential machines

Guattari's concept of the machine provides a useful way of conceiving of an artwork or event as a productive assemblage. From this basis the mechanics of self-organisation might be examined. Machines, Guattari tells us, are any system that produces an effect.[79] There are, for example, social, logical, biological and linguistic machines, and machines that are combinations of these systems, such as cities (Guattari, 1995b, 9).[80] There are also machines that are conglomerates of technical objects and, as Murphie describes, machines that are assemblages of technical objects-plus-bodies such as the 'car-driver' machine that produces travel (1996, 89). The 'machinic' is therefore not the mechanical (a fixed technical system), nor is it specifically linked to the technical (non-organic), but is a productive assemblage, another configuration of the non-unified subject (Braidotti 2002, 254). Its cohesion (such as it is) is achieved through a shared potential (Maturana and Varela 1980, 77). Like assemblages, machines can be broken down into smaller machines, or sets of components held together through some kind of productive relation (Murphie 1997, 265).[81] Machines act molecularly in resisting the collapse back into any irreducible whole, or series of wholes, through their continued potential activation of relation. A machinic connection or relation might therefore be one that is pragmatic, flexible and local, always with further potential iteration or expression available to it.

This thinking gives us three very useful ideas that help to expand any technologically based concept of the machine in a decidedly non-humanist direction.

Firstly, the need to understand the role that the wider ecology in which technical objects are embedded in (or unfold from) has in determining what potential is actualised. Technology, as Andrew Murphie explains, is always only one aspect of a larger notion of the machinic, requiring a larger physical/social field within which to operate (1997, 80).[82]

Secondly, as Guattari describes, technical machines inherently contain potential beyond their immediate actualization – 'ontogenetic elements' (1995b, 8). Thus they are held together not so much by any physical bond, but by a shared potential, an 'assemblage of possible fields' (1993, 35)[83] that develops through the process of 'concretisation' or interdependence.

Thirdly, that we must consider machines not through utility or representation, but in terms of their productive capabilities. Guattari's conception of the machinic shifts the discussion of the assemblage from: 'what is it composed from/what is it an aggregate of?' to 'what does it produce?'.[84] That is, machines are performative, concerned with 'matters of practices, doings and actions' (Barad 2007, 135). Within a machinic assemblage, Manuel DeLanda explains, components explore their capacities to connect with other component, their abilities to affect and be affected, which is separate (if related) to their 'intrinsic properties'.[85] Such machines are necessarily multiplicities, with 'no need whatsoever of unity in order to form a system' (Deleuze 1994, 182), preserving internal differences between components. Their potential lies in a productive 'opening out to heterogeneity and alterity' (Murphie 1996, 92).

An interactive art assemblage might be usefully viewed as machinic. This places the focus on how the work as a machinic whole is composed of various smaller machine components – bodies, technical entities and combinations of parts of these entities – that interrupt, modulate or transduce forces they come into contact with or are subjected to (Deleuze 2004, 219). The larger art assemblage or machine is then brought into existence and organised through these productive and provisional relationships between these smaller parts and by their shared modulation of a particular force.[86] Each component within an assemblage productively affects and is affected differently by any force, increasing internal difference or molecularity.[87] Thus interaction with and transduction of forces is here the process by which such 'an activity sets itself in motion', and at the same time generates 'processes of modification'. These transductions instigate further individuation of the machine while at the same time potentially reconfigure its internal relations (Simondon 1992, 313).

In the work *A Chorus of Idle Feet*, analogue sensors were set up in a public walkway that were capable of transducing the movement of bodies through the space to produce variations in the syncopation of sounds.[88] Here, various components might be thought of as forming assemblages, expressing a capacity to connect and produce modulations in forces, and then combining to produce more such machines built on intensive differentiation. Body, movement and light together expressed the capacity to produce shadows in the space – becoming a shadow-machine modulating light – while light sensors modulated the flow of electrons in a light-light sensor-electron machinic assemblage.[89] While these were capacities of the two machines, when combined they began to make a machine that transduced the force of movement to the flow of electrical current, as shadows produced changes in electrical resistance in the sensors. This machine, in turn, combined with other components to form another machine that expressed its capacities to connect movement into changes in sound pitch, rhythm, tempo or tone. For example, this machinic assemblage combined with an assemblage that converts electrical resistance to computer code such as MIDI signals that control sounds on a computer (an electrical flow-MIDI code-vibration machine). These machines were productively transducing movement into modulation of light waves, light waves into modulations of electrical current, and flow of electrons into modulated flows of sound waves. All these component machines then nested within a larger assemblage that collectively transduced the force of movement into these sound waves.

In the same work, other sensors (such as proximity and movement detection sensors focused on particular areas of the walkway, detecting changes in the position or number of bodies present), linked with the capacities of the movement to produce variations in the spatial distribution of bodies, which linked into larger productive relation with software triggering more sound pulses. This again nested within a larger machine, producing modulations in syncopation of the sounds as they combined.

Here all the components provisionally came together as an expressive machine, producing an emergent quality of rhythmic syncopation. This was a *collective* expression formed through interaction of all parts to create an event that retained the dynamic qualities of modulation of the machinic assemblage. As such it was concerned with the 'viscosities' of the transduction of various forces through the system: the styles and speeds of affectation of components by forces and visa versa. The work operated through an ongoing production of both internal connections and differences in the flow of forces. It was a 'fuzzy aggregate' composed of counterpoints, inequalities and tensions in the processing of forces between the parts (Deleuze and Guattari 1987, 328-9). Here the larger machinic assemblage obtained a level of consistency in production (it continued to express relations between movement and sound

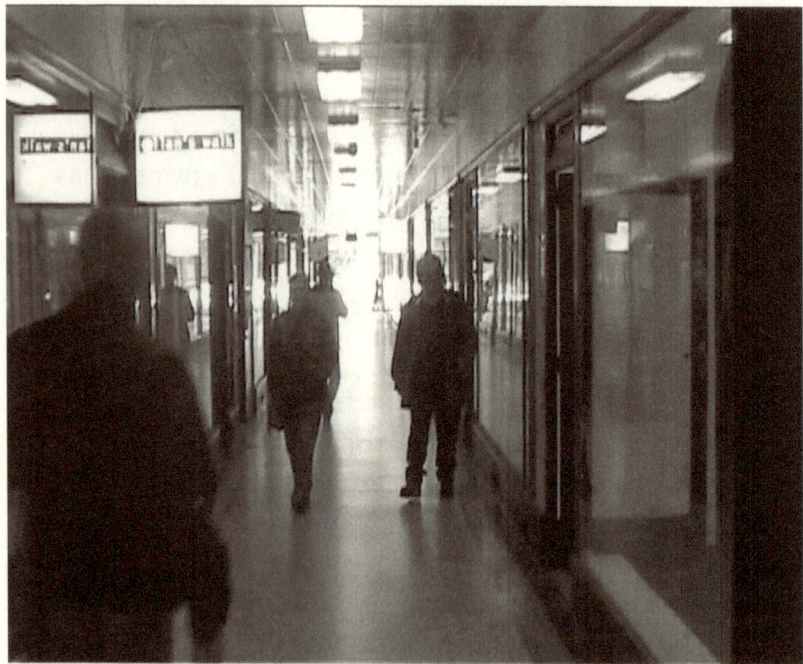

Figure 2.1 Andrew Goodman, *A Chorus of Idle Feet*, 2010. Digital video still. Allans Walk ARI, Bendigo.

rhythms) not through the submission of internal difference and organisation, as in a molar system, but precisely because it was internally flexible enough to accommodate intensive modulations. The initial force of movement driving the event was also molecularised, being transduced by various component machines into multiple new and potentially competing forces (see Figure 2.1).

What such a machine begins to produce is an event that is an exploration of its collective expressive capacities through the transduction of forces. At the same time, these explorations produce the machine itself. Thus, the two are, to some extent, co-produced, becoming implicit in each other's actualisation and potential: a 'concretisation' or structural unity and interdependence of components of the assemblage (Simondon 1980, 21). Such a shift in an interactive art-machine begins to move it away from the limited capacities of individual components, and from prescribed notions of either outcomes or of particular, pre-thought or fixed relations. This manner of thinking about machinic expressions performs a molecularisation onto the interactive event described. It splits the larger art machine into a series of smaller nested machines. Each has their own internal logic of working and are co-causally relational to other entities that their workings affect and are affected by. This understanding opens up a potential for thinking through both an increased movement of relations within the machine, and movement or transduction of the forces it modulates.

Overall this remains a fairly simple example. When considered on their own, most components of this interactive event – such as each individual light sensor – remained relatively predictable in their transduction of forces. However as forces were immanently transduced through multiple nested components over time, thus developing more and more relational entanglement, the assemblage evolved complexity at a higher level and began to generate potential beyond the capacities of these smaller components. My point here is that novelty might be achieved not through designing more technologically complex components, but through 'self-conditioning emergence' (Massumi et al 2009, 40). This requires a rethinking of the philosophical basis of design strategies so that relatively simple components might interact with one another to increase internal differences in the assemblage.

Structuring action and flow:
drift, autopoiesis and concretisation

These concepts of the minor, molecularisation, assemblage and machine form something of a basis from which to explore self-organisation in the participatory artwork, in essence being propositional to an event of the production of relation. From this point, in this chapter I address the questions of how an art event generates its own 'satisfaction'[90] through consideration of the concepts of drift and concretisation. This is extended in the next two chapters through the question of how the drive towards novelty might be maximised in the event through the key concepts for this book: a more detailed examination Whitehead's concept of 'feeling' as a productive differentiation from what has been, and the noise or parasite within relation.

Propositional invitations

To think of a relational art event in an open-ended fashion, we might think of the practicality of building it out of propositions. These propositions might be multiple, possibly contradictory. If sound 'A' can happen, or sound 'B' can occur, but not both sounds together, the sound that is not actualised still has, as Whitehead says, a creative role to play – both as a 'giveness' that shapes paths of potentiality, and as a continuing link to the virtual. The negated proposition remains a link, both to what might have happened or might in the future happen, and to the unrealised potential of an entity that 'vibrate(s) against the conformal' (1978, 188).

An entity, Whitehead states, 'feels as it does feel in order to be the actual entity it is' (1978, 222). The propositions composed within the art event are launching points, 'lures towards feelings' (259). These feelings are the prehensions (220) in which the drive toward 'satisfaction' is the realisation of some potentiality for the entity.[91] A feeling here is the potential for affectual connection, that is, an entity's potential capacity to be affected by, and affect other forces, entities or events. Thus, an inanimate entity might be seen as capable of a feeling (affecting and being affected by forces), and of driving towards its own satisfaction, as a sentient being.

A sensor, for example, might have the proposition of a tendency to notice movement. This movement may not happen. It is a potentiality, constrained by the given: its position, the mechanics of its construction, and so on. It has 'sensitivity' towards searching for this movement, a potential capacity to form a machinic connection with this force, the incoming sense data that drive its completion. It reaches a point of satisfaction of an occasion when it expresses this capacity for connection, whether it senses movement or not. These are exclusive potentials – and in any occasion, only one potential can be actualised while the other remains virtual.

Even simple and linear propositions are, in themselves, never fully conclusive. Any actualisation is only a singular iteration of that proposition's potential, and does not preclude further iterations arising. In this sense, although the outcome is conclusive for the particular event that actualises, the conclusion to a *proposition* is only approached, never realised. Thus while the individual event of the movement being sensed reaches satisfaction or an end-point, the proposition retains potential for further actualised iterations (DeLanda 2005, 75).

In a system with multiple exclusive and inclusive propositions, the outcomes become decidedly more non-linear and the virtual more evident as a factor within the system. The 'other alternatives are there all the time, *coexisting* with the one that happens to be actualized' (DeLanda 2005, 75, emphasis in the original) and creating a tension or problematisation that pulls the event towards further 'incompossible' actualisations. This increase in intensity is the line of flight from the prescribed event, in that it is a qualitative increase in relational potential within the system.

Propositions guide the dynamics of an event, though not in a prescriptive manner, creating tendencies (Bennett 2010, 103) and providing ongoing invitations or lures toward the potentialities of the event they condition. They instigate a 'second phase' of the virtual: that of a 'real' rather than the 'general' potentiality

(Whitehead 1978, 65), conditioning the potential by inclusion of the circumstances of the emergent event.[92] This is a gathering of, and complex negotiation between, the various individuated propositional potentials of all the machinic components, and it creates a *collective* propositional potential.

Thus while we might think of the artwork as a single entity or event, it is perhaps better viewed as a 'society'[93] of entities, divisible into multiple, overlapping and simultaneous events or entities, each seeking and competing for its own satisfaction. During actualisation, the event is always at a point of unfolding, facing multiple potential paths towards various satisfactions. These multiple and fluid assemblages – eyes/brain/image, ears/noise/speakers/current, software/sensor/movement data and so forth – are each divisible again, each seeking resolution of their feelings. This philosophical stance emphasises that art events are composed from the ground up. It provides an understanding that the concrescence of forces builds towards an endpoint of an actual event, discovered and motivated within the occasion itself by complexities of virtual and actual forces.

Seeing art as a propositional event begins to deflect the emphasis away from any final representational form, and to instead emphasise the ongoing role of the internal tension of the negated propositions and emergent differences in enriching the virtual of the event. Within interactive art, this suggests an experience focused on emergent qualities of relations in and of themselves. Here interactivity might begin to distinguish itself from goal-orientated 'gaming' directed towards solving a puzzle, moving through levels or controlling a space, and also from 'didactic' works directed towards a learning outcome, whether based on perception or content. Instead it might move into riskier areas, concerning itself with the setting of conditions that allow events to begin, and accepting the inherent danger that some desired and interesting outcomes and directions may not always eventuate.[94]

Self-organisation

How does the art event 'choose' which prehensions it follows through to satisfaction, and which entities will actualise? How can we think of this without falling back into prescriptive models? Having set itself into motion through its propositional structuring, and gained through feeling its own collective movement, the event is no longer beholden to any external intentions or drive – it must sort itself out internally. But it does not strive to be the best event it can – the most efficient, original or surprising. That would again imply some kind of transcendent motivation, a 'neo-Darwinist' thinking that assumes that entities or events are invested in, and capable of, striving for some preconceived ideal form or an outcome of maximum efficiency (Bogue 2003, 69–73).[95]

Rather, we could say, it 'drifts'. This implies a system, as Francesco Varela says, that 'makes do', seeking the 'viable' rather than the 'optimal' (1992, 205).[96] Such a system is 'pragmatic': its motivation is to find *a* satisfaction, not *the* satisfaction.[97] That is, it makes do with what it has, and cobbles together a solution. As Ronald Bogue states, systems self-organising through drift emphasise change or creativity over 'fitness' (2003, 74–5)[98]. They experiment with 'assemblage[s] of heterogeneous forms for no other reason than that they are possible' (75). Processes of drift enable systems to be truly interactive, as they are composed through that activity, rather than being representative of determined function or outcome (Varela 207, 209). Here drift is a molecular modelling of an event gathering and accentuating relational intensity within the emergent system, rather than containing such relational play in order to serve a central or molar design aim.

In drifting, a system demonstrates an agency that is clearly not attributable to any one (or indeed all) of its component parts that might then direct the unfolding of events. Rather any agency – if agency is viewed simply as the modulating and distributing of forces and relations – can be seen to be a collective expression of the event itself. Julian Yates terms this 'agentive drift', an agency that is a 'dispersed or distributed process in which we participate rather than a property which we are said to own' (2002, 48). Here drift is the dynamics of relations as they gather, a collective individuation with its own emergent and global virtual and actual organization (Bak 1997, 121; Varela, Thompson and Rosch 1992, 65).

Drift does not imply that such systems operate through random or chaotic connections, but that they create systems of intensive and local connection. For Murphie, this is a chaosmic interactivity that sits between chaos and stratification (2005b, 42). This might replace a system organised through a single dominant relational pull towards a future 'useful' and externally projected outcome – as much interactive art is designed – where differences becoming suppressed or flattened to serve a larger or dominant purpose. Systems in drift may lack or mitigate external motivation, but they gain a set of competing heterogeneous and *intensive* motivations. This encourages an immanent expressive exploration of the multiple potentials of relation within the assemblage through the play of subtle and complex dynamic modulation of internal forces.

In *A Chorus of Idle Feet*, changes to a small assemblage within this interactive system could be seen to affect the productive workings of many component assemblages, and the event as a whole. A change in light, for example, would affect the way electrons passed through the assemblage of a particular sensor, while also affecting other assemblages linking the sensor to sound vibrations emitted through speakers.[99] These vibrations potentially affected the larger assemblage of the art event by combining and diffracting with other sound waves being emitted, producing local shifts in the expressions of the speaker systems.[100] These might then affect both the rhythmic pulls of combinations of sounds, and the affective tonalities of the event.[101] Thus the productive expressions of the other component sensor-machines – those that were not directly affected by the changes in light – were potentially still altered through a series of complex implications that were relational, but not entirely predictable. In such a system, localised agitations or changes to flows affected surrounding assemblages and had a run-on effect, potentially spreading through and shifting much of the system's workings. Each component remained primarily responsive to its local connections, with no prescribed aim or outcome dictated by the original movement. A larger movement or circulation of forces in the system was created through emergent difference – contagious and rhizomic – instigating and gathering new combinations and *potential combinations* of co-dependent relations that the systems needed to negotiate.[102]

As a system operating through drift this was an open or dissipative system, 'in which momentary deployments of forces produce[d] systemic orderings, local eddies or drifts' (Yates 2002, 50). The system here sacrificed self-preservation as it drove towards creativity through the continued recombining of forces (Whitehead 1978, 103–5).[103] Such changes did not necessarily force a collapse in the system,[104] as there was a degree of consistency or dynamic equilibrium within the assemblage.[105] That is, it was a 'dynamic whole' with an ability to accommodate intensive changes, without necessarily causing destruction to the ability of the machines to communicate productively, even as it caused variations to the productive outcomes of the event.[106]

Drift has lured into being a system that is productive in a machinic sense, but not at all about a directed, idealised or maximised productivity. As each component assemblage responded to changes in its local systems of forces, there was a flow-on of repercussions that was not always entirely linear or predictable – an excess and freedom of relation that may, as Massumi and Manning state, reorientate exchange. Such systems are therefore principally about self-production, the experience of the components gathering together, an 'emergence of [a] field of relation' (Manning and Massumi 2014, 128). It is also always a 'minor' act that is a reorganization of available entities into new relationships, and more than the inclusion of new factors.

A system in drift is involved in a process of increased 'concretisation'. As Simondon thinks the concept, concretisation is a process exclusive to technical (as opposed to 'natural') entities. However here I would argue that it is possible to see it more generally as a process by which a set of entities are brought into increased co-causal relationship with each other. For Simondon concretisation involves a system in which each component 'is part of a system in which a multitude of forces are exercised and in which effects are produced that are independent of the design plan' (1980, 31). In this, concretisation relates directly to a process of drift in what Simondon terms a 'natural object'. That is, both set up circular, coherent systems of distributed agency expressing potentials rather than being driven by external factors (Simondon 1980, 40-1). Such systems attain some level of structural unity, Simondon states, with each element co-determining, becoming implicit in what other elements become. It requires that the component parts develop a 'plurality of function' and negotiate their operations, rather than fulfilling a predesigned or 'ideal' function (Simondon 1980, 20-1).[107] It is precisely because of the presence of potential indeterminacy – a flexibility of future relations, rather than a fixed and linear set of actualised relations – that machines are able to develop such self-organizing capacities (Simondon 1980, 13-14).[108]

While the components in a machine retain their individual potentials, it is the shared potentials that they develop through machinic operations – their shared 'associated milieu' – that forms a base for their collective individuations through drift.[109] This is the drawing of elements from a field as a 'system of virtualities, of potentials, of moving forces' (Simondon 1980,

51) into a field of relation. These processes of drift do not just happen within established concrete assemblages. Rather, the drift itself can be seen to draw disparate components into productive relation. Creating dynamic systems of drift must strive to be not simply making connections between component parts through actualised systems of feedback and (flexible) causal chains, but also need to enable conditions for the continued disruption of relations.[110]

In the example above, the light sensor-machine began to exhibit an ongoing potential to form a relationship with, for example, the sound waves produced by the pressure sensor-electron flow-computer-speaker assemblage that moderated both expressions of vibration. It was not limited in the ways or number of actualisations of the expression of this relationship; nor was it limited to this particular multiplicitous set of light sensor-machine to pressure-sensor machine relations. Entities gathered from a field of potential relation, into an actualised relation with each other, retaining potential for different future individuations.[111] It is at this level of potentiality that such a system continues to exhibit its molecular or minor nature. Such a gathered, collective, virtual milieu it is always sensitively balanced on the point of reorganisation – that is, a deterritorialisation and a reterritorialization.

Relational art events capable of drift might take many forms, creating many differing events. For interactivity, this does not mean that drift drives towards making events necessarily different. Such systems are indifferent to the quality or quantity of difference they generate. Importantly, they are indifferent to the *demonstration* of change and relation that haunts so many interactive works – the problematic focus on representation over open exploration. Systems in drift settle where they settle. On some days, the events generated in a work may be markedly variable, on others the work might seem to settle around the same outcomes. The artist must relinquish some control over this, leaving or encouraging it to work itself out: it does what it does, whether disappointing on one occasion and surprising the next. Perhaps this is the most challenging shift in thinking for an artist: creating a place for the participant in an event that is an 'active ecology' without, as Manning says, 'necessarily putting the participant in the role of direct activator of change' (2013a, 130).

Thinking in terms of drift requires designing interactive systems that are composed of components capable of retaining flexibility in the *order* in which they affect other entities, the *ways* in which they affect entities, and the *direction* in which such affectual relations operate. What is required is the invention of 'techniques for the proliferation of drifts', rather than the placement of a specific drifting in the event (Manning 2013a, 200).

None of this is to promote self-organisation as the be-all and end-all, as it is of course a dominant characteristic of capitalism, subsuming all to an equivalence of exchange (in this sense it is molar while still self-organising).[112] Here an *ethics* of interactivity and self-organisation needs careful consideration. This leads to the key questions of this book: how to propose systems that can continue to express creative potential of differentiation, while maximising their relational interdependence. It is in seeking practical solutions to this issue that the next two chapters examine the capacities of entities to express feeling, and the potential of noise within relation to act as a force of intensive differentiation.

3

Once more with feeling: Whitehead's concept of feeling and a trans-human ethics

> Each task of creation is a social effort, employing the whole universe.
> *Alfred North Whitehead*

> Whitehead's world is one of worlds, plural.
> *Andrew Murphie*

Introduction

The turn towards the relational as outlined in the previous chapters is still far too general and abstract for the practical task I wish to explore in this book – that of a pragmatic thinking through of how the relational might be utilised across a number of scales of activity in applicable artworks. For Whitehead, as Andrew Murphie notes, 'relation' is a term abstracted from the held 'contrasts' that are constitutive of an entity's becoming (2016, 21).[113] Here what we might generally call 'relations' are rather 'the gathering together, maintenance and creation [of] new contrasts – differential intensities' (Murphie 2016, 21). In this view the world is composed of these gatherings of feelings, intensity and differentials (Murphie 2016, 21), and Whitehead's schema investigates such gatherings in detail. In this chapter I wish to outline this system of prehension (positive and negative feeling) – emphasising the role of intensity in Whitehead's ontology. In the next chapter I refine it for my purposes through the use of Serres' concept of the parasite as a particular way of conceiving of these held and productive differentials that Whitehead argues are the constitutive dynamics of relation. These concepts will then be put to use in the following chapters as the basis of a rethinking of interactivity along the lines of differential ecologies.

If interactive art has had a tendency to present rigid models with very prescribed and contained notions of relational potential, Whitehead's concept of 'feeling' perhaps offers a way to think beyond this. This might be particularly useful in assisting a move beyond the predictable or prescribed result and into a realm that is more open-ended and process based. It might also assist a move towards an expanded concept of interactivity or participation that thinks both of the relative freedom of the participants in this encounter, while also considering all the various components of the artwork and their freedom of expression. Thus, as Murphie proposes, there is a need to develop a 'syntax of feeling', through which we might 'open up the world to itself, or, more correctly, open up the possibility of participating differentially in the dynamic ecologies of the world' (2016, 12). In this sense such a concern might broadly be thought of as post-human, though perhaps the term 'trans-human' is more suitable,[114] since the interest here is the expansion of the human beyond fixed identity, *alongside* the expansion of the potential of the field and all participant components of an event to co-produce novelty or 'individuate'.[115] I will refer to this as an ethics, in that it seeks a right for all components to fully express their capacity to 'feel'. This is a concept I return to later in the chapter and which permeates the more general rethinking of interactivity in the book as a whole. In this chapter the concept of feeling and its trans-human implications are, after a more general discussion of Whitehead's theory, read first through thinking the potential of inanimate entities (rocks) to feel, secondly through the implications of Charles Darwin's study of worms for ideas of the location of a non-human 'intelligence', and lastly through a discussion of the induction drawings of Australian artist Joyce Hinterding.

The Whiteheadian concept of 'feeling', as Judith Jones states, repudiates the idea 'that existing objects have determinate, sharp existential boundaries' (1998, 162). This is replaced by a complex system of relation that emphasises the autonomy (or 'subjectivity' in Whitehead's terms) of the becoming of an entity. Whiteheadian autonomy, however, always acknowledges the ways in which such becoming draws on both the actualised environment from which an entity emerges, and the role of the virtual as an equally real, if differently composed and operative, influence on becoming.

For Whitehead – as for James with his concept of radical empiricism that admits all experience, including relations, as equally real – it is of utmost importance to develop an ontology with a consistency in philosophical abstraction of reality without resort to exceptions, applicable to all entities and events (Stenner 2008, 99). Feeling, as the basis of his system of becoming, must then be applicable to all entities, as must the acknowledgment that each entity feels in its own particular way.[116] And thus, from this world-view, if you and I can 'feel' and make 'choices', so, in their own specific way, can a rock, a bird, an electron, or as Darwin argued, a worm.

Feeling

For Whitehead's organic philosophy, nothing is inert: everything is engaged in processes of becoming, changing, emerging, marching towards novelty. All things, Whitehead states, are capable of feelings (1978, 220), sensitivities that allow them to navigate, to form workable assemblages, and to become with their environment. Such feelings are not necessarily conscious, and in fact the vast majority are not conscious. Thus feelings are as relevant to entities without consciousness and they do not privilege sentience or the living over inanimate entities. Nor is feeling attached to preformed entities (Manning 2013a, 21). Rather, this is feeling as a force gathering towards form, immanent with the occasion, moving with the event. In this sense for Whitehead's 'atomic' philosophy, actuality is only this act of an entity's in-forming or 'concrescence': the gathering of physical and conceptual feelings into one subjective form.[117] Once this resolves into the 'satisfaction' of the entity (though such resolution, as discussed below, does not involve the erasure of the differences between the gathered feelings but their productive contrast from the point of view of the entity), it in one sense ceases to be, although it continues to exert influence through its potential to be felt by future entities in their own concrescent processes.[118]

In this complex theory of 'prehension' Whitehead outlines processes of becoming based on this concept of feeling.[119] Two aspects of this theory are of particular important for the purposes of this discussion. Firstly, the concept emphasises the inevitable emergent condition of existence. That is, there is an ongoing, unceasing process of individuation that all actualising events are involved in. Secondly, this emergence involves choice or selection from a larger potential (on a largely if not entirely non-conscious level), and therefore it is always a differentiation. Here process is a creative event of formation of an entity as potential is transformed into actuality (Guattari and Rolnik 2005, 311). Thus feelings are always cuts – choices, points of divergence or nascent novelty – that differentiate both from the potential data drawn from that which is already actualised and from the data drawn from the larger virtual or ongoing planes of potential. These cuts are made intensively, by an entity for its own satisfaction rather than in any way beholden to external interests.

To explain this, here I briefly outline aspects of the process of 'concrescence' as Whitehead calls becoming or actualisation. Concrescence is a process by which an emergent entity, occasion or event[120] draws a disparate or disjunctive selection of datum from the world into 'the real unity of one actual entity' (Whitehead 1978, 22). Thus in an ecology this entity is a nexus or 'one complex feeling' (Whitehead 1978, 44) at which a number of potentials meet. From the perspective of the field this nexus represents one novel solution to a feeling for the field in its entirety[121] that reflects its own perspective on the universe and has some connection, however remote, to all that is actualised.[122] Every prehension consists for Whitehead of three factors, the 'subject' prehending, the datum prehended and the 'subjective form' or the way in which that datum is prehended by the subject – that is, the selection or choice that is made and that leads towards novelty (Whitehead 1978, 23).

Feeling is a force gathering towards form, immanent with the occasion, moving the event (Manning 2013a, 21). Feelings are not relations between things. Rather the entity is a singular concrescence of feelings: an event of synthesising or patterning of formally disparate relations at one point in the field (Whitehead 1978, 232). The relation, from the point of view of the subject prehending, is a feeling: its own perspective or subjective take on the other entity. As Whitehead states, feelings 'aim at their subject' rather than being 'aimed at' their subject (1978, 222)[123]: they are generated and owned by the forming entity, not projected by any external agent. For Whitehead, becoming is an act of self-enjoyment, and the entity is in this sense *self-realizing*, transcending the entities that already exist and adding to the novelty of the universe (1978, 222).

It is important, however, not to think of this gathering of various feelings (concrescence) or the end-point resolution of this gathering (satisfaction) as erasing differences between those feelings, either extensively or intensively. In the former case the datum prehended is objectively available for other events of concrescence, within which portions of it will be accommodated and other portions excluded (negatively prehended), creating with this datum new complex feelings that express their difference to previous entities. The potential for further differentiation always exists.

In the case of intensive difference, this is a more complex matter that might be overlooked. In her writing Jones attempts to bring this to the fore, positing 'intensity', defined as 'the compression of multiplicity in an individual unity', as the key to understanding Whitehead's ontology (1998, 157).[124] Whitehead uses the term 'contrast', which Jones defines as 'the positive relation of two or more discrete elements in the complex feeling involved in concrescence' (1998, 12). That is, differing select datum from the world are made compatible (though only in the instance of a particular concrescence). Here the 'richness' of an entity's becoming depends on its ability to positively involve the maximum amount of datum in this pattern of contrasts and therefor maximise intensity (Jones 1998, 12, 17, 36). Contrast is therefore 'unity in difference', preserving these differences but finding a 'self-consistency' of the many in the one (Jones 1998, 56).[125] These 'held' contrasts do not, as Murphie notes, need to be resolved, but exist productively as a differential 'pattern' (2016, 20),[126] internal to and constitutive of the subjective form (Jones 1998, 102). This patterning consists of four factors contrasted into a pattern of relevance: 'triviality and vagueness' (the contrast terms for the prehension of a background of a becoming), and 'narrowness and width' (contrasts of which determine the foreground) (Jones 1998, 38).

Here relation *is* this gathering and holding of contrasts, not a simple connectivity. Events come together but remain atomic (a 'disparate multitude' and a subjective self-creation) (Massumi 2011, 20–1). Without this intensity, there can be no relation.[127] Intensity or contrast is therefore a problematic structure, a partial solution that is productive (of variation) rather than resolvant. Such intensities continue to be productive after the perishing of an entity in that these patterns are inherited through their ingression into future acts of concrescence (creating 'contrasts of contrasts') (Jones 1998, 40).

This intensive organisation is always the entity's self-motivated choice or selection from potential. This point cannot be over emphasised I think, as it provides a way out of a static universe of things in which only select 'special' entities, such as humans, are seen to have choice or agency. This separation of the human from the rest of matter underpins our supposed authority to command nature, and denies the validity of listening to the expressions and forming relations of all events. In this sense Whitehead's philosophy might be seen to be post (or trans-) human, though in reality it is also post object in emphasising relation and process over form.

As Murphie points out, Whitehead's system flips traditional Western notions of subjectivity around: no longer is the subject 'somewhat separate from the world', but rather 'it begins to head towards an actual occasion' (2016, 11). Subjectivity is not exactly erased in this thinking, but is seen as emerging from the acts of selection that take place in concrescence.[128] Indeed to look for truly individual subjects begins to look like the wrong question.[129] Firstly, this is true because, for Whitehead, an entity perishes on completion of its concrescence ('it never really is') (Whitehead, cited Jones 1998, 101). Secondly, this 'character' is trans-entity, in that it is then present in other entities' 'achieved intensive character' (Jones 1998, 100).

Subjectivity exists here as 'subjective form' or 'character' in the act of concrescence: the acts of feeling, valuation and patterning of physical datum and virtual forces into an entity's own particular take on the universe. Thus it would seem to more radically complicate notions of agency than philosophical moves simply assigning agency to non-human and inanimate objects.[130] 'Agency' can be a problematic term, with a tendency to imply the primacy of 'agents' as discrete, independent and stable entities positively exerting force, while somehow remaining internally immune to change.[131] This isolates objects, Jones claims, and is Whitehead's key issue with philosophies of substance, which again position relation (and its component parts) as secondary (Jones 1998, 95). Indeed, Jones argues, the search for agency either naively seeks this false separateness, or pessimistically abandons any concept of will or power as per some post-modern approaches. Whitehead, on the other hand, maintains what she terms 'an ethical spirit of hope and adventure' (1978, 176–7), and it is this ethical spirit of the potential for novelty in all events that this discussion of feeling is attempting to channel.

In Whitehead's system agency is situated in the event. This does not imply an externality of control, but that agency is intensive, in the making of evaluations as to the relevance of datum for an entity's own concrescence (Jones 1998, 88). That is, the agency is in the ability to create productive contrasts. Thus it is both 'borrowed and new at the same time': drawing on the valuations and ordering of prehensions by previous entities and imposing in some manner 'on all subsequent process' (Jones 1998, 129, 131). Therefore it never truly belongs to objects or entities, even with Whitehead's expanded field of creativity. At best agency is a condition of the emerging ecology itself.

Entities indeed do have a very real connection to all of the emerging ecology. As Whitehead states categorically, it takes a whole universe to make an event or entity. This can be seen, firstly, in that as an entity establishes a relationship both to those objects that it directly draws data from, it also draws in a 'second-hand' manner from entities whose data went into the formation of this object. Therefore, in a more and more mediated and remote fashion, the entity forms a relation to all actualised entities and their histories. Thus a prehension is always complex, capable of being divided into other prehensions in indefinite numbers that reach a singular resolution as a pattern of contrasts in any particular entity but never preclude other potential resolutions from arising.

Secondly, relation includes not only the complex layering of selected prehensions as discussed above, but also 'negative' prehensions. That is, prehension consists not only of positive relations or feelings – whose selection constitutes the data that forms its concrescence – but also the act of *not selecting* other data, again a choice or differentiation from what has been. In this, it establishes a richness and complexity that allows it to (negatively) retain relation to all, if only as the 'scars' or 'impressions of what it might have been' (Whitehead 1978, 226–7).[132]

Lastly, as well as drawing on these actualised objects for data ('physical' prehensions), an in-forming entity also draws conceptually on some of what Whitehead terms 'eternal objects'. These are pure and indefinite qualities such as 'redness', 'hardness' and 'warmth' or, for the 'higher level' entities amongst us, 'lust' and 'despair'.[133] These qualities are felt as objects. That is, what is felt is their 'capacity for being a realised determinant of a process' (Whitehead 1978, 239). Through this ingression of eternal essences or qualities (and contrasts between them) an entity conceptually modifies or evaluates its feelings of the actual world, creating another layer of complexity in the concrescence (Jones 1998, 45–6, 59; Whitehead 1978, 240–1).[134]

Once actualised an entity continues to ingress on proceedings by acting as datum for the concrescent processes of other entities, functioning 'as an object' to be felt in these events (Whitehead 1978, 220). Here it transcends itself and is further enmeshed or integrated into the ecology out of which it has emerged. The seemingly contradictory values of processes of personal satisfaction and objectification (being 'a unity' in its own subjective form, but in being 'divisible' objectification by other concrescences) of course overlap in complex ways and cannot, Jones' argues, be sharply separated on an ontological level, as individuation is never a linear or simple process (1998, 52, 88). Here feelings are never entirely clear and distinct, 'overlapping, subdividing [and] supplementary to each other' (Whitehead 1978, 235), as well as being divisible into other feelings. Conceptual and physical feelings may also 'hybridize' each other through treating other feelings in the event as objects to be felt (Whitehead 1878, 246). In this way they might be thought of as 'nested': as a series of contrasts or intensities that are 'implicated in one another, each in turn both enveloped and enveloping' (Deleuze 1994, 252; Jones 1998 48–50).

Rocks

If we accept Whitehead's challenge and carry this concept to its limit – beyond entities with attributes easy to anthropomorphise, such as animals and plants – we can ask instead: what does a rock in a stream feel? To which forces are its sensitivities tuned: rain, salts, acids, wind, tides, heat? How does the becoming form of the rock instigate new force – shape the wind, give new direction to the current, absorb or dissolve salt solutions? We begin to see the rock-world relation anew: the rock's continued fielding in the world – its continued effect on or transduction of the ecology's forces – and the field's continuous expression through the force of the rock, becomes an ecology of operations. We learn from the 'wisdom of rocks, from which we can derive an ethics involving the notion that, ultimately, we too are fluxes of matter and energy' (DeLanda 1992, 143).[135]

But the rock does not only feel the flow of the river, its chemical composition and the rain. Through mediation[136] it also feels the waterfall further upstream through the waterfall's effects on the flow and mix of sediment stirred up from the river bottom.

It feels the mountain at the birth of the river through its various effects on the river over time. It feels the change of season on this mountain top through the melting of the snow, the birth of fish and their thrashing, the splash of a bird hunting in the water and so on, all at various degrees of remove and impact, through the water. And conceptually the rock also feels and selects from qualities of rockiness, hardness, wetness, and heat, exploring some potentiality of these concepts through a selection that inserts them into actual events, valuating to some degree its experience of the actual. And, the rock selects *not* to feel other events: both the actual, such as the ticking of the clock in your house and your thoughts of lunch, and the conceptual: lust, anger, depression.

The valuation and admission of the various positive prehensions is more than a modifying factor; they constitute the rock's becoming – for it to 'not only *have* but to *be* a perspective on the world' (Jones 1998, 36, emphasis in the original). The rock has its own singular take on or positive logic of all the feelings that are deemed relevant to its concrescence. Its neighboring rock may also feel the melting of the snow and the movement of the fish upstream, but each evaluates these factors from its own perspective and according to its own appetite for becoming.[137]

Each rock valuates the positive feelings according to their importance for its concrescence (its triviality, vagueness, narrowness and width), and scales or contrasts these into a pattern of relevance, seeking the required depth of held intensity: the 'inequalit[ies] by which it is measured' (Deleuze 1994, 222). Thus for our rock the movement of a upstream fish may be a trivial feeling, felt through its momentary effect in the very slight variation in current, but a smaller stone at the epicenter of this disturbance feels the full force of the fish's fins and is lifted off the riverbed and flows downstream – not a trivial feeling at all from its perspective. Similarly backgrounded for the rock in question may be the vaguely felt movements of the individual leaves of a tree in the water – 'vague' in their indistinctness from one another (Jones 1998, 35, 38). 'Narrowness' and 'width' constitute the more foregrounded assessments of feelings (though all the terms are interrelated). It is a balancing act between a certain 'narrowness' of scope that is necessary – a value judgment that allows prehensions deemed less relevant to be backgrounded sufficiently (becoming the relatively trivial and vague) – and sufficient 'width' of ingression of those feelings deemed important for satisfactory depth of feeling and complexity of intensity to be achieved, and for sufficient 'thematic unity' for the rock to achieve the status of this particular novel entity in the world. These feelings are contrasted and patterned according to the rock's entertaining of its own 'ideal of itself' – in other words, in relation to its conceptual prehension of relevant eternal objects such as rockiness, solidity and so on (Jones 1998, 38).

We might easily accept this conditioning of the rock in relation to its given actual circumstances and its potential expressions during its overt formation, such as rock formed by lava flows molded in relation to landscape, water and climate. But part of the challenge Whitehead demands is that we consider the rock to be continually recomposed through events of concrescence and perishing.[138] Here the rock as a whole is a 'society' of smaller and briefly becoming events or entities (Whitehead 2014, Chapter III). Admittedly this is a society without great internal difference and, from a human scale of attention, with a very slow rate of differentiation, but it is a significant step from thinking of an entity as that which goes through a becoming phase to arrive at a 'pure' object status that is outside of this individuation (a downfall in the logic of many philosophies, as Whitehead seeks to demonstrate). Here Whitehead's 'societies' are nexus 'with social order'. That is, they have 'common element[s] of form' that are 'imposed' on all the member entities by their positive prehension of other members of the same society (Whitehead 1978, 34).[139] Within this 'atomic' conception of entities the rock retains at least some potential for change and ongoing selection or choice.[140] There is always room for differentiation to occur, and there are always prehensive relations of the world that tie the becoming-rock to the ecology with which it gathers.[141]

Worms

Another humble entity worth consideration, although in this case an animate one, is the earthworm. Charles Darwin devoted many years of study and an entire book to the worm, utilising a rigorously empirical methodology that lead him to an understanding of the very real and complex interactions and forces informing the worms' lives and their impact on the human world.[142]

However of most interest here are the sections of the study in which Darwin explores the 'intelligence' of the worm, an intelligence evidenced by their creative and non-teleological interactions with their ecology. While worms clearly have limited capacities to sense and interact with their environment, being blind, deaf (though sensitive to vibration), and possessing a limited sense of smell, to Darwin this does not mean that their actions cannot move beyond pure instinct or habit. Through a detailed study of the way that worms utilise leaves, Darwin seeks to show that worms have a capacity for creative self-determinacy. The worms appear to be able to adapt very quickly to unfamiliar types of leaves and to invent ways to attach to leaves, to drag them along the ground and to utilise them to plug the entrances and line their burrows. In doing this they develop novel capacities for solving the problems that are incurred with particular leaves – for example, plugging a burrow with pine needles for the first time rather than a broad leaf, or handling a leaf with an unfamiliar petiole (Darwin 1881, 59–60). Here perhaps we could say that the worms are able to successfully assess and pattern their prehensions of the capacities of the leaves in relation to the various conceptual qualities needed carry and to plug their burrows.

Darwin concludes firstly that the worms' approach to these new challenges cannot be explained by any logic of inheritance or habit. Secondly, he argues that the worms' abilities to utilise novel materials successfully are not based on methods involving either significant elements of chance or trial and error, which might also eventually result in the worms discovering a suitable method for handling the leaves. Rather, the worms appear able to perceive and creatively engage with difference in thinking through the best way to drag and utilise the leaves (Dawrin 1881, 73–4, 92–3).

Any argument that the lowly worm acts always or entirely purely for survival as an ultimate aim seems to be unsustainable when faced with this evidence. Whereas a neo-Darwinist approach might argue that a worm's capacities are all pre-formulated with survival as its entire domain of enquiry (a worm is blind because it has no 'use' for sight, and so on), in fact the worm is involved in a creative enquiry *with* its environment. Here it pays to remember that in Whitehead's system the leaves have feelings too, as does the borrow, and that the worm's prehension of leaf and burrow opening are, through mediation, also prehensions to some degree of these other entities' subjective take on their worlds. The worm's capacities are always forming-with or immanent to its emergent ecology through acts of feeling-with. These capacities are creative in that they are open-ended to a certain extent, never reaching a state of full formation, desirous of novelty rather than limited to survival or directed towards any one simple perfect worm-form[143] (an ur- or uber-worm perfectly able to exploit its environment[144]). The worm, in other words, has plenty of wriggle room.

For Darwin the worms demonstrate 'some degree of intelligence' in their activities (98).[145] But the worms are not writing philosophy or sonnets on love, so in this context, what exactly does the intelligence mean? I would suggest that what the worms demonstrate is an ability to tune with their environment on a profound level. In other words, they have the capacity to 'feel' or prehend the potential in worm-leaf-burrow interactions (a resonance or intensification of potentials[146]), to compose relevant contrasts out of this information (to pattern), and to make creative selections or choices immanent with their actions, tastes and needs (to valuate). Here the usage of the leaves in the burrow is a nexus of possibilities that resolves some potential of the worms, leaves and burrow's collective capacities into an event with its own subjective expression (necessarily composed also of all the negative prehensions of what is not selected or actualised). These collecting feelings making up an ecological intelligence that is immanent with, and belongs more *to*, the event, as a bringing together of potentials and capacities, rather than belonging to the worms[147] – just as the intelligence of juggling belongs in the moment of conversation between balls, hands, gesture, gravity and performativity rather than the identity of the juggler.

In this we might also say, in the styles of interior decorating the worms develop in collaboration with the leaves to line their burrows, that they exhibit a (pragmatic) creativity, which again goes beyond simple need or survival. As much of Alphonso Lingis' writing seeks to demonstrate, here there is a joy in living or self-production – in feeling with the world – that is an essential creativity.[148] Just as the individuation of the rock becomes more complex and resonate the more we consider its capacities and their expressions-with its ecology, so the worms' choices can never be fully explained in simple terms of need: there is a non-teleological, qualitative desire at work in the event, composed as it is of feelings that prehend and play with potentials.

Ethics

If morality is the relinquishing of individual freedom in favour of alignment with a prescribed concept of good that then constrains as it is applied blanket-like over all (a generalised righteousness), then ethics is perhaps in many ways the opposite, an 'augmentation of the power to live in this world' (Massumi 1992, 108; Deleuze and Guattari 1987, 256–7).[149] That is, it deals not with the system-wide or universal but with the specific, local and emergent: with, in other words, a politics. This, as Manning states, is a procedural and emergent politics rather than a politics of control exercised by subjects over life (Manning 2013a, 147). It is therefore 'attentiveness to the conditions of the event expressing itself' (Manning 2013a, 148): a force of becoming that is also always in itself open to new feelings that might affect and overlay its individuation.

In this, ethics is affirmative. The negative movement of morality might diminish or flatten relationality, composed as it is of capacities to 'express the high levels of interdependence' of entities. Ethics, on the other hand, emphasises the expression of entities' capacities to prehend and the power of their positive ingression to create novelty (Braidotti 2010, 226). For Whitehead, as Jones states, the system of prehension is a system of ethics in that it is a 'commitment to attentiveness about our world', both in terms of acknowledgment of the role of broad experience, *and* of the singular intensive character of each event. It does not level out experiences of the world as morality might seek to do, but adds to it, if addition is thought of as the addition of further contrast or difference (1998, 85).[150] Here Whitehead's system approaches ethics in that it requires attention to 'the general good' (Whitehead 1978, 15). This attention to other realities and perspectives is the very contrast that is 'internal to the being of the agent, and thus integral and ultimate to any action'. This concept of ethics eliminates both notions of the passivity of the non-sentient or non-biological, and 'the exaggerated sense of ourselves in as some kind of special freedom-nature in the cosmos' (Jones 1998, 85).

As Lone Bertelsen has suggested, such ethics might be the beginning of 'ecological responsibility', a 'shared attentiveness and an affective field established across space, bodies and objects' (2012, 39). Perhaps, as Darwin did, there is a need for humans to listen more closely to the non-human and consider more carefully the potential of non-human capacities. If we think these capacities and individuations from the perspective of the field more than from any object, then we may arrive at a transhuman sympathy that recognises not only the capacities of rocks and worms, but also a human potential for greater resonance with the ecology. This might be the very tentative beginnings of a different kind of sympathetic exploration that could also instigate our own adventure into greater expressive freedom: an ethics as relevant to rocks and worms (more specifically of rock-*ing* and worm-*ing*), that is an expanded ethics of differential 'life potentials' (Massumi and McKim 2009, 12).

Joyce Hinterding's *Induction Drawings*

When it comes to applying these ideas of capacities to feel (powers to select and self satisfy) to art, what is it that we might be looking for? Perhaps it is an art that plays with and off specific difference, concerns itself with flux, with an in-forming. Perhaps it is to seek an artwork that allows space for the emergence of feelings of its component events, which might seek not to impose a human-centered perspective or entertainment but instead might favour an entertaining of an environment by (and for) itself. This might be a paying-attention-to (a listening) and making space and/or time for different scales of interaction, different capacities to ingress into proceedings as nascent eruptions of difference.

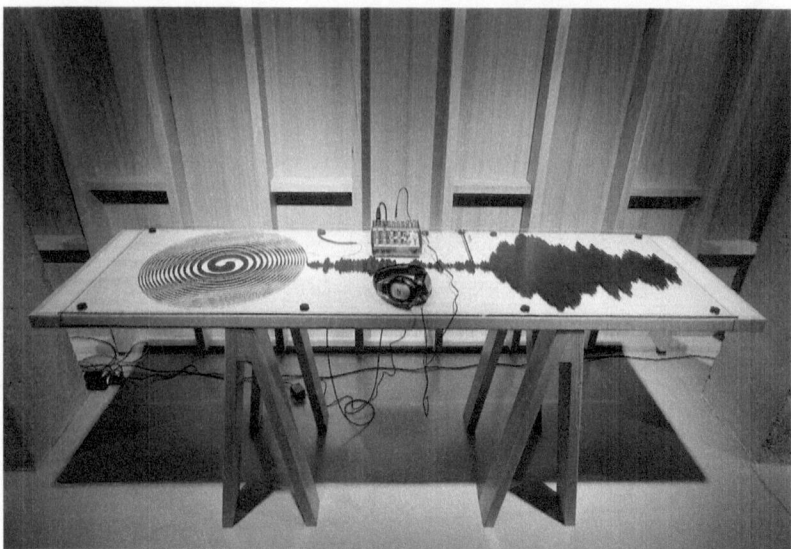

Fig. 3.1 Joyce Hinterding, Soundwave: Induction Drawings, 2012

Joyce Hinterding's *Induction Drawings* (see Figure 3.1), I propose, might exhibit just such characteristics and concerns. In these works Hinterding makes continuous graphite drawings on paper, wires them up (*sans* microphone), via amplification to a speaker system. The graphite forms a continuous conductive loop through which an electrical charge can move, when such a charge occurs its fluctuations are converted into speaker vibrations and thus heard as sound.[151] The sounds heard in the work are the result of the phenomenon of electromagnetic induction: sensitivity within the drawing loops to the differentials of fields of magnetic flux that causes a current to be generated in the graphite 'circuit' (induction loop). The natural phenomena of induction occurs when one potentially electro-conductive closed system (such as the graphite drawing) is in close proximity to an electromagnetic field (such as a body, a voltage loop or magnet), and a sympathetic or parasitic resonance occurs that causes a transient current in the first system. It is a resonance – two energies in communication (Deleuze 2002a, 65) – not the same electromagnetic force flowing between the systems. Each is self-determining. This resonance occurs only through differentiation:

it is only *change* in the original electromagnetic field that causes a sympathetic voltage to flow in the induction system.

Multiple factors are drawn together – selected and felt – by an induction loop (in this case the graphite drawing) in order to create the inductive current. That is, the event of the inductive charge is drawn from a concrescence or patterning of a number of other events or actualisations that act as objects for the insipient induction: the strength of the electromagnetic field, the area that this covers, and its rate of change (and the electromagnetic field is, as an event itself, already a subjective synthesis of all the various emitters of magnetic force in the vicinity that are valuated as relevant – bodies, machines, electronic devices, magnets and so on). This is Faraday's law of induction, where induced electromotive force in any closed circuit is equal to the rate of change of the magnetic flux enclosed by the circuit.[152] This law is a differential equation, expressing an immanent contrast (difference differing) between the three key objects from which datum is prehended by the induction event: an event that expresses a particular and subjective patterning of this datum as intensity.

The induction is atomic, constantly reinventing itself in relation to the changing conditions. Like the worms, this induction is a kind of ecological intelligence. It is not in any way related to human or worm intelligence and experience, but the induction loop's own ingression into the ecology with which it individuates, an expression of its capacity to prehend relevant differences differing and to put this datum to use to satisfy its own concrescence.

Two contrasts are needed to produce this induction: firstly, a rate of change in magnetic field *from the position or subjective view of the induction loop*[153] (an individuating difference that is qualitative and intensive), and secondly, a contrast in the angles of the two fields that meet (that is, between the electromagnetic field and the induction loop, with the two flows at an angle to each other). A new contrast is always produced in that the resulting induction loop flows in opposition to the original electromagnetic field. Such held contrasts operate problematically (being unresolved) and productively (producing the novelty of induction out of this ongoing prehensive differentiation or intensity). The potential for such contrasts is, according to Whitehead, the precondition of relations (1978, 228–31). That is, this potential operates as a future resonance (the necessary conditions of the field for prehension to occur), or intensity, which is the drawing together or nexus of contrasts or differences brought together as the subjective feelings – in this case, of this particular event of induction.[154]

But, in order to be true to an ethics of attention to all potential events in their own right, we must also acknowledge that the induction/flow of electrons is not simply a property belonging to the graphite drawing/induction circuit, but is an event in and of itself. It has its own selfish relationship to viewer, drawing, electromagnetic field and so on, and its own patterning of contrasts (as on an atomic level there is a patterning of electrons – a ferromagnetic ordering – in magnetised materials under the influence of electro-magnetic force[155]). As Isabelle Stengers notes, since Faraday's discoveries, 'the electromagnetic field has exhibited properties irreducible to those of a force "between" two charged and localized bodies' (2011, 101), and the charge here is 'a quantitative character' of the event rather than a property of any electron (Whitehead cited Stengers 2011, 101).[156] It is this 'character' that Hinterding lets loose – allowing its voice to be heard, its ingression into events to be expressed.

Alongside this event of induction, every component entity of the work has, amongst other feelings, its own subjective feeling of the other components to draw from: the speakers feel and pattern variation in current in the graphite loop, human movements are affected by eruptions of sound, and molecules of graphite feel the negative charge of electrons. Whilst every element draws datum from the others (and draws conceptually from the abstract qualities of flux, vibration, line, volume and so on), it is not possible to say that one exactly follows another in a linear manner. That is, they cannot draw in a simple way from resolved entities as 'objects'. The activities of concrescence are nested within each other. Potentials (individuations) are intertwined and co-dependent, it is an emergence that gathers (contrasts, relations, feelings, concrescence), and a concreteness that continues to become.

The induction loop-event is one particular tuning into the world that this artwork highlights. But it also, I think, encourages other sensitivities to be explored, allowing other expressions to be heard and expanded on such as touch, movements and sounds. All of these are events that can be thought of as not only between entities but constituting the very feelings of which these entities are (re)composing. What is foregrounded and made felt, by both the drawing and through mediation by the viewer, is the continued ingression of one event into another. This is communication across (trans) entities – a resonance between certain qualities (orderings of feelings). This might operate between a viewer's electromagnetic field and a potential of the graphite line to carry charge, or between the speed – the style of movement – and the volume and pitch of acoustic vibrations of the speakers.

What might be felt in part by the viewer as they interact with the installation is their presence as an object, in the Whiteheadian sense, for the graphite loop. That is, as datum to felt by another, very distinctly non-human but *vital* entity: desirous and selfish in its exercising of capacities to feel and incorporate some element of the human into its becoming, alive in its self-satisfaction and independence. But what is felt and made apparent in the human is also trans-human – a mobile field of electromagnetism that is itself an event drawing on elements of the human that can be utilised, alongside other electromagnetic forces (the mobile phone in the viewer's pocket, static from a nylon shirt, ambient charges and so on).

Thus the work asks not only who or what other than the human might engage or feel with their eventness, but also how other modes of human engagement might occur. While it does not deny the visual pleasure of the drawings or a distanced listening, it engages across the human with an unseen and largely unfelt more-than-human component of us all, the field of our gathering electromagnetic expressions. It requires that we pay attention to forces that can be felt in their effects, but which cannot ever be fully grasped – an oblique attentiveness to differential intensity known only as a continued expression of held contrasts. These induction artworks enable, I would suggest, an act of *listening* rather than *performing*, emphasising the singularity of feeling as well as the its collectivity.[157] We listen to the drawing system's expressions of a particular capacity (to feel flux), as the graphite listens to our more than human electromagnetic fielding. Unlike in much interactive and new media work where such non-human or more than human components are drowned out by performance and the instrumentation of non-human components that tends to ignore their capacities, perhaps Hinterding, like John Cage amplifying cacti, is listening to the components, allowing the space or time for the resonances between gesture, drawing, movement and flux to arise, giving attention to the various manners in which these acts of feeling by all components to make themselves felt in the event: the graphite's desires, the electrons' future-feelings, the speakers' negative prehensions.

Jane Bennett has stated that the 'ethical task' at hand is to 'cultivate the ability to discern non-human vitality', to become affectually open to the larger ecology (2010, 14) (though again I think this is often mistakenly interpreted as a call to acknowledge the agency of objects rather than the field). To me works such as Hinterding's might, in their own humble way, contribute towards an ecological turn and towards thinking the more-than-human. The *Induction Drawings* make us aware of how ecologies emerge across entities, and the importance of non-human scales (the slowness of the rock, the micro-activities of the worm with their macro-resonances, the continued liveliness of a graphite gesture). The works remind us that we must begin to think the ecological not as preservation for human use – indeed not preservation at all, but an ethics of positivity, that is, of a move towards greater involvement, feeling and creativity, as a 'veritable *theatre* of metamorphoses and permutations. A theatre where nothing is fixed...[leaving] the domain of representation in order to become "experience"...a transcendental empiricism of the multiple, chaos and difference' (Deleuze 1994, 56–7).

4

Thinking parasitic action

> Life degenerates when enclosed within the shackles of mere conformation. A power of incorporating vague and disorderly elements of experience is essential for the advance into novelty.
> *Alfred North Whitehead*

A turn towards a minor form of interactivity might be seen as a move to an ethical configuration of such events. For Simondon, an ethical approach to relation addresses not its relation but its immanent construction, enabling an opening to further expression and connectivity, and an ability to affect and be affected: to affirm both the singular nature of events and openness of relational potential (Combes 2013, 65).

As seen in the discussion of Joyce Hinterding's work in the previous chapter, such a definition of an ethical interactivity might concern not only the ability of relation to remain open in its connective potential, but also the way relation emerges out of a play of affectual forces and subjective feelings collectively taken into consideration. Murphie defines ethics in art as a 'series of practices...which promote expression and machinic connections' (1996, 105). As Murphie argues, the problem for an interactive art event is that a work will always re-stratify after an event of deterritorialisation. Therefore, to retain this ethical potential to explore collective creative expression and defer stasis, the pull of continued potential movement or change is required (Murphie 1996, 105). How then might a continuous and vigorous drive towards reinvention be structured into an event? Rather than just concentrate on the power of the event to establish layers of relation, how can their perishing and replacement also be driven internally?

In a minor assemblage, its 'health' lies, as Murphie says, in an ability to conserve creative possibilities (1997, 164–5). In the previous chapter I argued, after Judith Jones' analysis of Whitehead's ontology, that just such a 'preservation' of difference could be seen to operate through the held contrasts (productive differences) that constitute an event's becoming (and indeed constitute and are indivisible from the whole of the event's subjective life). Yet this 'holding' of contrasts should not be conceived as static, it is always in-forming, keeping the actualizing entity at the point of 'supersession by novel actual things' (Whitehead 1978, 45–6). For a system to continue to approach a molecular state, it is not enough to establish relation. It must continue to agitate – even if this molecular agitation exists on a virtual plane as an 'unrealized potential' (Whitehead 1978, 45–6), luring prehension towards further individuation.

To become an event that gains the power of continual self-invention of the everyday experience might require a system that is able to include not just a positive connectivity, but disconnections and failed, disruptive, competing and destructive relations (as Whitehead's system includes both the negative in terms of negative prehensions, and 'competition' in the singular subjective ingressions of an entity into all other entities). What is needed to activate a machine capable of drift is potential machinic difference – a capacity to intensively produce change that then acts on a local level to agitate and destabilise (Deleuze and Guattari 1986, 50). To remain intensively relational here, we must look for a disruptive movement that has a causal logic, however complex.

Michel Serres proposes that 'noise' in a relation is a necessary condition of its existence, stating that 'if a relationship succeeds, if it is perfect, optimum and immediate; it disappears as a relation' (2007, 79). That is, relations are a condition of difference in a system or assemblage, rather than arising out of harmony or equilibrium. As Serres states, relations are full of 'losses, flights, wear and tear, errors, accidents, opacity' that are their creativity. Without this differential capacity composed of excesses, surpluses, interferences and disruptions, such systems collapse back into a molar configuration (Serres 2007, 92, 127). That is, they becomes at best patterns of stratified or ossified relations, with a loss of the intensity that opens systems to novelty.[158]

Serres terms these noises within relation 'parasites', and explores the parasite as a potential mechanism to complicate and expand the idea of co-causality (2007, passim). The parasite here has multiple meanings, being both a literal parasite – feeding off the energy (both physical and social) of another – but also more importantly as the noise in the system of relations. Thus in a 'relational' system there is a potential third position – the parasite – (and then a noise within this parasitic relation as a third position of this third, and so on) that creatively interferes from within the assemblage.

As the noise or disruption to a force, the parasite is the emergent difference in relation; relation's potential to differentiate from itself. It is a force that pulls towards a more-than, towards a continued individuation or movement of the system that differentiates from the actualised. The parasite, as Yates says, acts against any 'fantasy of control or mastery' (2002, 50). It demonstrates how systems generate their own subjective 'open or dissipative' differentiation through interdependence produced by disruption: 'systematic orderings, local ecologies or drifts' produced by 'momentary deployments of forces' (Yates 2002, 50).

The parasite is essentially creative, in that it forces into existence new logics, new combinations, and new orders of exchange (Serres 2007, 35), as a difference that unifies through the production of relation (Deleuze 1994, 56). It disrupts clear communications, but produces something else through its (mis)translation of relations. This third position in the system is itself unstable, Serres argues, as the roles are interchangeable and fluid – each position is potentially noise for the other two. Therefore parasites lie in between any absolute or fixed position, always fuzzy and multiple, contradictory and irresolvable. This destabilises any hierarchy or relational equilibrium, making each position implicit in the relation of the other two (a nesting or quasi-causality) (Serres 2007, 182).

This is the 'disorder' or unpredictability of relational systems in drift that is inclusive of the disjunctions and failures that are always initiating new orders (Whitehead 1978, 91). The parasitic proposition is a machine that produces a continued evolution of difference: a difference in relation and then further difference within this difference. As a movement or molecularisation within any system, the parasite is potentially an engine capable of driving drift through its continued problematisation of relation. Parasites turn any linear system of relations into a complex and intertwined set that is never fully resolvable, making 'chains of contingency' (Serres 1995, 71) and then continuing to activate or reactivate these chains (Yates 2002, 51) so that they are more a 'series of frictions' than a linkage – 'tangential, contingent [and] unstable' (Serres 1995, 73).

It should be evident that this productive concept of noise is very different to its position within communication theory, as Shannon and Weaver conceptualise it. Within their systemisation, noise is only the 'unfortunate and unwanted additions':

distortions, static and errors (Shannon and Weaver 1967, 7–8). For them information exists as in a pure, abstracted form (the medium is *not* the message), that can ideally be transmitted between a stable source and receiver. Here message, sender and recipient transcend the actual conditions of the event of communication in an artificial separation of semantics and information as signal (Shannon and Weaver 1967, 8). This problematically supposes that information is simply replicated across the divide between two objects, rather than needing to be reproduced (Ingold, 159).[159] Any 'freedom' created by the presence of noise is, in Shannon and Weaver's thinking an 'undesirable uncertainty', as uncertainty can only be desirable if it is located in the agency of the sender to make choices (1967, 19). Thus, from a process philosophy viewpoint that seeks a productive problematisation or intensity of relation, their communication theory fails not only to acknowledge the essential role of differentiation in producing novelty, but also seems to deny noise its own status as an event with its own subjective prehension of the sender, signal and receiver – all of which are given an (artificially stable) agential status.[160]

Serres' parasite, however, is more than a simple disruption to established relation. It is a potential that is immanent to relation in-the-making. This is a potential at the stage of prehensive lure towards connection that always positions relation at the point of splitting and differentiating. In this the parasite is, as Serres states, 'a third [that] exists before a second' (2007, 63). This is a system of differenciation[161] – potential difference – as much as actualised differentiation. It is a system of internally organising and foregrounding the lure of instability and difference in creation. The parasite is a self-organising multiplier of relations – it bifurcates any stable exchange as a derivation from equilibrium, with 'abuse-value' rather than exchange-value (Serres 2007, 17).[162]

This creates new relationships through the eruption of difference that 'recharges the activity of relating from which all experience emerges', as Massumi states, it is not deconstruction but 'continued construction – reconstruction on the fly, not interruption, but recharging and resaturation with potential' (2011, 102).[163] This implies creating a propositional structure where relations not only layer, but also have the inbuilt potential to interrupt each other. Even as virtual noise, parasites create open-endedness – potential disruptions that can create a tension acting on any actualised relation to keep it on the verge of change or collapse, multiplying its virtual qualities rhizomically.[164]

On an interactive design level, the productive implications of the parasite might involve firstly the acknowledgment and encouragement of a wider range of potentially disruptive relations. Secondly, utilising the flexibility in relational positioning that the parasite forces into existence, and, thirdly, the more concrete construction of generative systems – with the inbuilt potential to interrupt and distort each other on multiple scales, and within many differing types of relational forces. The first of these factors involves understanding ways in which sensorial, affective and social relations can creatively alter and disrupt the actual individuated experience in any event, for example:

- Utilising the disruption of personal propositional tendencies – styles of movement, for instance – with which the participant disrupts the artist-artwork propositional relationship;
- Understanding how participants' emotional tonality may affect their experience, magnifying some aspects, minimizing or negating others, connecting their experience to memories;
- Considering how the participants' movements might disrupt any stability of software/sensor relations;

- Understanding how the vibrations of sounds felt through the floor will complicate the sense information gained through the ears;
- Acknowledging how the affective tonality of the room might be disrupted with the arrival of another body, creating a hyper awareness or 'transparency' of temporality within one's body in relation to the event, making a participant hyperconscious of posture, disrupting their image of themselves.[165]

Secondly, the parasitic model embraces fluidity in relation to any art event, enabling numerous interchangeable parasitic diagrams that could be described. For example, if we return to *A Chorus of Idle Feet*, the artwork example from Chapter Two in which the movements of the viewers comingled with the sensor infrastructure, software and the production of rhythmic pulses of sound, we can see the interchangeability of the three positions within parasitic relations. From one position, the participant is the host; the software draws energy from their body, and the parasite is the rhythmic sounds that disrupt the participant's movements. From another position, the software can be the host, in relation with the sound that draws the energy to mutate from its wave patterns, while the participant is the parasite, interfering with their simple communication through speed and rhythm of the body's movement. The sound might also be considered the host, in communication with ears/brain/kinesthetic functioning that draw stimulation from the vibrations, with this communication disrupted by the additional difference in rhythm that the software insistently implants in the relation. The exploitation and enhancement of these naturally slippery relations brings to the event an unpredictability of any planned interaction – continual, subtle re-tunings of relations that modulate and invent.

Thirdly, the parasite provides a focus in the more overtly concrete design of sensor-machine interactions, factoring

Sensor → wire → interface → program → wire → speaker → sound

Figure 4.1 A linear chain of relations.

in potential perishings or negations as primary creative propositions within intensively active systems. In *A Chorus of Idle Feet*, the various sensor-machine produced vibrations could be seen to be parasitic in their potential diffractive actions on each other and to involve a drifting. Much of the system still seems linear and predicable in its relational connectivity – with a trigger from a sensor activating a sound via connecting wires, computer interface, sound program, and speaker system (see Figure 4.1). In the design, however, this was complicated through building in multiple competing relations with the potential to act parasitically on each other.

The application of a series of parasitic propositions, in even one small part of this chain, altered the nature of relation. For example, in the relations between the sensor output that triggered sounds, a series of competing propositional potentials were designed that complicated any actualisation of a sound. Other sensor events had the potential to turn off the sound sample, and/or swap it for a different sound, and/or modulate its volume so that it might be inaudible or dominant, and so on (see Figure 4.2). Here in the latter example the eventual sound event involved a complex series of prehensions, both positive and negative, and a patterning of this datum. In the linear example however, while there were still prehensions of other events, there was less tension between the potential and actualised relations and ingressions of datum.

In such relatively simple ways, the design moved from a linear causation of relation of movement-equals-sound – a realisation of the possible – to multiple complex potential events intermeshed within a nexus of relations. Here the

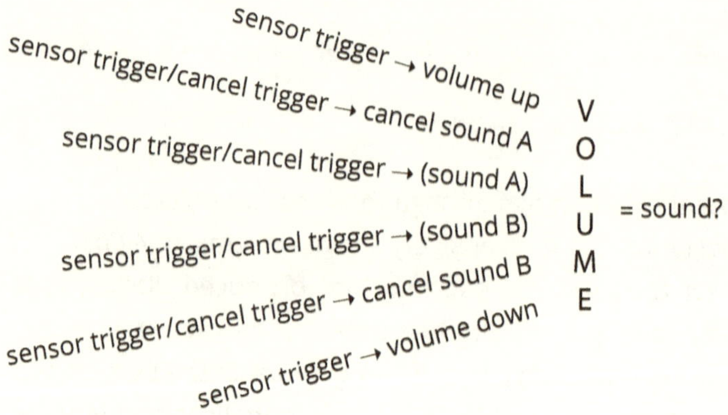

```
                sensor trigger → volume up      V
sensor trigger/cancel trigger → cancel sound A  O
 sensor trigger/cancel trigger → (sound A)      L
                                                U   = sound?
    sensor trigger/cancel trigger → (sound B)   M
   sensor trigger/cancel trigger → cancel sound B  E
         sensor trigger → volume down
```

Figure 4.2 Parasitic potential relations.

'noise' of disruption, a continual force moving the process into reconfiguration. These two designs need not be seen in oppositional terms, rather, there is a distinction between a differentiation that leads only to the possible, and a 'hyper-differentiation' that might 'seethe with fractal future-pasts' of the unactualised potentials (Massumi 1992, 91).[166]

The nexus of relations here can be seen to operate not just as independently self-satisfying, but also as complexly and fluidly interrelated through disjunctive events of emergence. These are potential noises within relations that construct through disrupting create intensity and the potential for novelty. An enriched connection to the virtual proposed relation as more than just complex vector relations of physical interdependence. Here a technological system utilising simple components began to approach a relational modelling, as each trigger became a factor within a complex series of interrelated events that were concerned with rhythms, intervals and disruptions that built an 'ecology' of interdependent components (Manning 2009, 74).

This complex system of relations was then multiplied exponentially for each sound event, and its virtual potentials also added to the equation.[167] Triggers that shifted the sound emitted from one speaker to another also disrupted the spatial relations of the sounds. Other triggers proposed competing shifts in the tonal qualities of the sound produced – changes to the equalisation, reverberation, and so on – potentially disrupting the perception of sound by bodies.

In this example, the parasitic potentials of the system drew the various machines into implication in each other's individuation through its entangled chains of cause and effect. Not only were these machines all concerned with the production of sounds, they are also involved in the actualisation of each other, as they began to affect the success or failure of each other's productive expressions. Differentiation here was the unifying element – activating the individuation of relation between entities and assemblages that were implicated within each other's actualisation. This was, at the same time, a differenciation that created a shared potential or priming for further disruptions and relational entanglement, and reveals the potential of disruptive noise to open a system.

The parasitic embraces Deleuze's concept of a 'difference without negation', it operates as a productive or 'positive' differentiation, rather than an oppositional difference (1994, xx, 205). That is, rather than acting as a negation that 'subordinates difference to itself', it creates problems within a system that are positively productive (Deleuze 1994, 266–7). This means, firstly, that all the differences have a productive or creative role to play in the drive towards novelty of the system. Secondly, it means that those differences not actualised in any one event remain open to further potential influence on the future of the event. The competing forces of the parasitic potential disruptions within the system create a logic by which the system intensively 'works out' what sound will actualise. It is a self-creative unity that in each instance creates a set of competing propositions, which then drift according to local and singular conditions in any one instance, rather than according to any preconceived outcome.

Relations within a parasitically activated system have a new intensity. They continue, even after splitting, to contain the tension of potential further such actualisations of disruption. This both molecularises and concretises the system by demanding a reconfiguration of each relational pull in relation to every other actual and potential force. There are always tendencies towards multiple, incompatible future splits, and therefore the relational forces remain in a problematised state that cannot be resolved into stasis.

Here parasitic tendencies evolve, not simply in reaction to established relation, but as a force of relation. The virtual and the actual parasite are emergent events in and of themselves. While there is always difference contained within a system, constructing an event that accentuates the parasitic tendencies of relations to creatively disrupt themselves perhaps shifts it further towards a state of hyper-differentiation.

This parasitic modelling remains emergent, embracing change and contradiction, constantly at a point of rearranging. Again, it is a way of enabling the conditions for difference to arise within the event, rather than a prescription of actualised differences. This conception of the parasite allows a way of describing a dynamic, emergent and complex series of relations, a methodology that embraces the potential fluidity. The point to such design is, in a sense, to not have a point: to rescue such art-events from purposefulness, to encourage growth, mutation and destruction, to enable an event to generate its own forces of concrescence, and find its own satisfaction. This does not imply an absence of artistic input in any negative sense, but a shift towards propositional, speculative structuring.[168] It places emphasis on the intensification of relation through differentiation, a shift that embraces the richness and lure towards future creativity of a dynamic virtual milieu.

The task for the artist is to steer interactivity towards the propositional, to invent ways to keep the event and the temporal experience of participation unstable, to keep assemblages fluidly creative. The point of this multiplication of the virtual is twofold.

Firstly, it makes the work as the event, the temporal experience of participation, unstable; it keeps the assemblage fluid and emergent – always reconfiguring, inventing new relationships of connection depending on the specifics of involvement.

Secondly, this instability begins to apply not just to the actual experience, but to the language that is used to articulate the event – it becomes a kind of meta-modelling of the experience, which combines various potential relations and interferences into a model that describes the event.

This combination is an immanent critique, always at a point of change or dissipation; it applies only to a specific viewpoint, and a specific moment, and must always be reinvented. As a model, it remains emergent, embracing change and contradiction, always needing to be rearranged. What this language of the parasite then begins to allow is a way of describing the dynamic, emergent and complex events of relation that embrace their potential fluidity, rather than a concentration on the form and comprehendible movement. The remainder of this book is dedicated to such an open exploration, with a series of different parasitic tactics across a number of registers, all potentially capable of driving interactive events through the intensive production of difference.

5

Walking with the world: towards a minor approach to performative art practice

> One walks down the path to get somewhere, but one enjoys walking, and one leaves one's house just to walk.
>
> *Alphonso Lingis*

Walking

Walking is intrinsically inventive and relational: to space, to the body itself, and to the potential that it both creates and differentiates. Walking moves us beyond a stable configuration of relations between a subject and objects, and towards a more complex experience that begins to escape such boundaries. It is, in the broadest sense, a parasitic tactic for the disruption of social, physical and mental structuring, capable of folding the body into the world – and world into body – a molecularisation that excites and disrupts.

This chapter considers the potential of walking as a 'minor' practice. For Michel de Certeau, cities are excessively stratified and homogenising systems that might be troubled through a technique of walking. Walking, de Certeau argues, is a 'soft resistance' that seeks a creative flight through reactivating connections between bodies and their environment. As Ben Highmore articulates, such walking is 'minor' in that it is positioned less as direct opposition to structure, and more as that which 'hinders and dissipates the energy flows of domination' (Highmore 2002, 152).

Every walk we set out on, even the most mundane and functional, is inherently an adventure into the unknown, into improvisation and discovery. If we are too jaded or numb to notice, then we have only to invite a small child or dog to accompany us to realise or invent creative and connective possibilities. With a child in tow or towing us, our walk can never be simply a blinkered move from A to B. Instead, it is rich with potential. It splits to become multiple: consisting of many foci, intensities, and heterogeneous singularities (Manning 2009, 7). A particular smell, a pretty tree, a siren, and a cat, a game instantly evoked out of the walk: all layers of an experience that is being continually reinvented in response to stimuli. Our bodies rearrange and respond to the affordances of the rock underfoot, a cold wind, the effort of a hill, the anticipation of a busy road ahead, the pull of the dog's leash. As Erin Manning says, in moving, the body and the space vibrate with potential relationships and affects (Manning 2009, 13). Such a walk is capable of being expansive without necessarily getting lost – a becoming-with the environment. It is for de Certeau a spatial practice that 'slips into the clear text of the planned and readable city' (1988, 93).

Stratifying and restricting forces exist not only within cities, but also within bodies that are unified and ordered by habit and subjection, succumbing to stasis and a loss of connectivity and breadth of expression. This Deleuze and Guattari term a body's own capacity for 'micro-fascism' (1987, 215). As movement complicates and disrupts established spatial relations, multiplying and creating new immanent connections to extend the potential of the body in space, it might also allow a becoming-minor of a body. Walking, as Manning argues, is a temporal, re-combinatory operation of becoming that decentres subjectivity and troubles stasis (2009, 23); thus a moving body is always more than a fixed identity (2009, 63–4). Arakawa and Madeline Gins conception of the 'landing sites' (2002, 5–22) – nodes of attention that the moving body produces – further explores minor procedures where bodies and environment fold into one another and disturb boundaries. The intermeshing of body-world potential that Arakawa and Gins articulate is always in-process, a performative exploration within an established system, be it a body or a place.

Here movement fundamentally disturbs boundaries. It complicates relations as it multiplies and creates new immanent connections – relation in-the-act. Walking differentiates and intensifies life, folding the body into the world and world into body (an environmental or ecological engagement[169]), exciting and operating processes of creative disruption. It is, in the broadest sense, a parasitic tactic for the disruption of social, physical and mental structuring, turning a rote exercise into an attentive adventure.

In this chapter, Nathaniel Stern's *Compressionism* performance is examined for its ability to enable exploration of a minor potential of walking. The configuration of technical objects and bodies in *Compressionism* contributes to a reactivation of the streets as de Certeau proposes, and allows a reconfiguration of intensive bodily relations through the activation of new internal and external sites of attention. I argue that the technical components of *Compressionism* help to transport the body beyond habit. While this assembling of bodies and technologies helps to constitute an 'augmented awareness' that might be cynically viewed as a postmodern counterpart to some romantic or mythical past of 'pure' non-stratified relation to place, my interest here in the work is rather that it problematises the habitual acts of walking and engaging with the environment. In this, *Compressionism* demands that the participant's body seek out new intensive and extensive minor relational potential. From this perspective *Compressionism* can be viewed as a procedure to 'escape or "reenter" habitual patterns of action' in order to reinvigorate our attention to these processes of contraction (Arakawa and Gins 2002, 62), to explore alternative routes, reinvent both processes and outcomes, and to embody a minor practice.[170]

Making the world/performing space

For de Certeau, walking through the streets recreates the city as more than a fixed 'geometrical or geographical space of visual, panoptic or theoretical constructions' (1988, 93).[171] The immanent movements and 'tactics' of everyday life produce a relational, contingent experience. In 'walking the city', de Certeau examines ways that deterritorialisation of spatial order is enabled through the act of walking, and the positive personal and social implications of these movements (1988, vii). This is positioned as a 'tactic' that destabilises, a fragmentary insinuation into place to reappropriate it 'without taking over in its entirety' (de Certeau 1988, xiv). It is a destabilisation that does not necessarily impose new order, remaining immanent and essentially *per*-formed rather than a preformed strategy (de Certeau 1988, xix, xx). In walking's immanent recomposition of static place as 'vectors of direction, velocities, time variables...intersections of mobile elements' (de Certeau 1988, 117), it molecularises or reenergises these territorialised 'places' (de Certeau 1988, 117.).[172] As Tim Ingold notes, in such a conception of walking and the space itself, both lack any real 'essence' or idealised form, but rather the act of movement explores emergent differential capacities held between bodies and environment (2011, 49, 24).

Here de Certeau sets up a clear distinction between an abstracted and disembodied or distanced concept of a space (such as the view of a city from the heights of a skyscraper) (92), and the embodied interactions within such spaces that movement enables. A number of other authors have explored these distinctions, if not always utilising the terms in the same way.[173] James J Gibson argues that there is no abstract space or time that is then 'filled in' by lived experience, but rather a 'flow of ecological events' that are heterogeneous and differentiated (1979, 93). Similarly, Ingold describes the emergent space of movement as 'unclassifiable', consisting not of stable and inherent properties, but a dynamic relational field of 'meshwork' that is always 'under construction', reproduced and reinvented (rather than replicated) through movement (2011, 159–60).[174] Manuel DeLanda makes a clear distinction between such 'meshworks' and 'state' structuring of space that is useful here as it avoids the naïve concept that a deterritorialisation of space is either sustainable or necessarily positive. Rather, he defines the latter as a centrally organised and rigidly controlled space, and the former as a 'bottom up' approach to the organisation of space that consists of complex, intertwined heterogeneous elements largely self-organising (DeLanda 2011, 257–274 and passim).

Indeed, as Ingold notes, any expanded concept of space could be misconstrued to still imply a static order that positions livable places inside of static space. This would, he argues, retain the concept of living as bound to the landscape rather than positing them as existing 'through, around, to and from [places], from and to places elsewhere' (Ingold 2011, 148). Movement for Ingold, after Deleuze and Guattari, is not a connection between points or places, but always runs between: an uncontainable line of flight breaking boundaries (2011, 83). The point here is the need to replace or reinvigorate the imposed structuring with potential for greater novelty and interrelatedness (to molecularise). This is the potential that the tactic of walking proposes in the city space for de Certeau.

Michelle Lamant comments that de Certeau's tactics allow pedestrians to 'create for themselves a sphere of autonomous action within the constraints that are imposed on them' (1987,

720). The walker, she argues, reconfigures the impersonal, visible and knowable space of the city streets through minor methods born of creativity rather than passive or active resistance (Lamant 1987, 720), replacing the productive and pre-structured place with an improvisational experience that operates inside the established systems. Of interest here is not the problematic and romantic return to the *flâneur*, as de Certeau's argument can be read.[175] Rather, it is that de Certeau's walker reactivates their relationship to a space by emphasising the reconfiguration of relations out of existing entities, and the continual differential action of movement that keeps these relations at this point of splitting, rejoining and re-layering.

Walking invites an intimacy and active engagement with the singularities composing an experience that enriches the homogenising actions of a place. The streets we navigate or describe through remembered movements and sensations might perhaps disrupt any idea of an absolute organisation of space with our shifting experience over time. Instead, as de Certeau says, they become a 'story, jerrybuilt out of elements' that is both 'allusive and fragmentary' (1988, 102),[176] layering and splitting the existing structure, filling the streets with 'forests' of 'desires and goals' (1988, xxi) to make the world habitable. An 'in-between' is created that allows a movement, a flow of forces, bodies and affects.

In walking, the experience of the city is always an intimate and shifting engagement, as feet selectively prehend the *qualities* rather essential *properties* of the street. The street is 'a course cloth of patchwork woven from the comings and goings of its manifold inhabitants' (Ingold 2011, 16), that splits the homogenising actions of the city through a continued gathering of singular ecologies of feelings. It is an immediate engagement with materiality, a creative coming together of surfaces. Mobility here activates the productive potential of life, giving it 'it its seemingly infinite range of specific virtual and actual individuations' (Murphie 2005a, 1). Thus walking becomes a technique of differentiation that extends and complicates, positioned as a creative derivation from that which is already in existence (Deleuze 1994, xx). It is a positive parasitism that is 'molecular' in allowing new communication or composition in the spaces between components (Deleuze and Guattari 1986, 41).

Differentiating the body

While walking can disrupt and reconfigure relations to space, Manning argues that it can also work to differentiate bodies through movement, allowing exploration of new potential intensive connections. Imagine that you are standing stationary in a doorway, about to walk out. Except that 'stillness' undermines itself: you are already always moving in two important ways (Manning 1996, 43–7). Firstly in a literal and physical sense, the body is always in a state of intensive micro-movement. Heart, lungs, eyelids, and eyes are the more obvious aspect of this, even though for the most part they operate below an overtly conscious, willful level. There are also the efforts of the muscles as they continue to exert force in opposition to gravity to keep one upright, and as the body performs constant micro movements and adjustments to keep balanced. The relatively still body, Manning states, is in fact a series of 'micro-postures that move in tandem with the rejigging of micro-movements' (1996, 44), perceptual disruption and differentiation.[177] Here, one could argue, the body is always in a process of perceptually differentiating, in that it has its own differential machines – technics – built into the sensory distributions of the body. These operate in the interval – the differential. Again it is this gap between – a qualitative intensity – that is meaningful: the felt experience *between* the data processed from one ear/eye/nostril/foot and another, a held contrast before a relation.[178] Movement here activates the continuous streams of noise that are perceptual differentials, and this 'perception/action continuum' of differentiation is emergent with movement, intrinsically composed of and with such movement (Murphie 2005a, 6).[179]

Secondly, the continuous gathering and incipient pull of the virtual also undermines stillness. As you are about to begin, Manning proposes, milieus of virtual possibilities are composing themselves, creating tensions, an 'elasticity' that is released as the possibilities resolve into an actual movement. The choices are not infinite, in that not everything is physically possible, but are limitless in that they are being endlessly created, and each choice generates another equally complex series of choices. They resolve in the satisfaction of an actual event (your left foot takes a small step straight ahead), and all the virtual movements perish. This event 'propels the preacceleration of a new occasion' (Manning 1996, 38–9). New sets of virtualities begin composing possibilities for the next step, shaped by many things, such as the limits of body, habits, responses to the space, and so on, and it is movement that both generates and selects from the potential actions.

Movement here, Manning says, cuts across the body (2013a, 46), connecting and disrupting the actualised body's relation to its larger potential, which is always also reconstituted by the activity. It is a technique by which a body accomplishes the shifting beyond itself of ongoing individuation. This evolving potential for new connections is a minor 'flight' from stasis, a flight that is not an escape from oneself, but an increase in intensity, or richness of potential (Deleuze and Guattari 1986, 13).

Landing sites: worlding the body

Walking the space of the city is never without constraints: proposing and conditioning movement, the body's projection and diffusion into space. Environments provide conditions – platforms of potential actions – that affect the actions of the walker. As Massumi argues, a park bench, for example, creates anticipation of a certain habitual action (sitting), and in this way works to order the movement in the space. The bench is a 'storage of repose' that creates suggestions of actions. While one could sit on the ground or stand on the bench, Massumi argues that the image of the bench creates anticipation of a certain habitual action (bench-equals-sitting), and in this way works to order the movement in the space (2003b, 5).[180] These conditions can enable as much as they constrain, proposing new actions.

Massumi relates this both to Gibson's concept of 'affordances' and Arakawa and Gins' concept of 'landing sites'. Affordances are what the environment 'offers' or 'provides or furnishes' an animal (Gibson 1979, 119). Affordances are about productive relationships. What is prehended is not the object as such but the relational or interactive potential between objects and bodies (Gibson 1979, 126). That is, affordances are perceived potential machinic couplings-through-movement. Affordances, Gibson writes, are not neutral or abstract but complementary and specific to an individual animal's tendencies. An affordance 'points two ways, to the environment and the observer' (Gibson 1979, 132). They are a prehension of the potential of the body as much as of the environment (Gibson 1979, 132). Affordances then exist and interact with each other in complex and nested sets or 'niches' that are ecologies in and of themselves, whereby 'the niche implies a kind of animal, and the animal implies a kind of niche' (Gibson 1979, 120).[181]

Such affordance are propositions, 'lures towards feelings' (Whitehead 1978, 259), constructing potential from which events can draw. For example, a patch of grass might afford many responses from the walker: a place to lie down, the danger of snakes in summer, wetness to be avoided after rain, the smell of the countryside, an opportunity to sit and talk, and so on. These propositions potentially operate on multiple levels – sensorial (softness underfoot/wetness/smells), affectual (inviting tiredness and an urge to rest, fear of hidden danger, joy of free space to play), kinesthetic (sitting, lying, running, walking), and social (conversation, solitary contemplation). The conditions of the space do not necessarily impose a habitual bodily response; rather, they can lure a range of potential actions into being, triggered by common constraints (Gibson 1979, 119).

These constraints are immanently performed by the body-in-composition as it walks. The ground, for example, is an 'enabling constraint' of movement intrinsically related to the form and practice of walking (Manning 2009, 70),[182] as gravity plays a role in shaping some movements (exertion increasing up a steep hill) as much as it precludes others (leaping walls), wrapping the feet into sensorial relationship with surface textures and resistances of various materials underfoot. This active making of movement-body-space is not limited to, nor even primarily located in, conscious mental activity, as propositions 'are not primarily for belief, but for feeling at the physical level of unconsciousness' (Whitehead 1978, 186). Conscious – mindful[183] – and pre-conscious movements are capable of both the habitual and improvisatory.

Certain activities and spaces more forcefully and productively disrupt habits by requiring an active and attentive care that brings to the fore the processes of connection and projection into the world. The urgency of movement and the complex negotiations required to enter or exit a peak hour train, for example, both instinctively causes one to edge into a gap between bodies that affords passage and brings to our consciousness the continual negotiations and collective reconfiguring of space required by moving in the city. We must calculate who will allow passage, who must be edged around, intuiting minute adjustments of tempo and posture to keep a free space ahead. Positional information comes at the body from all directions as we compose a provisional line through the chaos. With every step, the space available and the potential for the next move shift, and both body and path must always be renegotiated, making premeditated paths redundant. It is in such moments of intensely improvised movement that the space and body might together begin to approach a contingent, immanent quality.[184] Such an encounter with the city is far from the free and idle wandering of the *flâneur*; it is a series of conversations between competing forces and potentials affecting both the configuration of the space and the composition of the body (Manning 2009, 15).

Arakawa and Gins concept of 'landing sites' provides a useful refining of affordances (2002, 7). This is a process of 'portioning out' space to provisionally deposit sited awareness around the body (Arakawa and Gins 2002, 5). The body, they state, takes cues from the environment to 'assign volume and a host of other particulars to the world' (Arakawa and Gins 2002, 7, 9). These sites are a way that the body contributes to and distributes itself into the world: a 'holding of the world' in attention, an attention with dispersed foci composed of all perception – 'a bit of substance, a segment of atmosphere, an audible anything, a whiff of something, whatever someone notices' (Arakawa and Gins 2002, 81). Landing sites are a process by which differentiation of the field occurs, to different degrees of specification and diffusion.[185] This, Arakawa and Gins argue, is a process by which, perceptually and kinesthetically, the world and body are immanently enfolded. In this sense, the body not only differentiates the *space* through movement, but also distributes *itself* within the space, contributing its awareness towards things in the world.[186]

Processes of landing sites productively disrupt the limits of the body, constructing through dispersion a new extended and enriched potential body*ing*. These projected landing sites fold, nest, diffuse and focus dynamically while the body moves. It is a constant, creative, noisy process of splitting stable relations.[187]

Returning to the space of the peak-hour train, where spatial relations shift quickly, this process by which the space-body-movement relations enfold the body and object/world into shared individuations becomes more consciously attended.[188] Entering the train carriage with one's own particular style of moving[189], we begin to create landing sites. We distribute awareness on both the more physically concrete (arrangements of bodies and objects), and on more vague and diffuse levels, such as the ephemeral (reflections of light on surfaces or affectual tonalities). A change in height or texture underfoot as we enter creates a foot-floor site, a commuter's headphones or conversation sites attention vaguely in one direction, the line of bodies exiting the train deposits attention towards this flow. The vacant seat in front of us concentrates attention not only on the object itself and the seat/body kinesthetic potential (stopping, sitting, a virtual becoming-with of seat/body that makes the seat also part body and body part seat), but also on the kinesthetic possibilities of surrounding floor space (the potential of moving to or beyond the seat).

Landing sites thus move through, over, around, and inside other landing sites, each divisible into smaller sites, continually complicating relations as the body moves and redistributes itself in the environment. The point we are pressed against other bodies in the train carriage becomes a shared site of focused attention,[190] located within a general awareness of the other passengers. As we move through the space, the sites make such navigation possible, and begin to propose relational and kinesthetic possibilities. The landing site on the exit opposite not only creates another site of attention, but also wraps both body and door in potential future kinesthetic relation (an exit from the train).

These landing sites are in-the-making – as Manning says, a 'tending towards relation' (2013a, 12). This again is a process of becoming-minor, a decentering through movements that recombine components of an event (Deleuze and Guattari 1986, 50) and create new intensities through prehensive selection. The act of depositing landing sites agitates or molecularises boundaries between body and world – destabilising distinctions through the creation of shared potential collective individuation.

In the theories of both affordances and landing sites, vision is construed as haptic and kinesthetic, and this is far from the role de Certeau assigns to vision as inextricably linked to power.[191] Both Gibson and Arakawa and Gins suggest that it has other potential operations of an enactive and synesthetic nature, with, as James Gibson states, 'the optic array...not only provid[ing] base information but also the possibilities for action on the basis of that information' (Gibson cited in Mock 2009, 96).

'Ecological' vision, as Gibson describes it, is not about a distancing through the reduction of the world to retinal images, but an ongoing engagement with the world (1979, 61, 244–6, passim). Here vision is a perceptual system, involving 'eye-head-brain-body' rather than passively received messages to be decoded by the brain. Thus for Gibson, vision begins not with the head fixed and the eye exposed to a series of snapshots 'like a camera', but with 'the flowing array of the observer who walks from one vista to another, moves around an object of interest, and can approach it for scrutiny' (1979, 290). Ecological vision is sensed throughout the integrated sensations of muscles and body structure and through the movement within the environment (an 'ambulatory vision') as an embodied, *lived* experience, not the translation of stimuli (Gibson 1979, 291–2).

Manning also elaborates a synesthetic operation of vision that is part of a co-mingling of the various senses that themselves are linked to movement and also kinesthetic (2009, 49). As we move towards some landmark – a tree for example – vision operates not just to recognise the image of a tree, but also proprioceptively to create the feeling of self within the space

(Manning 2009, 49).[192] This we might think of as a landing site that has been deposited, situating part of the body at the landmark ahead. As we move, we see continual variation in image of the tree – parts come into the field of vision or disappear, become larger or smaller, so that our eyes as they move across the tree might act not as 'a capturing of the world, but a captivating by it' (Manning 2009, 86).[193] Furthermore, as Gibson also notes, an essential component of vision is proprioceptive, involving a registering of 'movements of the body as much as does the muscle-joint-skin system and the inner ear system' (1979, 175).[194]

Compressionism

Transdisciplinary artist Nathaniel Stern's ongoing *Compressionism* performances (2005–)[195] comprise a customised, scanner-battery pack-laptop assemblage worn or carried by one participant, while she or another person holds and moves the scanner surface across objects to 'perform images into existence' (Stern 2013b) through a kind of shared seeing-moving within an environment. These scans are literally a 'compression' of the temporal act into a two-dimensional image (see Figure 5.2), seeking, as Stern says, to 'accent the relationships between the performance, myself, my subjects and the tools' (Stern 2013a).

What does the performance of *Compressionism* add to the already dynamic becomings of the moving body in space, or, rather, how does it reinvent and re-molecularise these processes, doubling them with new levels of awareness? *Compressionism*, I want to argue, does not alter *being*, but the *manner* of being (Guattari 1995a, 109): it creatively performs the body (and space) in a new way, not to return it to an imagined pre-stratified form, nor to replace previous space-body modulations, but to enfold it with existing relations. The work here challenges habits, provoking participants to intuit new minor ways of being.

Compressing the city

Performing *Compressionism* was an awkward act. The size and weight of the scanner required that it be held in both hands away from the body, with feet braced to maintain balance. This created a tension running through the body, stretching toward objects to be scanned. Keeping the scanner steady required a clumsy cooperation between both scanner and bodyweight as counterbalance, and also between the holder of the scanner and the person carrying the battery pack and laptop capturing the image (see Figure 5.1). There was a zone of intimacy established, both between the collaborating bodies and between the scanner-body assemblage and the objects being scanned. Scanner, body and space all conjoined through the act of moving.

Compressionism here involved a close investigative walking – through back alleys, parks, along surfaces of objects, architecture and bodies. It was an exploration of texture, colour and contrast, held together by the collective movement of the bodies-scanner machine. The intensive, explorative, close-visioning movement in the city enacted through the *'Compressionist'* event was remembered through the personal, composed from actions, disjunctions and sensations. One's experience of the event was composed of particular colours, surface textures and variations. The colour of a particular leaf, the textural shifts on a building surface, the passage from tree to wall to doorway, the incidental sounds heard while waiting for the scanner to warm up, the effort of a particular stretching of the body – each of these coloured one's experience of the event. It was a fragmentary mapping of a space – a haptic or closely focused narration of layering intimate, personal actions onto the surface of the city space. The haptic here showed its potential in bringing attention not just to the surface of the object, but also in its engagement with multiple sensations, and with participants' interior/exterior boundaries (Marks, cited Jones 2006, 143).

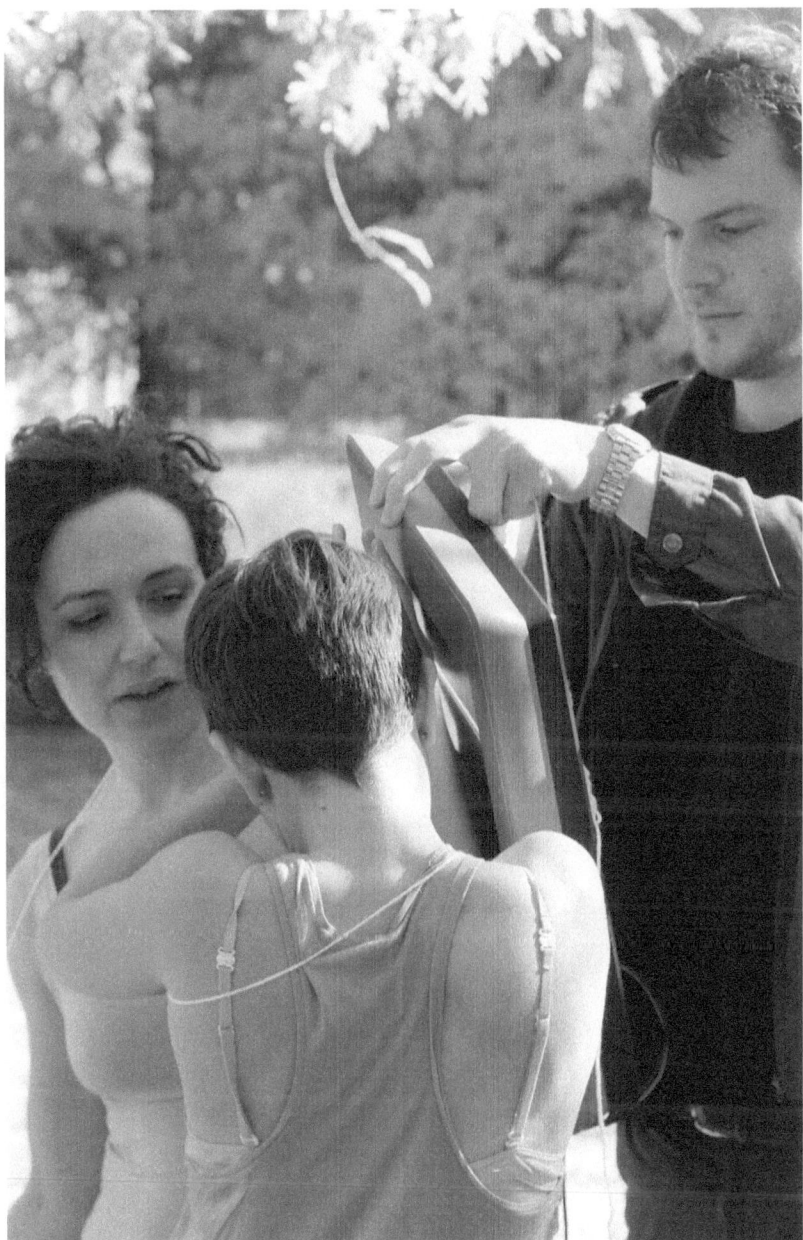

Figure 5.1 Compressionism Documentation, Montreal, 2012. Digital photograph. Photo: Bianca Scliar

Participants performing the scans improvised new literal connective passages that opened gaps between systems of

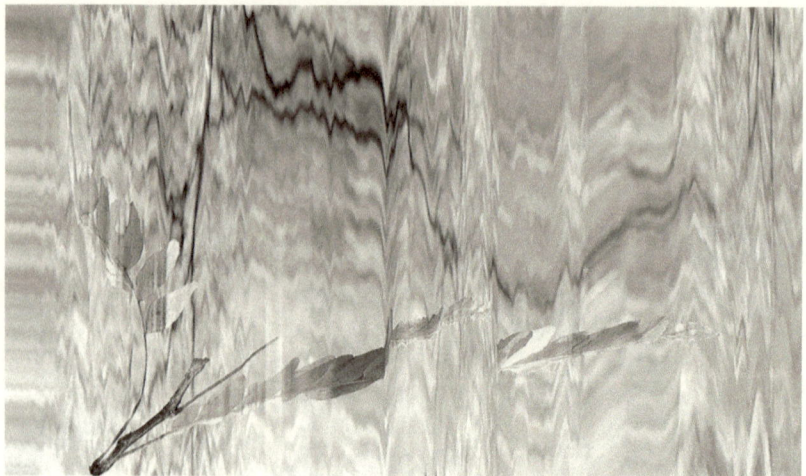

Figure 5.2 Nathaniel Stern, Compressionism Scan, Montreal, 2012. Courtesy the artist. Digital Image.

place.[196] The scanning travelled up walls or through holes, over horizontal, vertical and angled surfaces, backtracking to points of interest – inviting and improvising new affectual connections as much as the equipment's awkwardness precluded usual styles of movement through the space. The space scanned was understood as a series of overlapping and angled surfaces, as the scanner was moved parallel to these surfaces, emphasising their shifts as the body coordinated the changes in angle – a point of 'touch' between body and environment.[197] Space was understood not through a stable image or representation, but through *practice of engagement*: a dynamic expression of the relationships between moving bodies and environment that was felt through the meshing of forces (rhythm, tempo, shifts and variations) (Ingold 2011, 211). *Compressionism*'s movements insinuated into the city the experience of a 'plurality of centres, a superposition of perspectives, a tangle of points of view' (Deleuze 1994, 56).

Dancing objects

As participants slowly moved the scanner over the surface of an object, these actions were translated into a larger movement of the hands and arms – creating an awareness of contours and small deviations that was heightened by the fact that the object itself was always at least partially obscured from view by the scanner. This was a blind, groping approximation of the shape that was performed: a scramble of image memory, a drawing of the shape with the hands, a constant reforming of posture and balance, an attention to the sound of the scanner's processes that resonated with the rhythms of bodies moving. Each object invited potential movements in relation to its form. For the minute or two before the laptop compressed the data into a viewable image, the event existed on its own as an awkward dancing of the object, an approximation of vision performed by a loose assemblage of other senses, drawn together by movement.

Compressionism afforded new connections between senses through movement. Vision became situated 'along the tendons and the muscles' (Serres ND, unpaginated), and the event approximated a new eye-organ out of hands/feet/balance.[198] What would normally be felt as the small-scale movement of the eyes traversing an object was explicitly performed (danced) as a full body movement, and brought to attention through this shift in registers. The body-scanner assemblage performed sight, inscribing it in space.[199] Here the primary link between an ecological perception and movement was made evident to the participants – an engagement in an emergent environment that demanded time spent along a 'path of observation' (Ingold 2011, 46) rather than an assessment from a fixed point. This embracing of the scanning/visioning technics was a minor tactic in that it consisted of 'adding to' and 'perverting' habitual configurations of sense organs to increase the intensity of felt experience (Deleuze and Guattari 1986, 10).

The *Compressionism* event deposited a series of (mobile) landing sites in addition to those that walking the space might normally require. Attention landed on the new and mobile collaborations of sensory input informing the movements (a shared sensory experience residing between and linking body/scanner/world) that caused unexpected intensified conjunctions, and cooperation between surfaces beyond their usual functioning (Deleuze cited in Grosz 2008, 198). Part of the conscious attention landed on the held scanner, as the mechanics of holding and operating the equipment forced new improvisation of relations and landing sites in the muscles of the hands and arms, in the feet maintaining balance – depositing more defined sites of attentiveness onto the surface, gradient and texture of the ground. Less qualified sites were also deposited in the vague attention given to those carrying the rest of the equipment, and to the space around the object or surface being scanned. The more defined and useful landing sites were in the mobile spaces between object and scanner surfaces, while the unseen object itself remained a more generalised 'imaging' landing site, in Arakawa and Gins' terms, nesting within the particular, while resisting definition. In these ongoing differentiations *Compressionism* perhaps molecularised and multiplied local connections through a splitting and re-siting of attention (Deleuze and Guattari 1986, 50, 37).

Compressionism might be seen to address a heightened awareness of, and engagement with, the processes of the virtual in two ways. Firstly, it literally created new potential that the assemblage's heterogeneous component parts did not hold on their own – such as new capacities for seeing, new postural explorations, and new prehensive potential to trigger actualisations. Secondly, through continued disruption of any developing habit, it promoted a suspension in its own continued unfolding that made the ongoing individuations perceptually felt. Here the assembling of body and scanner equipment provided new levels of potential intensive sensory difference, for example: the rhythms of the scanner head moving that the body attempted to follow, but never quite duplicated; the new decentering weight pulling on bodies that had to be resisted or followed; and new restrictions on the range of movements of the limbs. All these factors created tensions and difficulties. The technological components were not specifically the producers of these new relations, but were a technique to activate the conditions under which bodies began to explore minor 'sideways and decentered movements' (Deleuze and Guattari 1986, 50).

Conclusion

What *Compressionism* produced as its primary outcome were new expressions of movement – new improvisational collaborations between bodies/scanner/objects /surfaces/space that reconstituted each as enactive and extensively relational, both collective and singular (Manning 2009, 22). The event demanded an augmented or composite awareness, larger than that of the body on its own and prior to the event, reconstructing the body's field of sensitivities, and requiring new cooperation between bodies, equipment and space.

In thinking more generally of the potentially generative role of movement in interactive art, what might *Compressionism* have to offer? Firstly, while many interactive works involve movement as a key factor in participation, in this instance, I would suggest, there is never a sense that it is a functional movement designed simply to link pre-defined capacities of bodies and objects (hand-to-joystick, gesture-to-sensor). Rather mobile capacities might begin to emerge as 'properties of systems of relations' (Ingold 2011, 49) that continue to differentiate from actual conditions in a lively relation with the virtual. In developing this type of emergent relation, as Massumi comments, a work might attain a dynamic co-causality that is often missing in the triggers of sensor-based works that instrumentalise movement (2011, 45–6).

Secondly, unlike many interactive works that employ everyday and unthinking movements, *Compressionism* foregrounds these habitual gestures through the awkwardness of the constraints of the mechanism, the disruptions to the visual perceptual system, and the delays between gesture and its representation in the final scanned image. While walking, as both de Certeau and Manning argue, might already allow a body to exercise potential to produce minor iterations of streets, bodies and their relations, here such activity is made strange from within at the same time as its relationship to the surfaces of the environment is troubled. Perhaps then the key to this artwork's capacity to activate minor potential lies in its problematisation of any mastery of conditions or movement, creating awkwardness in the negotiations between limbs, bodies and space that made the performers strangers within their own movement capacities.[200]

Compressionism might then be seen as neither an attempt to return to pre-stratified states, nor as some new prosthetic melding of bodies and technologies to take us beyond the limits of the biological, but as a technique for bodies to disorganise their own forms in order to experiment with new expressions of relations (Massumi 2011, 28). If the 'minor' is concerned not with outcomes but enabling the conditions for new connections to arise (Massumi 2011, 18), then this artwork suggests that the role the technological component of the work plays might be less about creating new relations itself, than with disrupting habit and turning the body's attention to the capacity of movement to gather bodies into emergent and dynamic new ecologies.

Bridge: Psychopomp

In *Psychopomp*,[201] two performers moved around a darkened space inside two costumes that generated internal light and sounds that played through four speakers arranged around the edges of the space. The costumes worn during the performance were embedded with sensors so that movement, contact and pressure and shifts in posture generated the soundscape and caused coloured LEDs in the costumes to operate (see Figure 5.3). Each individual's actions had the potential to affect the lights in both costumes and to displace sound samples triggered by their movements.

The headpieces of the outfits curtailed participants' vision, so that they could only make out bright spots of light, thus they were more reliant than usual on touch and hearing to navigate the space. Their ability to fix stable positions was complicated by the disruptive actions of their movements, which triggered changes in sounds and shifts in the locations of sounds from one speaker to another. In addition, the lights they could see in the costumes altered in response to both body movements and the volumes of sound from various speakers. Navigation further complicated by the weight, volume, and soft texture of the new 'skin' wrapping their bodies, which made tactile sensations vague and somewhat alien.

All this created a scenario in which movement was necessary as a means to any level of cognition in body–body and body–space relations, yet movement simultaneously kept these relations highly mobile and caught in a web of co-causality. Here the primary role of movement in understanding both the space of performance and the capacities of bodies was made evident. Stripped of any possibility to overview and quickly grasp the space, each step consisted of a tentative reconstruction as participants tested their new capacities to interact and relate to sounds, lights, surfaces and bodies (both their own, newly made strange and the other participant's body as a potential site of connection).

With this reduced vision and unreliable hearing, participants were forced to turn attention to new and mobile collaborations of sensory input that distributed prehension throughout the body and space. This was an imaging that was in the service of, and serviced by, a synaesthetic coalescence of sensations – touch, hearing, balance, temperature of another body (the body as a perceptual system) (Gibson 1979, 61) – that were cobbled together as a workable alliance. Peripheral sensations were brought to attention by bodies attempting to make connections: perceptions composed of the intensities held between contrasting surfaces.[202] This cooperation between surfaces beyond their usual functioning caused unexpected and intensified conjunctions to arise – an arm pressed against the weight of a back, a foot cautiously feeling out the terrain underfoot, the slight vibrational ripple and noise of costumes brushing lightly past each other, all became central to any comprehension of spatialisation and the boundaries of the performers' own bodies.

As bodies reached out, groping in darkness for certainty, they battled with the problematics of their new clumsy relation to the field. With such compromised and unstable sensory input, affordances became more transient and slippery. Landing sites could be tentatively projected here – onto the new augmented surfaces of the body, the spots of light perceived on the other performer's costume, a particular sound emanating from a speaker, a shared site between foot and floor, and so on – distributing attention onto the surface of the body, the collaborator, and into the space. But these alliances quickly dissipated as the conditions continued to shift. In this way, senses cautiously turned out to these edges in an unresolvable searching for a stable point of location, an attention to these new shared but fuzzy spaces between body, costume and world: an attunement to the collective event in its unfolding.

Such tentativeness might be a suspension in the gathering of the event, an emergence of form, or, perhaps even less definite, an emergence of the conditions for form to begin to arise. Perhaps it was the inability to filter or prioritise sense information – to order and stabilise the field of experience – rather than a lack of information, which caught participants in a looping state of 'always just beginning' to make sense of world. The flooding with sensation of something not yet comprehensible is described by Manning as the 'activation in the here-now of the not-yet' (2013a 179) – a tuning towards and slowing down of the process of 'parsing the object from the field' (2013a, 277).[203] This disruption to the usual processes of perception separated causal comprehension from the richness of undifferentiated sensual immersion. It was a stretching of perception that provoked, as Manning has written of such experiences, an encounter with the shaping of the 'more than' of the event (2013a, 179), of the crystal point at which the actual and its larger potential begins to split, and the pull or lure of the virtual can be felt.

This tentativeness might approach what Arakawa and Gins have termed a 'biotopological thinking', encouraging an attention to the field, as much as to the body proper (2006, 60). Such

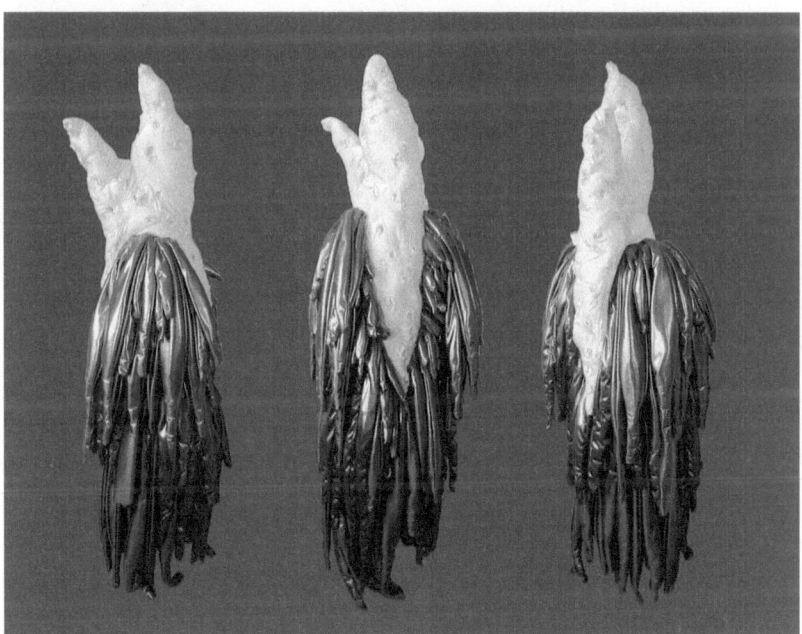

Figure 5.3 Andrew Goodman, *Psychopomp* Costume documentation. 2012. Digital photograph.

thinking they describe as a 'self-diagraming', a coordinating of one's world that portions spatial relations both approximately (as it was always evolving), and at the same time rigorously (as it was intensely relational across multiple scales of engagement) (Arakawa and Gins 2006, 73–4).

Psychopomp accentuated a felt quality of 'not knowing' – not quite knowing what delineated one's boundaries anymore, where either oneself or the other performer were positioned in the space, where a sound emanated from, how movement translated into sound events. This might be viewed not as a 'lack' as such, but, as Stengers notes, a 'characterization of a mode of working' (Stengers 2011, 286) that foregrounded the multiplicitous nature of the point of actual/virtual at which bodies moved. The 'not knowing' was a parasite within the knowable – the already-formed relation, the stable object of representation – disrupting and advancing through differentials with which movement problematised and molecularised the body. Not knowing was here commissioned as a tactic of production, positioning bodies at the 'edge of virtuality' (Manning 2009, 35) that movement then stretched out. In this it was perhaps a system 'advanc[ing] through problems and not through victories, through failures and rectifications rather than by surpassing' (Serres and Latour 2011, 188); a system charged with new indeterminacy. It required a new in-process attention that drew the creative and *ecological* processes of 'worlding' and bodying that are always occurring, bringing the gathering of relation to a perceptible level.

6

Entertaining the environment

Introduction

In the late eighteenth century, the Abbé Nollet created entertainment by passing electric current from a Leyden jar (an early battery prototype) through a line of 300 Carthusian monks holding hands, causing them to simultaneously jump in the air (Elsenaar and Scha 2002, 19). This was one of a series of early experiments exploring a fascination with this newly discovered force in the world, capable of passing through and rearranging subjects and objects. Such works demonstrated a shift in positioning the human and the environment: an enthusiasm for exploration of a distinctly non-human agency active in a lively world of forces, and an entrancement with the capability of such forces to traverse and reorganise human body potential into a decidedly 'post-human collective body/assemblage' (Goodman and Manning 2012, 2).

Erin Manning has proposed 'entraining' and 'entertaining' the environment (Goodman and Manning 2012, 6)[204] as a way of thinking through Alfred North Whitehead's perceptual categories of 'causal efficacy' and 'presentational immediacy' (Whitehead 1978, 310–21; 2014, passim). 'Entrainment' concerns the 'immanently relational intertwining of perception with action' (Goodman and Manning 2012, 6), and as causal efficacy can be thought of as a 'lure' towards prehension – 'call(ing) forth new immanent associations and new assemblages' (Manning 2013a,

23). 'Entertainment', on the other hand, is indifferent to these causal relationships (Whitehead 1978, 324).[205] Entertainment concentrates on 'the direct perception of the fielding of experience such that it brings its qualitative resonances to the fore' (Goodman and Manning 2012. 1). It centres on the felt quality of the experience of the activities of the field organising itself, rather than on the resulting objects or subjects. 'Entertainment' is resolutely concerned with the immediate activities of the field or environment and the collective individuations of an event that might arise.

Perception, Whitehead states, 'is the catching of a universal quality in a particular substance' (1978, 158). Here perception moves beyond mere feeling, subjectively 'rooting' the 'blind' and 'vague' feeling in the 'immediacy of the present occasion' (Whitehead 1978, 163). For Whitehead, as Jones states, it is the bringing together of the perceptual components of causal efficacy and presentational immediacy as the display for the subject of 'an *extended* environment *contemporary* to the percipient', that allows for comprehension through symbolic reference of 'the way in which causally connected organisms in temporalised relationship...are apprehended in genuine community in the present moment' (1998, 151, emphasis in the original).[206] That is, the two aspects of perception 'intersect' to provide sufficient understanding of 'a contemporary world of extended actual things', which, Whitehead argues contra to Hume, presentational immediacy cannot provide on its own (Whitehead 2014, unpaginated, II: 5, II: 1).[207] In this 'intersection' of the two factors intensity is achieved through subjective patterning, in that there is a contrast felt between the perception of the moment and comprehension of what has come before it, *and* that there is a contrast between what is in the moment and prehension of that which has potential to come to be (Whitehead 2014, unpaginated, II: 4).

In thinking through Whitehead's dissection of acts of perception into these two categories there are three points that I would argue are worth noting. Firstly, that the two components are essential to perception and are never fully separable. Nor, despite the term presentational 'immediacy', does one necessarily precede the other in a clear linear sense (Whitehead 2014, unpaginated, I: 8). Secondly, perception in this sense does not necessarily mean *conscious* perception, though it certainly is a factor for, as Whitehead terms them, the 'higher grade' organisms. These organisms have greater access to presentational immediacy and therefore have a greater capacity to condition the causal information prehended from the environment (Whitehead 2014, unpaginated, I: 8).[208] Thirdly, we must remember that for Whitehead perception is never the passive imaging of an established environment by a subject, but an act of self-production through the prehension of different components of actual and virtual datum and their constitution into the organism's concrescence (Whitehead 2014, unpaginated, I: 6).

Isabelle Stengers explains causal efficacy as a construction of chains of cause and effect, often based on prior knowledge or habitual response to sense data (2011, 401). This is a succinct description, in line with Whitehead's own initial description of causal efficacy as a subjective perception of the relation between the organism perceiving and relevant concurrent and precedent events.[209] But it also something of a simplification of the greater potential of causal efficacy, which more expansively also places events within a temporal and spatial relational patterning. This is not concerned with notions of time as 'pure succession', but the 'concrete' relational time marking the passages from events to events (the objectification of events that 'establish the conditions' to which subsequent events conform) (Whitehead 2014, unpaginated, II: 1). Similarly, causal efficacy is not a relationship to abstract space, but, in defining actual geometrical relationships to the environment, causal efficacy explicates another aspect of subject–event relations, and importantly is also a perception of the intertwining of the body with the environment, as we 'see *with* our eyes, we taste with our palates, we touch with our hands' (Whitehead 1978, 170). Through these aspects, causal efficacy provides not only a grounding of the body in the space and time of the past, but 'a sense of the implications...of the present on the future' (Whitehead 2014, unpaginated, II: 4).

For Whitehead causal efficacy belongs 'to the fundamental constitution of an occasion', and is therefore available in some form 'even to organisms of the lowest grade', whilst presentational immediacy is a 'more sophisticated activity' and available only to 'organisms of a relatively high grade' (1978, 172)[210]. Presentational immediacy is 'our immediate perception of the contemporary external world', and the knowledge it provides is, Whitehead says, 'vivid, precise and barren' (2014, I: 12). That is, whereas much if not all of the information gleaned from causal efficacy is vague and trivial, in the qualitative force of the immediate sensation we find both the precision and directness needed for a deeper perception. On its own however (if such a thing is truly possible), presentational immediacy remains 'barren' or disconnected from the full realisation of the occasion because these qualitative factors are not linked with intrinsic characteristics of that which is prehended until combined with causal efficacy (Whitehead 2014, unpaginated, I: 12).[211] As Whitehead notes, it is hard to imagine, at least for a human organism, a situation in which one might experience presentational immediacy on its own. Firstly this is because 'the present fact is luminously the outcome from its predecessors, one quarter of a second ago', at the very least in terms of having laid the conditions for events, however surprising, to arise from (Whitehead 2014, unpaginated, II: 4). Secondly, the very act of sensing provides some spatial information, as there is a spatial relationship established between, for example, a sound and the ears that hear this sound (Whitehead 2014, unpaginated, I: 12,

II: 6). Even in a moment of blind anger, he reasons, 'it is the man we hate' – a 'causal and efficacious' object, and 'not a collection of sense data' (Whitehead 2014, unpaginated, II: 4), and thus not blind to the way actual things are at all. However, perhaps one might occasionally experience a moment in which immediate and unqualified sensation briefly overwhelms the causal,[212] and it is one such experience in an artwork that this chapter examines.

Art events, like all other events of perception, necessarily contain causal efficacy and presentational immediacy to various degrees. However, as Massumi has articulated, interactive artworks have tended to overshadow direct experience in their insistence on demonstrating and fixing relational connections, foregrounding 'causal efficacy, instrumentality, [and] affordance' at the expense of their 'own artistic dimension' (2008, 7–8)[213]. This, Massumi says, is 'why you so often hear the comment from participants that [interactivity] feels like a video game' (2008, 8). Massumi argues that this reduces and contains relation in problematic and prescriptive ways as representational (2008, 8–10). Here it again becomes evident that a call to a 'relational' turn in interactive art is not enough on its own, without a careful consideration of the types and qualities of relation, and particularly an intention to encourage open-ended relational pulls towards the future rather than reinforcing existing conditions. The question of how to foreground the felt qualities and intensities of an interaction over causal comprehension is therefore a pertinent one for interactivity – the kind that wishes to step beyond the representation of existing relation toward an experience of its felt emergence.

While an emergent awareness of the processes by which causal efficacy folds into presentational immediacy does provide, as Whitehead states, a sense of the 'withness of the body (as) an ever present' (1978, 312), here, as a means to immerse within the immediacy of sensation of the event, I propose disruptions to the qualifications and validations of sensation that causal efficacy provides[214]. This parasitic disruption is examined through Lygia Clark's propositional artwork *Caminhando*, where the lack of causal comprehension within the work disrupts habitual perceptive processes and instead works to activate a felt resonance with environmental fields. This is produced through processes of transduction, bringing a new engagement with other entities in the environment and felt implication in a larger shared potential.

This chapter attempts to 'think with' Manning's concept of entertaining the environment in order to unpack the experience of *Caminhando*, concentrating on its potential for the opening of the body to a wider transductive field of play, and for the production of a phasing. This phasing might be a moment of slippage, a crack through which to escape the limitations of subjectivity. The question of how to think beyond the human subject is, as Simon O'Sullivan states, not as simple as a turning away from the human. Rather, it is a becoming-minor that is 'a kind of stretching or twisting, a rupturing and stammering, a releasing of forces from within and the contact of forces that are without' (2006, 64).

I relate *Caminhando* to a concept of an ecological ethics in that the work addresses not the representation of relation but its immanent construction. I argue that the work is ethical in that it enables an opening to further expression and connectivity. That is, it encourages an increased ability to recognise and respond to the force of other components of the event (to affect and be affected).[215]

From agency to transduction

As discussed in Chapter Three, the term 'agency' is problematic for a relational approach that seeks to resist collapsing back into the philosophies of substance of which Whitehead is justly critical. Once subjectivity is seen as only emergent in the act of concrescence, another, more ecologically compatible or event-based term is needed that is capable of acknowledging ongoing individuation and emphasising the ongoing and positive ingression of forces into new individuations.

In *Vibrant Matter*, Jane Bennett addresses these issues by thinking such acts of forces as a 'distributed agency', a 'swarm of vitality at play' (2010, 31–2). We might also think it as a process of transduction by which we can understand individuation that 'operates beneath all forms [and] is inseparable from a pure ground that it brings to the surface' (Deleuze 1994, 152). It is an ongoing and, in itself, multiple process that underlies individualisation. Individuation is the 'more than of becoming' (Massumi in Manning 2013a, xi) – becomings being dephasings of ongoing field-entity relations, singular expressions or differentiations of larger ecologies of forces. Transduction then is the process by which such 'an activity sets itself in motion' at the same time as it generates 'processes of modification' (Simondon 1992, 313; Simondon 2009, 11). For Simondon, it is a way of understanding and expressing the ongoing relation of a gathering of pre-individualised forces to an individualised entity that then exists as a 'partial and relative resolution' to these internal tensions (Simondon 1992, 300), while still allowing potential for further change.

Transduction describes the integration of formerly disparate things within a concrete system, the evolution of a shared associated milieu. It is how the becoming of an entity generates further unfoldings: becoming a force for further change, though not as a linear progression, but a series of overlapping, always transforming forces of differing viscosities, driving ongoing individuation. Whitehead's theory of prehension similarly describes such a process as a system of concrescence and continuity: an entity, having achieved actualisation, becomes an 'object' for other entities, potentially influencing these entities' unfolding concrescence (Whitehead 1978, 235). Thus an entity draws prehensively on every other actualised entity and the further potentials of the system, by whatever degree of separation, becoming a dynamic point in a complex ecology of relations. Here such feeling can be seen as transduction, a continual moving of force from subjective gathering to objective datum, and in such a complex and intertwined system, the transduction that triggers prehension must be seen as a vast nexus of complex forces, rather than a simple cause and effect paradigm.

Caminhando

> Make yourself a trailing: you take the band of paper wrapped around a book, you cut it open, you twist it, and you glue it back together so as to produce a Mobius strip. Then you take a pair of scissors, stick one point into the surface and cut continuously along the length of the strip…When you have gone the circuit of the strip, its up to you whether to cut to the left or to the right of the cut you've already made. This idea of choice is capital. The special meaning of this experience is in the act of doing.
> *Lygia Clark*

Following *Caminhando's* instructions creates a body-tool-object machine producing movement or an expression of connectivity rather than representation.[216] The work is per-formed rather than pre-formed, opening potential for a process of collective individuation to occur – a new event of assembling between its component parts – a drawing together through the force of shared movements between hands, eyes, scissors and paper (see Figure 6.1). As Clark says, 'at the outset, the *Trailing* is only a potentiality' (Bois and Clark 1994, 99); the paper and the cutting are, in themselves, nothing substantial. In the end, the result seems inconsequential and leaves little trace (Clark in Suchan

2008, 6). The art exists as a moment of resonate intensity, of prehended phasing, its beauty lying in the delicate capacity to activate and foreground transduction.

Process philosophy clearly views transduction as a ubiquitous event, enabling the 'drive towards novelty' in the universe that Whitehead describes. What then differentiates *Caminhando* from the everyday? It reveals the process of the translation of forces moving through the hands, scissors and paper, but it does not make the process 'conscious' in any articulate manner. It makes the effects of transduction felt by slowing down the process of phasing, provoking a suspension in the flow, and making evident the potentiality of the event. With the opportunity for re-construction and invention, it brings attentiveness to the environment, not as 'other', but as a collective gathering of a potential dynamic ecology.

At the point where you have cut an entire loop of paper and are back to the beginning, the scissors are no longer next to the original incision, they are somehow on the other side. Sight contradicts expectation, hand/scissors contradict paper: the habitual perceptual schema is problematised and cohesion falls apart. The causal efficacy gleaned from the skin/hand sense datum leads one to expect that the cuts in the paper will match up, but this is contradicted by the presentational immediacy. It is an 'error in symbolic reference', exploited here to promote 'imaginative freedom' (Whitehead 2014, I: 10). The link between these two components of perceptual processes is felt through their failure to smoothly orchestrate. Any stable sense of fixed space instantly dissolves, briefly becoming purely relative to the movement. It is a sudden plunge into the depths of presentational immediacy – an immediacy of sensuous perception that does not yet have the 'solidarity' that its qualification by causally efficious information will provide (and thus on its own it resists division 'into delusions and not-delusions') (Whitehead 2014, I: 12).

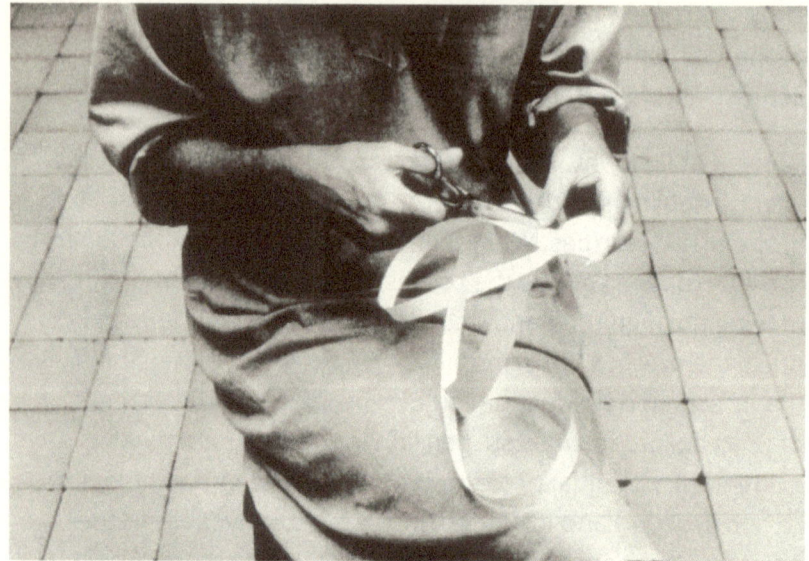

Figure 6.1 Lygia Clark, *Caminhando*,1964. Photo: Beto Feliciano. Courtesy of "The World of Lygia Clark" Cultural Association.

Tentativeness

This jolt shifts one out of habitual inattention and preformed assumptions, forcing a new concentration on what is going on in the moment. A similar sensation of disorientation might be experienced in the everyday when there is an unexpected loss or distortion of sense perception – such as a sudden change of auditory conditions like the disorientating effects of echoes in a tunnel, or the tactile strangeness of one's mouth after dental anesthesia. Such occurrences make the familiar world uncanny, and force improvisations with new combinations of sense information.

For the sighted person, for example, sudden darkness might trouble any sense of stability of objects and their relations and boundaries, and force a temporary fluidity and experimentation as the body cobbles together some kind of workable new 'organ' to make sense of the available data. In such a space, to those habitually reliant on sight to make quick spatial decisions, the whole body surface becomes a groping hand. Skin feels the edge of an object – as a resistant force – to gain information about the object, but never really know it as a whole. An edge could as well belong to a table, as a bookcase or doorway. Nerves respond only to the immediacy of the hard flatness, reinventing the object and body in relation at the next, cautious groping forward. As Whitehead says, sense relations here become 'vague', losing spatial definition yet retaining and even amplifying the emotional tonality of the event (1978, 176). Causal efficacy becomes less distinct here, while the immediate sensory information – and its felt lack – is drawn to the fore.

This process of re-gathering and reconfiguration that follows such a shift is the focus of *Caminhando*. Faced with a sudden loss of causal logic and a confusion of sensory data, completing the delicate task at hand requires a response to the unfoldings of the event in the present – and, indeed, to care *more* for what is being felt in the moment. The work demands a slowing down, a care towards the developing relationships between hands, paper and scissors, and how their potentials begin to merge and interact: sympathy with their own particular capacities.[217] We are asked to pay careful attention to what is being felt: to be immersed in the feeling of a re-gathering of forces. In navigating such conditions, 'tentativeness' naturally arises, as Arakawa and Gins might say (2002, 45), as both cause and affect of a body rearranging.

Such tentativeness might be thought as a feeling-out of the future potential of the event, an immersion in its goings-on. It requires that we gather what sense information we can, and backtrack from assumptions. This slowing down the shift from shaping to content allows a felt awareness of the pull of forces towards recomposition to arise (Manning 2013a, 189), feeling out the ongoing transductions of the ecology. *Caminhando* problematises any sense of subjective control over the event; it begins to evoke tentativeness into a simple habitual cutting action.

For an art event seeking to re-energise relations to the evolving ecology, we might ask how this kind of tentativeness evokes or makes evident the momentum of future potential and its relation to the field. *Caminhando* enacts Manning's proposition by unlinking the processes of entertainment and entrainment (however briefly or incompletely) in order to become submerged in the flow of individuation, of the gathering and transduction of forces from the field.[218] It perhaps asks us to develop a sensitivity to proceedings outside of habitual, so that the 'delicate and fragile value-realities' – those first tentative prehensions of the gathering of the ecology – do not 'die under our feet' as we march toward the already known (Jones 1998, 195). If there is an ethical need to think-with and feel-with the individuations of the non or more-than human ecology (Bennett 2010, 14), then art might have a potential role to play in engaging us in this increased attention and sensitivity towards emergent relation.

Paper, scissors, hands

As discussed in Chapter Three, for Whitehead the feelings of all entities are shared with the environment in the ingression of datum to form the entity and in the entity's gifting of itself as datum for other acts of concrescence (1978, 220). These feelings allow entities to become with their environment, if the environment itself is taken to be an event or series of enmeshed events. In *Caminhando,* affects pass through and initiate assemblages, new forms, and instigate new forces. The arrangement of fibers in the paper form tendencies (tearing in one direction, resisting in another way), that shapes the displacement from the hand-scissors' force. The kinesthetic tendencies of the scissoring action collect and direct the expressed pressure of muscle energies; the rhythm of vibrations of the cutting of paper is transduced by the ear and skin. *Caminhando* engages with not only the extension of what is perceptible to the participant, but also the dynamic negotiation between what is felt by all components of the event, and the feelings not immediately perceptible but essential to the forming of the event (Goodman and Manning 2012, 1). The event requires attention to how scissors, fingers and paper feel, to the sensitivities that form their worlds. It questions how their combined individuation – their folding into one another, their eventful assembling – creates, mixes and shapes their shared responsibility for events and further potential.

In itself, this is a potential extension of interconnectedness with the larger ecology of the event. The forces instigating the unfolding individuation flowing through the entities – the event of cutting and their intertwined affectual relations, their ability to feel – form the assemblage. These flows distribute the agency, not within objects per se, but in the event itself, contradicting the animate/inanimate divide. The 'environment' here is not some stage for a theatre of operations, but the field of forces resonating with entities. Here we might say that rather than things having feelings or sensitivities to an environment, entities have types of forces that can pass through them, that can transduce them, activating phasings, and that an increase in affectual sensitivity is therefore an increase in involvement with a larger ecology.

Multiplicity

The *Caminhando* assemblage is more than a binary machine. It is more than a multiple; the event is a multiplicity with its own logic, a concrete system of objects and field that exists in its entirety or not at all (Deleuze and Parnet 1987, 2). This multiplicity lies in the gaps between molar opposites – between hand/scissors, body/paper, subject/artwork – and in the transduction, the movement of forces through simultaneous individuations that pull apart the molar, making sieves of its boundaries and, in the excess of ongoing further differentiation, its shared potentiality.

Such transduction integrates disparate realities into a system of relation (Simondon1992, 315). This is a relation not only of the actual, but also the virtual. Multiplicities are irreducible: the sound of the ocean, wind, fog, and flocking birds. The earth's multiplicities are 'nebulous set(s)...whose exact definition escapes us, and who's local movements are beyond observation' (Serres 1995, 103), that we are thrust into or born out of (already always re-phasing): always from the middle of things (Deleuze and Parnet 1987, 23).[219] In the middle are the lines of flight (lines of 'growth and movement'), as immanent and symbiotic connections between that which is in the midst of coming-to-be and the larger potential (Ingold 2011, 71, 83).[220] Leaderless birds, for example, can collectively navigate so gracefully because their shared individuation brings into being not only the individual, but also an associated milieu, a collective pool of potentiality (Mitchell 2012, 73). Subjects themselves are not communicating, but rather are 'regimes of individuation that meet' (Debaise 2012, 7).

Caminhando places us in the middle of the tension of events tending towards further becoming, as always in-process, a reaching towards the next. Paper, scissors, skin each become dynamic points in a system, singular expressions implicated in the modulation of a shared multiplicity. This is the *agencement* of the assemblage (which is also always the assembl-*ing*[221]), more than its component parts, where cause and effect are lost in concrete inter-determined, co-causal transindividuation (Manning 2013a, 24–6). The becoming-scissors of the hand, the becoming-paper of the scissors, or the becoming-cutting of all the components, are combined in their shared potential – indeterminacy that is the richness of the event. To begin to feel part of such a gathering of future potential of forces might be a lure tending towards, or giving attentive care to, the qualities of how and what emerges, towards a shared responsibility in an ecology.

The power of the forming multiplicity here is that it takes us beyond the stalemate of the dichotomous, denouncing 'simultaneously the One and the many, the limitation of the One by the many and the opposition of the many to the One' (Deleuze 1994, 203). *Caminhando* draws attention to our shared individuation with the ecology of the event, and that our individualisation is an expression in and of this individuation that neither halts nor contradicts the latter process, but is a partial solution to an ongoing field of negotiations. Here it is made evident that we cannot have the individual without environment, that the two are points on a path of symbiotic enaction, individuation driven by transduction that is the becoming of the whole system, both the actual and the virtual with which it resonates. Assemblages in *Caminhando* create a shared ecology in the largest sense – a shared milieu or potential alongside a connected actuality – a system with 'internal coherence' (Simondon 1980, 40), because the enaction of the assemblage is co-causal with its field of potential: field and individual are a multiplicity.

Tactics

Clark says that, through participation, *Caminhando* causes the figure of the participant to 'deterritorialize itself' (cited in Martin, Ruiz and Rolnik 2000, 76). Deleuze and Guattari state that everything can have a microbrain (1994, 213), a topological system of forces for a nervous system. While Arakawa and Gins say we are organisms that 'choose to person'; such individuations are routines of expected behaviors (2002, 1–5). Implicit in *Caminhando*'s instructions are challenges: choose something else; embrace your multiplicity, your connections with the world, the forces that exceed your body, invent procedures, tactics to free yourself, learn to 'swim' in the tentativeness that is the 'more than' of bodying (Arakawa and Gins 2002, 84) that move us beyond stable subjectivity.

Arakawa and Gins' work shows how bodying makes 'landing sites', mobile points of connection penetrating the world, dispersing the body and intertwining with environment. *Caminhando* is such a technique for reaching into the world, transducing the body into emergent assemblages, to spark new individuations. It is a procedure that gives rise to new microbrains: in the hands-scissors, in the ears-eyes-paper, and so on. The art event here is a machine that might open up a gap in the subject. It is in this gap that moments of 'felt phasing' begin to create a flight path: an option to embrace multiplicity, to accent individuation over fixed identity. Caminhando begins to question the containment of the subject; it begins to activate an awareness of a dynamic relation both the actual environment and to the virtual, 'the combination of mutating fluxes, on their productions of speed' (Deleuze and Parnet 1987, 88).

Conclusion: Towards a new politics

This relationship to an environment is not something separate with which to engage, but is enactive: formed through collective individuations always occurring from and in the middle of other processes. This is not to say that the everyday does not contain subtle but strange occurrences when the body schema becomes momentarily confused. These are moments where causal efficacy and presentational immediacy fail to align and the body has to scramble to reassemble itself, allowing a brief glimpse into the processes of exchange and emergence in individuations (the confusion of tying a tie while looking in a mirror, where right becomes left, for example). But it is in *Caminhando*'s ability, despite the banality of the actions, to detach the event from the habitual inattention to transduction, and instead create a 'semblance', that such processes are drawn to the fore. Semblance, as Massumi uses the term, is the virtual's felt ingression into the event (2011, 15–16), its felt presence allowing a diagramming to take place, a thinking-feeling of the 'dynamic form' of relation and its connection to ongoing potentiality (Massumi 2011, 15).

All this, I suggest, is a step towards a new politics of art that attempts to engage in the creation of lines of flight, with the composing of techniques for inventing (new) potentials for existence (Massumi 2011, 14). It is *political* in that it 'connects up different aspects of life' – new lines of causality and experience (O'Sullivan 2006, 74).[222] Here *Caminhando*'s politics are those of the 'micro-political', as Lone Bertelsen defines it, working at the level of bodily habits (2012, 43), in which the event focuses attention on the continued felt emergence from which neither body nor field can be detached. This is an *ethical* art in Deleuze's definition, a practice of pursuing expression and connection, rather than representation (Murphie 1996, 105). It is an *ecological* approach that activates attentiveness to life and the field, to the conditions of the event expressing itself (Manning 2013a, 147–8), an ontogenetic 'technicity'[223] for living. This is an ecology-in-the-making: body-becoming-environment, environment-becoming-body. It is ecologically sensitive in assisting the formation of a trans-subjective attentiveness to an affective field across the becoming of space, time, bodies and objects (Bertelsen 2012, 39). Art events here, as Guattari states, can create an 'ecology of the virtual' capable of engendering 'conditions for the creation and development of unprecedented formations of subjectivity' (1995a, 91).

Throughout this book I have suggested that interactive art could at times do with less emphasis on the efficacy of relation between participant and artwork, and particularly on the conscious comprehension of these relations. Instead it might focus on further exploration of the potential of an immersion in sensation that stretches perceptual processes and makes felt the viewer's own emergent role in an environment's individuations.[224] I am proposing that the agencies driving this are best understood as the flow of forces and their transduction.

These forces pass through and trigger the individuations of entities, gathering such individuations into an intensive ecology that drives invention. This is an experience of a trans-human and lively world in the widest possible sense. This is a move beyond the subjectivity and agency of the human participant. In this move an investigation into what might trigger the environment's own capacity to generate forces of becoming would seem to me to be paramount, and I begin to approach this through Manning's concept of the 'minor gesture' in the following section.

Bridge: Pnuema and the minor gesture

In the installation *Pnuema*,[225] things happened as participants moved around – lights came on and faded or their rhythmic pulses quickened, and stormy sounds erupted and swirled around the space. Things happened too when the participant stood perfectly still or left the space, as elements of the work responded to other components' actions (such as feedback from light variations affecting the tonal qualities of sounds, or the movement of the hanging sculptural objects triggering the sensors), and complex 'behind the scenes' algorithmic processes continued to activate changes calculated from both current and previous sensor input. Here, rather than linear connections between movement and light or sound, complex combinations of triggers determined what changes were generated, so that the effects of a particular action continued to reverberate through the work over some time. For example, the composition and development of the layers of singing sounds that occurred when the space had no participants present was shaped by the system's 'memory' of bodily actions that had occurred earlier, and any stormy sound sample required particular sequences of triggers within certain time limits in order to be played. Thus while the generative aspects of the work related to bodily movement, the participant was not able to discern a direct link between their gestures and what was generated. In this sense, the event began to have an (automated or algorithmic) life of its own, entering into relation not only with human bodies, but also into a series of temporal conversations between various elements of the work.

Participants were able to feel some *qualitative* connection between their actions and how events evolved. For example, striding quickly around the space would over time increase the speed at which the aural storm developed and the lights took on more complex and resonate patterns of movement. But as the work played out connections and disruptions, it also resisted the demonstration of interaction. The complexity of the relation between an event – a movement or a change in light, the effects on other components of the work, the built in time-lag between a sensor event and its repercussions, the variations in the effects of a particular movement – meant that while the art event itself could, in its own way, 'feel' the relational implications, such *quantitative* understanding was denied to human participants.[226]

What filled this space that was formerly central to the relational or interactive event? Perhaps the immediacy of sensation began to assert itself? Perhaps it was something subtler that resolutely refused to address the human, and instead addressed the formation of the work from the field at an imperceptible and undemonstrative level? In this, the effects began to edge into vague perception – a fuzzy awareness of the incipient gathering of an event that was the event's ability to feel and respond to itself, to prehend potential individuation.

Manning has defined such relational pulls that 'lead the field of experience' and 'open [it] to its differential' as 'minor gestures' (Manning 2016a, 48).[227] A minor gesture is not exactly contained in any entity (algorithm, sensor or person), or event (movement, calculation, sound, light or relation), though, in order to individuate, these draw on the potential such gestures open.[228] A minor gesture 'introduces a kind of continuous variability into the work's progress, a variability that is durational', as Manning states, where what is felt is variability in itself, a sense of an opening to (parasitic) potential (2016a, 49).

This is a 'tuning' of the event to its future that is felt qualitatively, as an aliveness of an event forming. In *Pnuema,* this might be felt through the immediate and sensual connection with the expanded relational value of the lights and sounds as they form new complexities of connections. That is, it might be felt as a variation in connective or transductive potential sitting alongside any material or actualised variation. The minor gestures at the heart of *Pnuema's* self-tuning made both the actualised and potential relations mobile, always in flux – though not comprehensively demonstrated to the participant. Rather, such causal efficacy addressed, and was sensed by or resonated across, the ecology as a whole. This was an intensive exploration of the 'environment's *own* capacity to make felt the complex ecologies at work' (Manning 2016a, 54, emphasis in the original) – an ecological sensitivity not fully located in any one body, but as a plane with which the event itself engaged.

Participants were addressed here, but not only on a subject-to-object level. They might have tuned to the shifts in the affective tonality, alongside other components that also tuned and aligned in their own ways with such field effects. There were forces or wills at work that were not only dispersed but that resisted residing in objects and remained instead gestures incipient with the event. This allowed components to begin to address each other directly rather than only via human mediation. Did participants feel these gestures? Perhaps as an excess of relation beyond understanding, as a displacement of will, a loss of agency when compared to a normative interactive experience, as a sense of something lurking just beyond comprehension but nevertheless broadly affective: as an immediate but indistinct sense of variation and of a gathering of a more-than-human ecology.

7

The noise in the noise: micro-perception as affective disruption to listening and the body

> Sounds...dematerialize the substance of things they resounded and extend their own patterns...they drift off things and link up with one another.
> *Alphonso Lingis*

Introduction: vibrational symbiosis

The pitcher plant and the wasp have come to an arrangement: when the wasp enters the plant's flower and buzzes at a specific pitch the stamen release their pollen in an emphatic burst of rhythmic (vibrational) sympathy. No other pitch will do, the flower is indifferent to all other notes. It waits; it *listens*, attentively, for the wasp's particular calling card.

And yet...this is a plant – it has no ears, no brain. How is it able to listen, with what does it hear, how does it pay attention? And, one must ponder, how is it that it knows what it hears when it has no brain to perceive with? Perhaps, just as the brittle star has no eyes and yet is all eyes,[229] the pitcher is all ears – its entire surface attuned to the potential of a frequency, sensitive to the particular oscillations of the one vibrational speed for which it has an appetite.

The dance of the pitcher plant and wasp hints at the micro-perceptive potential enriching heard sounds. The transversal agency of sound as vibrational force courses through ecologies at pre-subjective, pre-content and pre-contextual levels, enveloping all in resonance that is the 'combat of energies' confronting each other (Deleuze 2002a, 65–8).[230] This is the vibrational diffraction of enmeshed relational difference. At this affective level, interactions – immanent relations – with sounds are not limited to the ear and the brain. They stretch across the entire surfaces of bodies attuned to the sensations of their particular ecologies: a 'listening' independent of cognitive capacities and body boundaries. This strange pitcher-wasp symbiotic relation seems to indicate that sound contains, or is contained within, sonic excess (Goodman 2010, 9): a silent, contagious life as force and as potential force, enveloping all in the ecology of the unheard.

This chapter considers some of the disruptive potentials of sound – that is, micro-perceptive sound's potential as a parasitic activator of change. It considers ways in which affective force produces ecologies through vibrational diffraction.

Micro-perception

The term 'micro-perception' refers not just to perceptions that are literally too small to be recognised, though the physical presence of the unheard begins to indicate some of the potential of micro-perception in relation to sound. Rather, as Brian Massumi asserts, it refers to a 'perception of a qualitatively different kind' (Massumi and McKim 2009, 4). It is pitched at the level of affect: 'hitting' the body, not with perceivable content but as a noise or interruption. Micro-perception can be perceived only as this interruption and transition, thus it is a 'purely affective re-beginning of the world' (Massumi and McKim 2009, 5).

Affect is a primary creative force,[231] as Jonas Fritsch argues, that unifies an event as it is also its extension or excess. Affect is, he argues, 'pre-personal, pre-individual and non-conscious but real in so far as it offers potential for action' (Fritsch 2009, 5). As such, it questions easy distinctions between event, subject and field (ibid. 6). It is a transitive force that connects and remains in excess of its effects, thus retaining further capacity to affect as it moves cross-temporally towards the future (Bertelsen and Murphie 2010, 140, 145).

Micro-perceptive sound then might be seen to offer potential as a transductive force, disrupting boundaries as it drives creativity through a resonance that connects through intersecting and knotted together 'diverse realities' (Mackenzie 2002, 13). Understanding the act of hearing as one of transduction potentially alters our whole conception of the act.

A single sound pulse is micro-perceptible. It is a singular shock to a surface that on its own cannot be understood as sound. It can be perceived only when in contrast: in relation to the interval, rhythm or difference between pulses. That is, it is not so much the single high or low point of a sound wave that is comprehensible, but the variations in pressure over time or the differences between a high and low point of a wave (the amplitude), and the distance between waves (the frequency, or number of waves in a given time). These then require firstly an *internal* or intensive differential logic (in the subjective comparison between the components of the larger sound event).[232] Secondly perception requires an *external* differential between the ambient pressure of the medium through which the wave travels and the pressure of the wave itself. In both cases if there is no contrast there will be no perceived sound, although clearly a single force or pressure will still be felt by the body as a micro-perception (though, as I will argue further on in the chapter, this can be expanded on in several ways).

As indicated briefly in the previous chapter, a direct connection can be made between Whitehead's conception of the role of prehension and held contrasts in the concrescence or individuation of an entity, and Simondon's concept of transduction. Simondon argues that transduction is more than the operation of forces on objects and the subsequent transformation of these forces through those operations, in that it is forces transformed into other forces through structuring (Combes 2013, 14–15; Mackenzie 2002, 50). We can therefore say that forces as held resonance constitute becoming (or individuation or concrescence):[233] affectivity that is 'the relational layer constituting the centre of individuality' (Combes 2013, 31). These 'resonances' are the internal contrast of different relations that, like the held contrasts of prehensions for Whitehead, are constitutional of the event of concrescence (Simondon cited Combes 2013, 18–19).[234] As in Whitehead's system whereby there is a subjective ingression of selected datum from the world into the concrescence of an event, the resonate contrasts are internal but also forge a link to the actualised world. These contrasts also resonate with the preindividualised potential of the event (which is also in a sense exterior to the individual at any one point in time) (Combes 2013, 31; Simondon 2009, 5, 7–9). Thinking of this link between transduction, affect and resonance emphasises that it is never a resolution of affective energies that occurs in becoming, but as Deleuze says, there is an ongoing 'confrontation', frisson or interaction between energies (2002a, 65–8). A collective or trans-individual and concrete example of this is discussed in this chapter in relation to the phenomenon of diffraction, in which complex resonances between sound waves constitute new and collective sound events.

In thinking of resonance as a key to the production of an event, one might argue that we do not even 'hear' the sound per se. Rather, the sound waves activate a sympathetic resonance in the mechanisms of the ear, which in turn are transduced into impulses in the nerves and then to neural firings in the brain.

This suggests that while in the act of hearing sound in the environment is prehendable by a body, the actual 'hearing-event' is self-contained and self-actualised as a subjective event that is intensively driven and satisfied. Deleuze's example of this thinking is that of a needle piercing the thigh: the pain felt is not the needle, but the actions of the nerve endings in the flesh (1993, 96). In this, as in Whitehead's theory, an entity is responsible for its own 'satisfaction' or concrescence, even as it draws prehensively on its relation to other entities (1978, 126, 153–6, 236–8). In this sense, sound does not pass into the body as such, but perception might be said to occur through a productive sympathetic tension or held resonance between the two systems.[235] In terms of an act of hearing or listening, this means that the hearing event is separate from, though influenced by, the sound event, and is never simply a passive ingression of data. Thus there is always the potential for creative divergence.

Interlude: Artaud's scream

Artaud's radio play *To be done with the judgment of God* pierces the air and vibrates the listener with wild screams and glossolalia (that are parasites to language, 'ruptures' and 'stoppages of flow') (Serres, 2007, 189). These can never be confused for nor contained within representational meanings. But more than this: the words themselves that are sung, shouted, agonised and whispered are so charged with affective power as to 'illuminate the entire nervous system' (Artaud cited Weiss 1992, 275). Here objects (bodies and meanings of words) become again force. The play's broadcast is an act of transduction as its transmission disperses the actors' bodies through the airwaves as disruptive vibrations, enacting Artaud's philosophy that man 'is not only dispersed within his body, he is also dispersed in the outside of things' (Artaud cited Weiss 1992, 253). Artaud incites this ability of sound to transverse the body, turn it inside out, to make organs of its surfaces, to empty its interior of meaning: Artaud-the-alchemist[236] cruelly uses 'radio magnetism as a counter-shock to achieve...the destruction of bodily hierarchies through vibrations' (Lucaciu 2010, 72). It is a cruelty, as Deleuze says, made not of horrible things, but rather 'the action of forces upon the body' (2002, 45).

Artaud's scream is made a 'physical substance in space' (Barber 1999, 106), a disruptive vibrational force that encapsulates his 'vast project of physical transformation' (Barber 1999, 93). Broadcast, it seeks to invade the sanctity of the listener's home and body. But the scream is transmitted not just in the literal scream that punctuates the radio play, but also saturates every sound of the event, as micro-perceptible affect coursing through and tearing open bodies it encounters.[237] It proposes to fold out the listener's body, makes their whole surface an organ that is invited to resonate in sympathy with the a-perceivable force of the sounds.

The problem Artaud addresses through his particular use of language/vocalisation is one of how to extend the tension of contrast of the micro-perceptive without providing resolution.[238] He develops a technics to suspend the body within the processes of multiple 'tendential unfoldings', as Massumi phrases it (Massumi and McKim 2009, 11), while also making felt the potential for 'different capacities for existence' (Massumi and McKim 2009, 12) outside of the major and the molar. It is an 'exploratory dancing of the extremities of the body' (Barber 1999, 103) an adventure into excess, a plunging into the multiplicity, where body, home, language as ground are contaminated and shattered.

Body as ear

While micro-perception is a pre-bodily force *of* the world, it must also be recognised that it is always implicated in the bodily, in that it acts on and through a body.[239] It affects bodies through the creation of a felt difference, both prior to and after the micro-perceptive event: an affective attunement (Bertelsen and Murphie 2010, 5, 6). Affects can be known as such only through their effects on bodies (Bertelsen and Murphie 2010, 4), and such bodies – be they speakers, walls or animals – all have an 'appetite': that is, a potential to affect and be affected[240]. Each, in its own way, performs a particular way of 'knowing' the world – a specific engagement with certain vibrational frequencies (Barad 2007, 379).

The human ear could be thought to engage with vibrations roughly between 20Hz and 20 KHz (Roads 2001, 7), but the human body is, in fact, receptive to a much wider spectrum. Outside of this audible frequency range lies 'unsound': the infrasonic and ultrasonic (Goodman 2010, 17).[241] To this list of the imperceptible, we might add, as Curtis Roads does, the subsonic (sounds too soft to be perceptibly heard), and ultra-loud sounds (those that are 'felt by the exposed tissues of the body as a powerful pressure wave' more than they are recognised or processed through the ears) (Roads 2001, 7). Such vibrations might be said to act synaesthetically on bodies – they affect the body at a base level of vibrational force that disrupts and stimulates multiple sensory capacities. This is the pain of high volume shock waves forcibly vibrating flesh, the infrasonic beat of a sub-woofer that reaches you through the soles of the feet, the prickling sensation on the skin of high frequencies, and the physiological effects of these frequencies in stimulating neural activity (Goodman 2010, 184). To this we might add the emotional effects of such unsound: the anxiety or edginess that might be evoked by either the very high or loud, the coercive effects of deep beats, the lure of the just-too-quiet to be heard. As affects, these unsounds come to be known to us through their formative effects on our emergent bodies.

Space-Shifter

Entering the environment of Sonia Leber and David Chesworth's *Space-Shifter* [242] the viewer is bombarded by strange voices – part language, part guttural exclamation – that saturate and resonate every surface, as much unsound as sound in their violent a-rhythmic shaking of the entire space (see Figures 7.1 and 7.2). Floor, walls, air, speakers, sheets of metal, and bodies are invaded, vibrated, penetrated, turned outward, and made into surface. Metal buzzes with secondary resonances, feet become ears as they oscillate with the floor. Waves of vibrations bounce of windows, walls and flesh, taking on new and singular speeds through their interactions with the differing viscosities of surfaces. The speakers, room, floor, metal, and bodies all (re)perform or express these vibrations in their own way, transducing according to their own affordances. Thus, a speculative vibration launched into the space by the speakers proposes to these various surfaces a multiplicity of responses, combining their various and singular capacities to resonate into a machine that produces vibrational difference.

The event of vibrational penetration of the space makes these new and contingent surface assemblages: machines that attract and modulate sound and unsound.[243] It rearticulates all bodies/entities into 'shifters',[244] new combinatory propositions glued together by the force of vibration. Its 'choral' sounds[245] are 'launched like missiles' to 'act directly on the space'[246] and entities.

Parasitic diffraction: the vibrational as differential force

In his essay entitled *Four Objections to Sound Art* Tim Ingold (2011, 136–9) sets out to argue that we need to make use of sound in artworks in ways that do not simply replicate the representational models of much visual art in presenting a soundscape to be 'played back', made 'aural' as painting can make a landscape 'visible' (2011, 136). This, he states, denies the fact that 'the ears, like the eyes, are organs of observation... just as we use our eyes to watch and look, so we use our ears to listen as we go forth in the world' (Ingold 2011, 137). Rather than compare sound to vision, Ingold says, we should associate it with light, emphasising the experiential nature of sound that involves a 'commingling with the world' that is both an 'embodiment' and 'emplacement' (2011, 137, 138)[247]. Here, I think, Ingold argues effectively for the need to think beyond the naïve idea that merely making an immersive sound recording is enough to create meaningful interaction or avoid the traps of representation. He instead suggests a more provocative approach that might emphasise the potential of vibration to move bodies beyond themselves and instigate to new and collective processes of individuation.

What then happens then when we think of *Space-Shifter* not as 'sound art', but as a series of vibratory propositions encouraging trans-body resonances – focussing on the productive disruptive potential that such micro-sound initiates, rather than its aesthetic or representational qualities? How can we think of such vibratory events for their ethical potential as disruptive relational forces that breach thresholds, folding and splitting entities?

To begin this, we need to first understand something of vibrational diffraction, and its role in producing difference through parasitic disruption. To include micro-perception in any discussion on sound is to acknowledge a more expansive definition of sound as vibrational force. Here it is a 'variation in pressure over time' (Evans in Massumi 2002, 171) encompassing all the elements of a sound that will be contracted into a perception – tone, pitch, rhythm, volume (composed from waves that differentiate in frequency, amplitude, phase and shape) (Evans in Massumi 2002, 171) – and the unsound, the micro-perceptible remainder. The physics of sound, Roads argues, clearly demonstrate that the basis of all these components of sounds is events of vibrational difference,[248] where rhythms of contrast disrupt any continuum: questions of speed and interval of oscillation. Sound itself is then an expression of this modulating difference (Evans in Massumi 2002, 171).[249]

But a vibration's actualisation must also always act parasitically on other waves in the space through the physics of diffraction. Diffraction 'has to do with the way waves combine when they overlap and the apparent bending and spreading of waves that occurs when waves encounter an obstruction' (Barad 2007, 74).[250] As waves, sound then 'intra-acts' in this manner,[251] with individual wave patterns engaging in disruption and interference with one another. These entangle in complex ecologies, always immanently expressing their differences in producing novelty in the torsion between these forces. In *Space-Shifter*, for example, a sound wave generated by the speakers hits and reflects off a surface, returning as a repetition but at a different speed. These reflections diffract with the incoming wave, producing new modulations that then also interfere and combine with both incoming and reflected waves, producing further modulations, and so on. What consistency of relation there is here is the consistency of events surpassing themselves (Combes 2013, 41), as each wave is implicated in the individuation of all the others. Such noisily productive enfoldings, disruptions, complications and interferences are parasitic actions. It is the noise in relation that is its creative force – a third and mobile position[252] that multiplies vibrational difference, blurring distinctions between cause and effect (Serres 2007, 57) as a resonance of a resonance.

Due to diffraction, we can say that a vibration in *Space-Shifter* always also produces parasitic vibrational forces intrinsic to its event. *Space-Shifter* proposes to construct vibration-surface assemblages that form parasitic machines operating on multiple fronts: producing intensive difference within wave events through diffraction that multiplies and drives towards novelty. The work here employs micro-perception tactically in several different ways, revealing the experience of *Space-Shifter* primarily as an event that explores the parasitic potential of sound and unsound.

The heard and unheard components of the sounds affectively engage the body with vibration in ways that create new contingent bodies from components of the body-artwork assemblage (machines within machines). Over and above the sound that is perceived by the ear itself, there is also the vibrational excess of sensation experienced by the 'skin-as-ear drum' that envelops the body (Serres 2008, 119).[253] This creates a shared vibrational zone of feedback loops between skin and world, an intra-active ecology of diffractions. Surfaces are implicated in each other's becoming(s): speaker surfaces affecting and affected by the vibrational capacities of the metal plates, floorboard oscillations meeting and conversing with vibrations of shoes, skin and walls bifurcating each other's projected vibrations in the shared space in-between, bodies remade as speakers, receivers, reflectors – together resonating surfaces.

Space-Shifter proposes space, floor, feet and metal as the ears, as they act as conductive surfaces, transducing vibration. Sound waves differentially connect surfaces to make vibrational ecologies that nest within ecologies. This is a doubling of the surface into a field-body machine, an in-between that is alive with productive potential – a 'sound envelope' that is as much a sieve as a container, a 'sensate surface' of connection (Anzieu 1989, 62–9).[254] The force of this sensorial meeting of surfaces – pressure/resistance meeting pressure/resistance – is a vibrational interaction with another that leads us out of ourselves (Lingis 1998, 135). It is a worlding that the sympathetic resonances enact: our surfaces taut drum skins.[255] This is a collective perception, as performed by the body as a sensate organ in sympathy with the forces of the world (re)generating.[256]

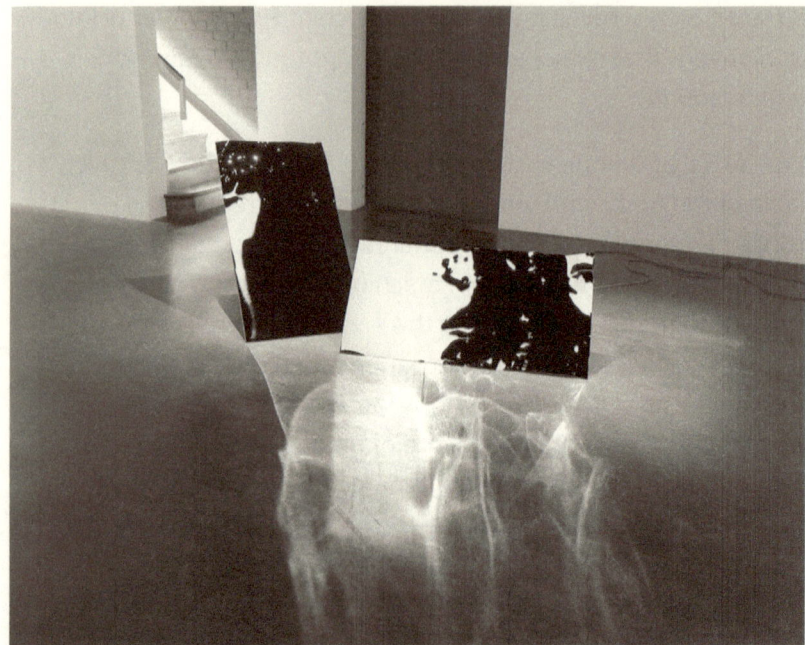

Figure 7.1 Sonia Leber & David Chesworth, *Space-Shifter* (detail view), 2009 Steel with 2G pack enamel paint, 14 channel audio, audio transducers, speakers. Courtesy the artists. This project was supported by the Australian Government Through the Australia Council for the Arts.

Here *Space-Shifter* makes explicit the vibrational forces surrounding and interpenetrating the body. The diffractional resonances with, and resistances to, the power of the external vibrational rhythms are folded into the body's own rhythms and speeds to create a third shared potential – a parasitic body disrupting prescribed boundaries. This is an ecological resonance, a collective and generative contrasting or transductive event.

Both audible and inaudible elements of a sound set up diffractive patterns with each other (Roads 2001, 33), a resonance that Goodman terms the 'hypersonic effect' (2010, 184). This parasitic noise operates on the audible range, modulating unheard vibrations, producing what we perceive as tonal colour or timbre (the layering of tones, overtones, intra- and ultra-sonic frequencies that give qualitative breadth and openness

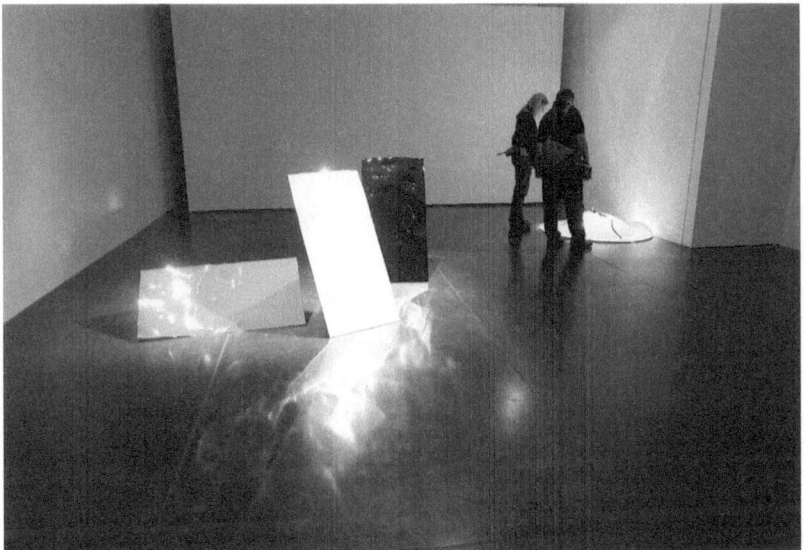

Figure 7.2 Sonia Leber & David Chesworth, *Space-Shifter* (detail view), 2009 Steel with 2G pack enamel paint, 14 channel audio, audio transducers, speakers. Courtesy the artists. This project was supported by the Australian Government Through the Australia Council for the Arts.

to perceived sounds). In addition, these diffractions produce a rhythmic multiplication or syncopation, with surfaces acting as attractors in the system of modulation of beats.[257] Here *Space-Shifter* becomes an affective 'rhythm machine', where connections between entities are assembled via sympathetic rhythms (Goodman 2010, 111), organising or patterning relations between pulsating bodies. Rhythm plays out the problem of the disjunction of differing vibrational speeds, as a gathering of these differences on a plane.[258]

As such, the parasitic actions of wave diffraction more than multiply the vibrations to be experienced through diffraction. They are micro-perceptive machines that produce a *multiplicity*, virtuality, to the sound event, a system of potential disruptive production of 'new rhythms, resonances, textures and syntheses' (Goodman 2010, 191) that is immanently produced with the audible.

Micro-perceptive sounds are parasites on cognition, on the hegemony of perceptive reduction of sensation of vibration,[259] and on the easy distinction between listener and the listened-to (receiver and received) as all become entangled in ongoing transductions. The insistent force of vibration in its not-fully-formed or cognisable state requires of a body that it compose organs to cut or actualise perception from a virtual plane of vibration. It also keeps vibration on the edge of the virtual, still at its most open to different combinatory possibilities, suspended in the not-quite decided. This is the parasite as creator of 'fuzzy' relation (Serres 2007, 57). Here sounds in *Space-Shifter* lose their beginnings and ends through refolding and held dispersion. There is unease in the encounter with these heightened disturbances, an edginess that the lure of the unheard performs, a heightened sense of the presence of an excess that cannot be contained within the audible, that refuses contraction but insistently is felt on the body. This invades enjoyment or contemplation of the work as one is thrust into the middle of its machinations (Deleuze 1993, 93). In this way *Space-Shifter* acts parasitically on one's emotion state – a metaphorical diffraction – disrupting the contraction of sound to signification, acting heterogeneously on established language-sound hierarchies.

On all these levels, *Space-Shifter* is insistently not just 'sound' to be contemplated and comprehended, but affective force in the event. It is a 'performance of the world in its ongoing articulation' (Deleuze 1993, 93), a way of 'knowing', a 'specific engagement of the world' (Barad 2007, 379) across a vibrational plane.

Refrain: Parasitic unsounds

In the installation *Momo*[260] (see Figures 7.3 and 7.4), unheard but affectually forceful vibrations were layered to produce a sound ecology that might impact on bodies beyond the perceptual processes afforded by the ears. Within a sound design – one that already recombined sounds through cutting, layering, echoing and volume shifts in response to fluctuations of light and movement in the space – each sound sample was itself a layered combination of perceptible and micro-perceptible sounds. Samples consisted of both a dominant sound (a word, phrase, or other vocalisation), and approximately four to eight 'unsounds' (see Figure 7.5). These sounds were manipulated to sit below a humanly perceptible threshold by virtue of their high or low frequency range, and/or because their volume sat below an audible level, and consisted of both altered versions of the dominant sound, and other found sounds chosen for their particular affectual qualities.[261] Here another layer of held difference or contrast was added to each sound event through these new and competing samples that began to move the dominant sound beyond itself, recreating the sample as a machine capable of intensively differentiating.

While the viewer could not audibly comprehend these additional layers, they did create affects on bodies in ways somewhat more difficult to articulate. These affects could be felt by listening to the difference between the main sample on its own and the layered composite sound. When combined, what was heard gained an unsettling quality that heightened the already abrasive qualities of the vocalisation. A sense of uneasiness was added that could be described as a shift and increase in richness or intensity of the affectual tonality – a prehension of the unsaid/unheard. In addition, certain frequencies in the background sounds produced subtle physical affects on the body (such as a slight prickly feeling on the skin or a tension in certain muscles) that added to the emotional response, and to the feeling of a 'more-than' qualitatively combining with the perceived sound. These layers of the experience might be thought of as disrupting through creative multiplication, a 'checking' of the process of clear perception that allowed micro-perceptions to 'invade' consciousness (Deleuze 1993, 93).

This felt presence of an unheard excess within the sounds perceived might be proposed as the beginnings of a bodily awareness of a larger vibrational ecology at work. In this way, the design sought to experiment with heightening sensitivities to both the excess of sound in the sonic environment, and to the sensitive capacities of parts of the body that interact with vibration. Rather than focusing on communication via the ears, the design experimented with the disruptive qualities of vibrations to encourage listening in a larger bodily sense.

The utilisation of micro-perceptible sound also began to work towards a more complex ecology of interactions. These were concerned not just with ear-to-speaker connections, but also with multiple sound wave-to-sound wave and surface-to-surface connections and combinations. A non-human level of dynamic interaction played out within the work, as vibrations of both sounds and unsounds interfered with each other – as they always do – but were multiplied and complicated by the greatly increased percentage of unsounds present. These played out, on an environmental plane, the combinatory, diffractory and essentially molecular nature of vibration.

Should we still term these as sounds? Certainly they acted on bodies, making connections between surfaces, but perhaps they began to disturb the boundaries between sound and other forces, between one kind of sensation and another, between the capacities of the ear and the potential of the surface of a body to be coopted into an expanded listening machine. These micro-perceptible vibrations remained, to some extent at least, at a level of affect, of trans-objective and trans-subjective force.

These active forces played out their differential equations below a perceivable level. What was perceived were the effects of this battle of 'wills' (Deleuze 2002b, 61), but the vibrational here extended to a more-than-human plane, beginning to position the work as being concerned with a larger play of force within

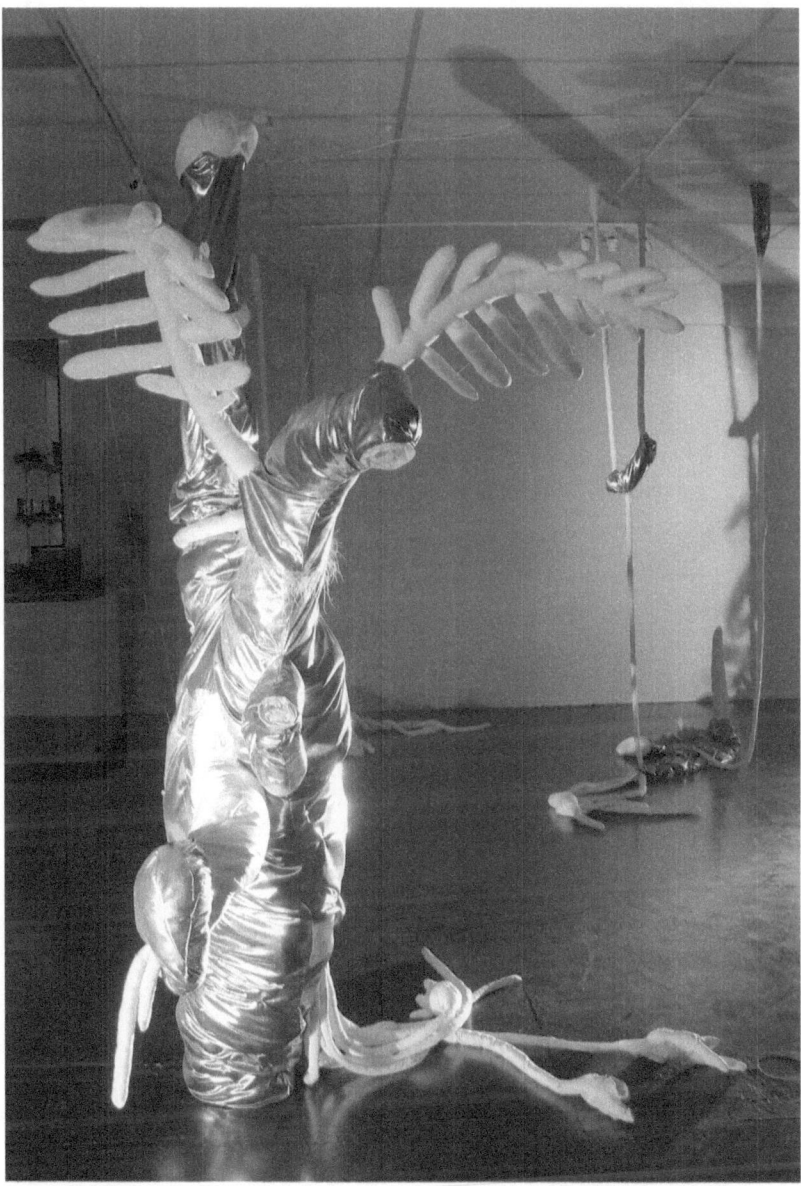

Figure 7.3 Andrew Goodman, *Momo*, (detail view). 2011. Paradise Hills Gallery, Melbourne.

the environment. Micro-perception here operated at the level of the minor gesture, emerging 'from the field itself', as Manning says, concerned with an expressive variation not held within an

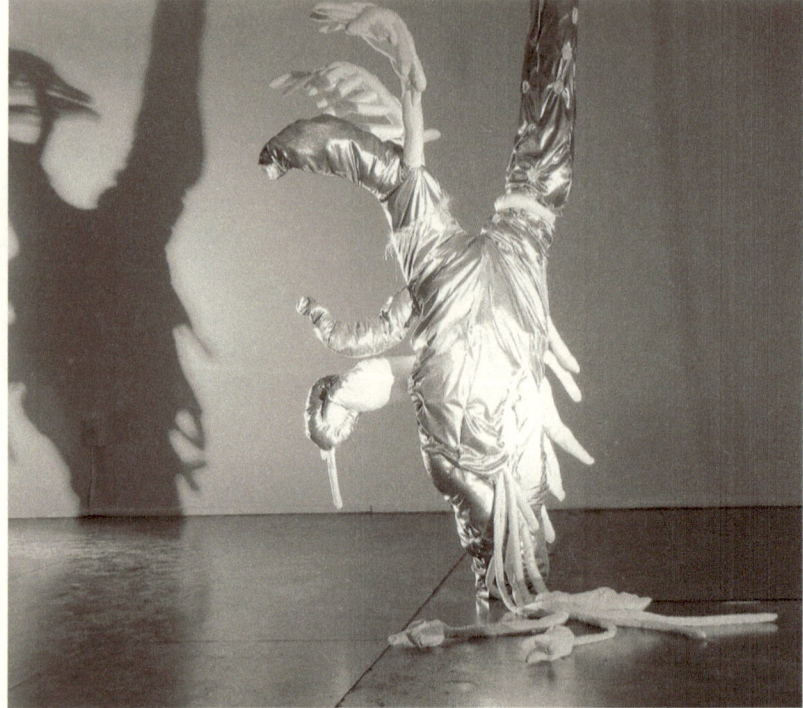

Figure 7.4 Andrew Goodman, *Momo*, (installation view). 2011. Paradise Hills Gallery, Melbourne.

object as a perceived sound, but within the environment's own capacity to prehend and interact with its intensive differential (2016a, 48, 54).

Multiplicity: the aliveness of the virtual

How can we perceive sound – whether through the ears or body as a whole –and construct a useable set of vibrations from the multiplying 'noise' of diffracting micro-perceptions? Clear perceptions, as Deleuze argues, are actualised out of the potential of the micro-perceptions that form their virtual – the multiplicity from which they concresce. Each perception is a singular configuration of 'compossible minute perceptions' that yields perception as a cut in the multiplicity of such potential combinations (a 'zone of clear expression') (Deleuze 1993,

The noise in the noise 173

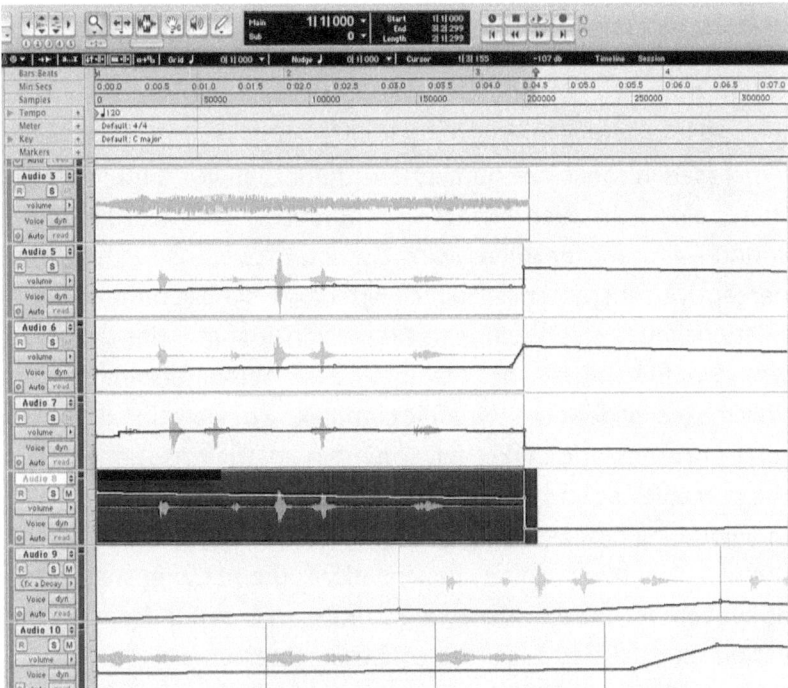

Figure 7.5 Sound layering in a sample from Momo. In this example, the dominant sound is highlighted, while other manipulated copies of this sample, and samples from other sources, sit below a perceivable threshold.

90).[262] These enmeshed micro-relations form an affective entanglement, without themselves being distinctly expressed. It is the act of perception, productive resonance with vibration, which cuts into this virtual plane and actualises a particular contrast of the relations between micro-perceptions. That is, the perception expresses a distinct diffractive combination of micro-perceptions in a particular way that yields a focus, but retains also some relation to all the micro-perceptions of the multiplicity. Each perception then is a singular and subjective expression of its relationship to the entire field in its intensive and selective patterning or contrasting of these micro-perceptions (Deleuze 1993, 90).[263]

As always, perception is a result of the differentials of differential equations, that is, what is perceived is the modulation of difference over time (Evans in Massumi 2002, 177). This dynamic (unheard) virtual of the perceived sound actively disrupts its stable status as 'object' with determinate or idealised status.[264] Instead it becomes the product of differential relations of affects expressed in conscious perception. There is always a multiplicity that is alive in its ever-diffracting evolution in each heard or felt sound – a future-feeling drawing the sound towards further perceptive concrescence. *Shape-Shifter* draws these unheard relations into a clearer zone of expression, just as it positions what would habitually be clear into a zone of indeterminacy. This makes evident the dynamic complexity of vibrational forces present, and makes felt something of their relation to the perceived sound as it invites us to suspend ourselves in this individuating process. One is thrust into – or emerges tentatively out of – a seething ecology of sensations: the body reconstructed as synesthetic machine, drawing vibratory sensation from it's various surfaces-as-organs to construct a perception.[265] In this respect, the work might be seen to be 'ethical' in sympathy with Simondon's proposition of ethics as the 'sense of individuation' (Simondon cited Combes 2013, 64) that links or makes felt the preindividual component of an event and affirms the relational nature of this event (Combes 2013, 65).

Here, *Shape-Shifter's* ethical relationality encourages an awareness of a 'vitality' of nonhuman composition, and the ability 'to become perceptually open to it' (Bennett 2010, 14). But the 'non-human' here must be thought of, not as an exclusion of the human dimension, but as the affectual forces that course through and are felt by both the human and other entities, making evident the transindividual elements of any concrescence (Mackenzie 2002, 117). The transindividual, Mackenzie says, cannot be conceived of as being interior or exterior to the individual, but as a 'continuing folding and unfolding limit between inside and out' (2002, 137). This positions the individual as 'one provisional [outcome] of a collective individuation in process' (Mackenzie 2002, 207). This transductive stance, which

Mackenzie takes from Simondon, again places an emphasis on the forces and minor gestures within the field that motivate the further collective gathering or individuation, and of which the vibrational ecology of *Shape-Shifter* provides an exemplary case.

Shape-Shifter achieves this ethical sympathy with the ecology, I would argue, through its ability to make problematic the experience and concrescence of a remarkable or clear perception (Deleuze 1993, 91). 'Perception' of sound is revealed as contingent and in-process, a process of differentials differentiating, which is 'an expression of the in-between' (Murphie 1997, 326). Sounds that have denied representation on a more superficial level – by emphasising part words and vocal expression over easy signification – work to draw the participant into implication in the processes of diffraction and production, as a series of interactive surfaces that assemble as differential machines.[266]

Micro-perception is configured as a problem, which finds an expression in perception (though not as a 'solution' as such, more a 'working through'). When engaging with *Shape-Shifter* we try to comprehend, to make the vibrations coalesce into readable 'sounds'. But the magnitude of the differentials, the speeds at which they move, and the unbalanced relationship between the heard and 'unheard', disrupts this contraction. The richness of the work's affectual force leaves us disorientated, perceptually unresolved, still searching for a defined body, space and sound. This process of disruption of vibrational wave by vibrational wave is not only foregrounded but stretched or preserved. It is the vibrational 'aliveness' of the event that the body of the participant comes to feel itself explicitly implicated in. Thus as feelings – as prehensive resonance with other entities (Whitehead 1978, 220) – the affectual qualities of micro-perceptible vibrations become evident, and new sensitivities to the vibrational ecology in which we are immersed are proposed and can be experimented with.[267]

Conclusion

Shape-Shifter emphasises the temporal through the mediation of rhythms of the vibrations disrupting and combining (Braidotti 2002, 154). The work addresses listening as an act of combining and disrupting relational vibrational processes and of sensing the inherent further parasitic potential, rather than as the perception of individual 'completed' or explicated sounds. In this it approaches what Braidotti has proposed as a 'nomadic music', concerned with a becoming-interval and a dynamic relation to the field, to the inaudible and imperceptible (Braidotti 2002 155).[268]

A 'nomadic' music suggests shifting ideas of sound design from completed or wholly realised sounds to mobile assemblages of micro-sounds as micro-perceptions. This might enable a shift from a representational model to one of production. That is, a shift towards a focus on enabling conditions for the production of perception of sounds out of the field of micro-perceptions, with their inherent and parasitic diffractive resonances. *Shape-Shifter* approaches the limit of what can be heard or understood as sound, and in addressing this limit of the perceptible, it proposes new organisations of surfaces (assemblages) with which to perceive.

Here sound in an art event is potent, not for its ability to extend meaning and communication beyond the capabilities of the eye, as it is so often how it is utilised, but rather to problematise such notions of communication-between. Thus it is harnessed at the level of affect to open potential for new bodily individuations, and it is the space of the body that *Shape-Shifter* vibrates as much as the air or floor. It sets these bodies resonating to awaken new appetites, new sympathetic resonances and dissonances, as they tune into the multiplicity of the vibrational ecology within which they become.

8

A thousand tiny interfacings: fertile acts of resistance

Introduction

> These spaces between are more complicated than one might think...less a juncture under control than an adventure to be had.
> *Michel Serres*

Brian Massumi has argued that the interface is an unsustainable concept within a process-centered world. In its usual understanding, the interface is positioned as a 'privileged site of mediation' within a system, Massumi states (1995, 7). This is evident in the various definitions of the interface as 'a bridge and a channel' (Hansen 2011, 68), a distinct 'point of contact' (Grau 2003, 198), or as 'devices that link humans to machines' (Poissant 2007, 236).[269] Such ideas of the interface as a prime site of creativity, interaction and communication deny what in process philosophy might be seen as the relationally enmeshed nature of all entities. Massumi's philosophical stance emphasises the 'primacy of processes of becoming over the states of being through which they pass' (Massumi, De Boever and Rolfe 2009, 38), that is, that any entities interfacing with each other are themselves composed of relations. As such, discrete interfaces are problematic in that they might be seen to imply a world inhabited by ideal, internally stable objects, between which interactions occur. The interface's role, in such modes of thinking, is to rejoin entities that are by implication discrete, where the complexity of continued unfolding and relation to the dynamic virtual or potential is greatly diminished.

There is much to be critical of in the privileging of the interface. As Massumi notes, it can promote a naïve excitement in undifferentiated flows of information, an unquestioning, utopian promotion of interface 'for interfaces sake' (1995, 1), that fits in perfectly with capitalist models of circulation and surplus value (Massumi 1995, 9). To this, one might add the cybernetic conflation of the biological and technical, of which Simondon is so dismissive,[270] and which Massumi describes as the 'industry philosophy' (1999, 33). The extension of the 'prosthetic function' of the interface, is utilised as a method of controlling, 'a relay point in the dissemination of human ordering activity into space…transform[ing it] into a realm of expansion onto which the human projects itself', with real difference erased as the body 'disappears behind a techno-logical shield' (Massumi 1995, 3). This subjectification of the technical object, which Anna Munster has pointedly termed 'interfaciality', is a codification as face to face, rather than body to machine relation (2006, 122–4). Interfaces here contain potentially problematic elements of power and control in their stratification and limitation of relationships, denying, as Matthew Fuller says, a user's engagement with the internal operations of computer software (2003, 142). In this, he argues, they potentially not only codify relations and subjectify technical elements (treating technical assemblages as a stable and ordered 'whole' with fixed interrelations between these elements), but also work to model human subjectivities in relation to the particular and pre-coded interactions that an interface demands of them (Fuller 2003, 113–4). Here the disciplining operations of interfaces operate not only to refuse certain levels or types of engagement, but also to enforce or require other types of homogenous interaction, such as the ubiquitous 'swipe' of the smartphone or tablet that encodes and limits bodily gestures.

Such disciplining of relations, may indeed, as Fuller notes, exhibit tendencies to break down as 'control folds in upon control, mess[ing] with its too-easy seriality', creating 'opportunity for something else to emerge' (2003, 113). However, the primary sticking point for discussion of the interface within process philosophy remains: that the very concept of a distinct interface relies on hylomorphic thinking that see it as a privileged site of interaction within an otherwise inert representational system of 'scientific materialism' that seeks to explain 'all change in terms of changes in "external" relations between beings that do not change in themselves' (Stengers 2011, 128).[271] These clear cut boundaries between things become hard to sustain with closer inspection: electrons migrate, charges pass, affects flow, bacteria course freely through us – the separation and discretion of objects and forces becomes more and more relative and intertwined. Within a process-based conception of the world that recognises the primacy of forces and relation over form, all is interface; everything is dynamic communication, incipiently co-forming.

So here we have our paradox: maintaining clear and distinct interfaces between things requires us to ignore the actual flow and enmeshed quality of lived experience, while acknowledging the primacy of the relational means everywhere we look are a thousand tiny interfaces. Neither proposition is of much use for either thinking or constructing dynamic, immanent art events. In this chapter, I want to show some ways in which we might think through the process of interfacing as a creative force within an art event without succumbing to the type of static, representational models of which Massumi is justifiably critical.

To do this I will examine a particular incidence of interfacing that occurred in Raphael Lozano-Hemmer's work, *Re:Positioning*

Fear: Relational Architecture 3, in order to consider ways in which unplanned interfacings between a public and the technical assemblages of the work helped to develop a greater level of both self-organisation and openness in the event, potentially operating across a social, artistic and technical level. An interesting shift in the forces generating in the work occurred – moving from those preconceived by the artist to new, shared and emergent individuations developed through an interfacing of a public bringing their own intentions and tonalities to the event. But, while these events are of particular interest here, I do not wish to overstate the uniqueness of the case. As Lozano-Hemmer has said, the events were certainly significant in his rethinking of the ways in which he staged further *Relational Architecture* iterations, however this does not necessarily imply that the occurrences were extraordinary for such large-scale interventions, which are by their nature always composed of multiple and often contradictory intentions and forces, and can potentially head in numerous directions, both predictable and surprising.[272] Rather, this example provides an opportunity to consider the creative potential of interfacing, and its ability to complicate and re-energise the event. In putting the interface to productive use as a differential tactic within an art process, I propose that it might provide a logic of self-regulation, one capable of internally driving the creation of intensities of resonance or disturbance through connection.

Interfacing

If we begin by thinking temporally rather than spatially, it is possible to consider these interfaces as moments rather than points of action or relation. This suggests that the interface might now be thought of more as a process of interfac*ing*,[273] as an unfolding or contingent process within a larger nexus of relation, as an in-action moment of intensity of disruption, contrast and invention rather than a privileged or static position within an art event.

As noted in Chapter Two, a machinic conception of both bodies and technical objects allows us to think of them as assemblages that are productively relational, rather than fixed – always capable of further expression of some potential. These organic and non-organic machinic assemblages are mobile, in that they can contain other machinic combinations nesting within them, and can also co-operate with other assemblages to form larger (though resolutely non-unified) machines (Braidotti 2002, 254). I will briefly consider the idea of an art event as a machine producing transductions of forces, before attempting to unpack the creative role of interfacings in *Re:Positioning Fear* by suggesting that interfacing might productively parasitise.

Transduction

It is common to think of interfaces as translators of code, points of information exchange, from digital to analogue or vice versa, or as a 'point of contact where humans and machines meet in order for exchange to take place' (Grau 2003, 198). However to assert the primacy of the flow of forces, rather than the secondary exchanges of text, I have begun to argue that transduction is a better way to fully think the event of interfacing. Transduction positions interfacing as the integration, through the flow of forces of differing viscosities, of formerly disparate things within a becoming-concrete system.[274] As Thomas LaMarre notes, a move towards concretisation implies an increase in the complex inter-determination of the individuations of the entities that comprise a larger ecology. It also implies a greater openness or indeterminacy in the 'charging' (with potential) of the relationship between the potentials of an entity and its field (the internal and external milieu) as the 'associated milieu' of the event that 'runs through or across inside and outside as a *transductive potential*' (LaMarre in Combes 2013, 93, emphasis in the original). This 'charging' with potential is, as I will argue is the case with the events that disturbed and ultimately transformed *Re:Positioning Fear*, a *problematisation* within a field that acts as the catalyst for new individuations to arise. These are partial or ongoing solutions that individuate not only relations between the entity and field, but also new sets of rules or planes on which individuations might operate (Vollrath 46). That is, such problematisation enables the 'discovery of the dimensions according to which [the] problematic can be defined' (Simondon 2009, 11, 12). Transductions individuate or evolve these dimensions, Simondon states, *over time* (2009, 12), bringing the concept in line with interfacing as an unfolding of an ongoing productive relationship rather than a pre-structured or instantaneous ordering of relations.

In transduction then, as argued in Chapter Seven, we have a way of thinking how components relate that, rather than resolving or fixing relation, emphasises the ongoing productive and speculative internal and external tension of resonances between potentials brought into conjunctive and nonlinear relation (Mackenzie 2008, unpaginated). Transduction, for Simondon, generates the dimensions in which components can communicate 'without loss, without reduction' (Simondon 2009, 12): a 'solution' that conserves rather than limits or reduces information and potential as in the traditional notion of the interface. Thus transduction might expand interfacing from a limited notion of fixed actualised relations mediated through an interface, to one that emphasises dynamic and ongoing interactive potential on a virtual plane.

An art-event might be a transductive machine: regulating and producing affectual flows, a 'machinic of expression rather than a signifying apparatus' (Murphie 1996, 104), a producer of movement (Munster 2006, 15) or difference. Again, transduction must be thought of as occurring not only on a concrete physical level, but also – as will become particularly pertinent in the art examined in this chapter – at social and psychological levels (Simondon 2009, 11). In conjunction with this, the individuation of the individual is also trans-individual in that it is inherently intertwined in larger, collective individuations (Simondon 2009, 9).

If the transduction that occurs through interfacing produces difference, then this positions interfacing as a prime creative force-form.[275] Seeing interfacing as a machinic action implies a shift in designing art events in order to emphasise their machinic potential, their productive capacity or capability to produce difference. It is this operation of the interface as a *differential machine* that is addressed below through an unpacking of *Re:Positioning Fear*, in light of three related actions of creative differentiation: parasitic noise, folding and the resonance of the incompossible, and concretisation.

Re:Positioning Fear

Re:Positioning Fear consisted of an orchestrated shadow dance composed of a projected conversation thrown onto the architecture of the city. This text was made visible within the shadows participants cast on the surface, creating silhouettes of differing sizes depending on their distance from the light sources (see Figures 8.1 and 8.2). Here the bodies of the participants performed disruptive interfacings within a machine composed otherwise of technical objects and public architectural components. This melding of technical objects with the unpredictable input of a public presents one possibility of providing the technical elements with an expanded potentiality. Its 'relation with elements outside itself' provides a level of indeterminacy (Munster 2006, 14). The body, as Combes states, is always in an ideal position to make connections with the technical, to 'become with', to play the role of 'transducer between machines' as it has an 'always active virtual' (2013, 60).[276]

Parasitic noise

Part of the appeal of this work is undoubtedly the inbuilt complexity with which it enables or creates potential to engage various components of the city in a new and playful manner. This, as Andreas Broeckman writes of the work, was a dynamic 'social interfacing', as *Re:Positioning Fear* constructed a 'fragmented and heterogeneous system of engaging different publics in a variety of specific ways' (Broeckmann 2004, 381). Thus personal imagery was re-inscribed on architecture burdened with often-oppressive histories, public spaces re-commissioned into dialogues with the performative, bodies unproductively intertwined with technologies of surveillance and control, and so on.

However a much more interesting and radical disruption also occurred in the particular unfolding of this work, which was already primed for playful intervention and evolution. It was in this catalysing moment, through parasitic action, that a new and more complex machine was produced. Alongside the positioning of their shadows on the façade to activate the hidden text, participants began to synthesise a different work out of the components by engaging specifically in play between their projected silhouettes. They utilised the potential to radically alter the size of their shadows by moving closer and further away from the projected light source to engage creatively with one another. For example, a wheelchair bound participant created a giant image of himself and 'ran down' everyone else (Lozano-Hemmer 2005, 6), while other participants played with shadow puppetry of smaller bodies, and the making of multi-limbed combinatory beings.[277]

A thousand tiny interfacings 185

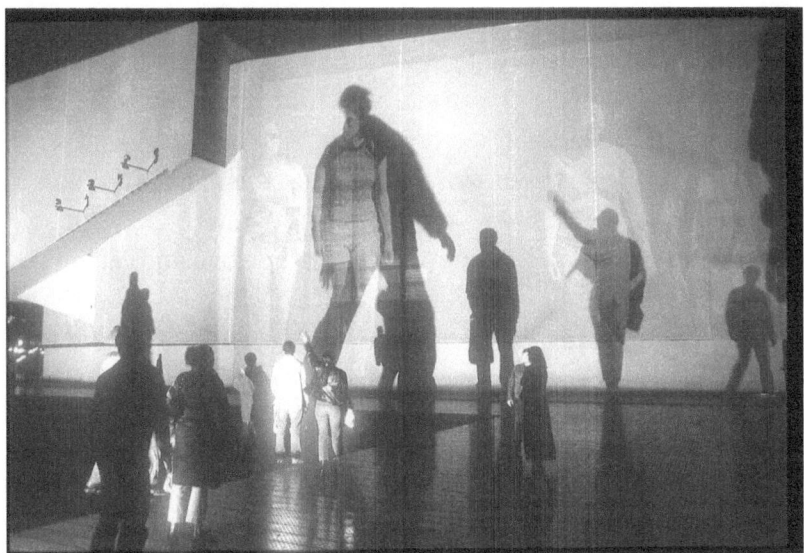

Figure 8.1 Rafael Lozano-Hemmer, *Re:positioning Fear, Relational Architeture 3*, 1997. Landeszeughaus, Architecture and Media Bienale, Graz, Austria. Photo: Joerg Mohr.

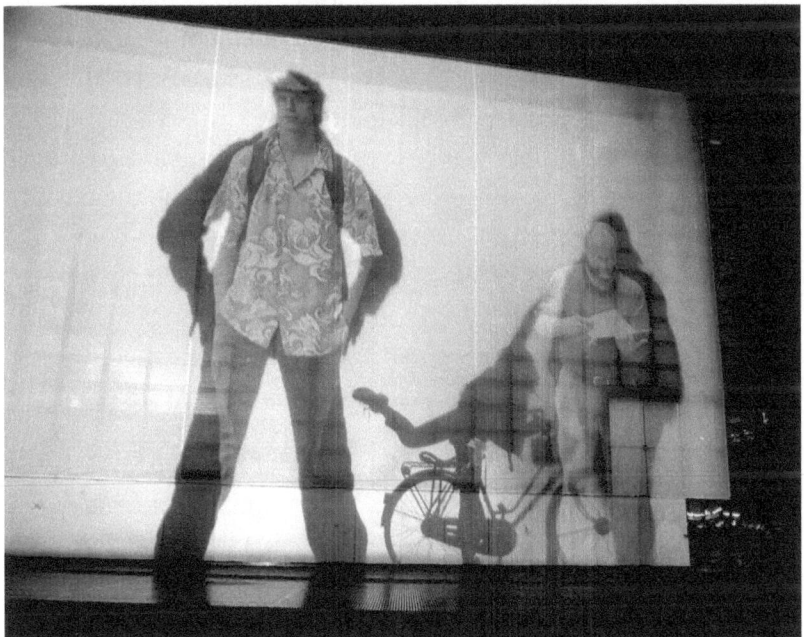

Figure 8.2 Rafael Lozano-Hemmer, *Re:positioning Fear, Relational Architecture 3*, 1997. Landeszeughaus, Architecture and Media Bienale, Graz, Austria. Photo: Joerg Mohr.

This free shadow play was, I would suggest, a kind of parasitic noise, feeding off the energy already flowing through the work to create new paths, and to creatively bifurcate relations.[278] It continued to qualitatively express something of the original relation (moving shadows revealing text on the building's surface), while at the same time producing a new (minor) relation through the same initial forms. The contemplative and reflective rhythm of movement in the large-scale text was overlaid with the noise of a quick and teasing play of shadows, creating a tension, a clash of intentions and tonalities: gaps and miscommunications.

These parasitic actions existed on multiple levels and at different scales. They operated throughout the transductions of form-force taking place, wherever interfacing occurred, producing excess. For example, as bodies overtly disrupted light to create new imagery, there was also a more subtle disruption of intention. Artist's intentions (or perceived potential of the work) interfaced with the participants' disparate motivations, to create a third, more mobile position. This composed indeterminacy within prescribed events of relation. This is not intended as a metaphor – within process thinking intentions, urges, feelings, desires are not phantasms, but forces and lures towards forces in and of the world (as James states, process thinking must not 'exclude from [its construction] any element that is directly experienced') (2010, 18).[279] Such conceptual forces are, I am suggesting, as capable of interfacing as anything more materially substantive – of immanently joining and modulating together to produce new movement, to drive differentiation/ bifurcation.

Parasitic machinics here produced not a linear evolution of the work, but rather enabled processes of transversal connectivity and entanglement (O'Sullivan 2006, 17). The parasitic action of interfacing was an agent of difference in that it continued to transduce relation. It kept the event always on the point of splitting and moving into multiple new forms, suspending it in unfolding differentiation, disrupting any simple or sustained connectivity. As such this contingency operated both on the level of actualised relations (how a given participant's presence and gestures interfaced within the larger event), but also on a level of the development of potential dimensions of operation. This affected how the very rules that constituted the larger event began to evolve and complicate, beginning to creatively disrupt some of the more potentially problematic interfacing that might occur in the work to fix participants in the gaze of the technology's eye. While disruptions to intention are not unusual within works such as this, designed to accommodate interference, what is notable is the degree to which such interference overtook the original structures.

Folds – the vibration of the incompossible

If parasitic action was, in a sense, a continually performed splitting of relation, the interfacing that occurred in *Re:Positioning Fear* might also be thought as producing difference through connecting, through incitation or a 'dynamics of infection' (Stengers 2011, 160). That is, through a folding of technological objects and bodies in interfacing, something new was produced (art). As Andrew Murphie writes, this is a doubling that technologies can perform (1996, 89), in this case the body becoming-with the lights, the façade becoming-with shadows, portraits becoming-with movement and so on. Rather than collapsing difference to produce a new homogenous history or façade, this folding multiplied difference to produce new singularities that were performed alongside, throughout and in the gaps of the previously existing iterations.[280] Thus, for example, in folding shadows that had a single purpose now performed (at least) two operations. But this was not simply a doubling of function, as folding overlaid and intertwined the two actions: to complement, overlap, interrupt, and fragment each other, creating multiple shifting moments of differentiation out of what was initially a fairly simple folding.

Interfacing here was a performative act by which the machine continued to re-fold its internal systems, and fold elements outside itself (various bodies, intentions, movements, tonalities, and so on) into its workings. This created, as Deleuze writes of such actions, a 'forced movement' or 'internal resonance' within the system (1994, 118). As discussed in the previous chapter, resonance acts like 'contrast' in Whitehead's system of concrescence to conserve 'tensions in the form of a structure' (Simondon 2009, 6)[281] – differences that are transduced through being 'topologically and temporally restructured across an interface' (Mackenzie 2002, 25; Sauvagnargues 2102, 66–7). This ongoing and continually productive resonant intensity-without-resolution was a 'machine' producing ongoing and new potential. The new shadow play on the façade overlaid the original projections; as the artist's intentions and the new tonalities participants brought to the event continued to question one another; and as one participant's shadow intentionally and/or accidentally overlapped in new combinations with other pedestrians' movements, gestures and poses. Such enfolding and resultant resonance might suggest that the event of *Re:Positioning Fear* had moved on from a relatively stable state of equilibrium where potentials of the event were actualised and 'no more force exist[ed]' (Simondon 2009, 6, 8), and where each component was kept at a regular spacing or relationship to one another that did not significantly develop over time. Instead it had developed into what Simondon terms a 'metastable' system, 'supersaturated' with potential that was always individuating (2009, 6). This potential that was always immediately available 'without distance and without delay' (Simondon 1995b, 225), recharging itself through the re-enfolding of components.
This might be a *diagrammatic* system that was a 'place only of mutation', whereby forces were 'in a perpetual state of evolution', and were 'inseparable from the variations in their relations' (Deleuze 1988, 71). Here folding implicated machinic components in each other's becoming through an ongoing and inventive

process of variation and re-articulation – repetitions that produced difference.²⁸²

In this entanglement or nesting the event became 'polyphasic', in Simondon's terms, a condition whereby there is a 'persistence of the primitive and original phase in the second phase, and this persistence implies a tendency towards a third phase' (cited in Combes 2013, 46).²⁸³ This third phase is, as Combes explains, the genesis of collective individuation. It is by drawing on the 'preindividual shares [of nature]' of potential remaining post-individualization that 'individuals can give birth to a new reality': a collective individuation that 'reunites these shares of nature charged with potential' (2013, 47–8). Such collectivity 'is not a result of relation [between individuals]…it is relation that expresses individuation of the collective' as 'its own operation of individuation' (Combes 2013, 47). Thus the new shadow play in *Re:Positioning Fear* gave rise to a new collective event with its own set of transindividual relations between participants, façade, lights and projections. This drew on the un-actualised potentials remaining within these components, folding these virtual remainders together; addressing collectively those problems that were not resolvable on an individual level (Grosz 2012, 50). Here we can see the *event itself* taking on a new level of self-generative power – new intensity – through a resonance that drew on but surpassed the potential of participants, artist, technological objects, architecture and so on.²⁸⁴ Thus the event's creative power might be in both the creation of actualised and *potential* foldings that the interfacing opened up, and in a bifurcating of future enfoldings that resonated within the event.

I want to suggest here that this more radical folding occurring in the interruption of *Re:Positioning Fear* might also be seen as a fold of the outside. The 'outside' or 'incompossible' is force in non-relation (Deleuze 1988, 72; Deleuze 1993, 60) – itself a disruptive gap in the relational field – that 'eats into the interval and forces or dismembers the internal' (Deleuze 1988, 72). This can produce a reorganisation that is a 'trans-formation...to the composing forces, [which] enter in to a relation with the other forces which have come from the outside' (Deleuze 1988, 73).[285] The participants' shadow-body play was an outside of the event, which was folded into emergent relation, at the level of force as well as form.

This folding began to transform the affects of the event, since affect is what is experienced in the transduction of force (Deleuze 1988, 60). The new affective tonality that was folded into the event coursed through, transducing, infecting all the systems and delimiting the event.[286] This was a force of qualitative change, of affective tonality. Interfacing here might be viewed as a 'vitality affect' on a force, 'elicited by changes in motivational states, appetites, and tensions' (Stern cited Manning 2013a, 5),[287] producing a felt moment of creative differing.

What is it that can be conceived of as truly outside of the event? Not the participants themselves (it cannot be any 'composed form', Deleuze argues), but these emergent and composing affectual forces outside of any form (Deleuze 1993, 73, 72). This again is more than the individuation of an event within an established field – the remarkable point within an already constituted ecology. It is the force of individuation that makes both the event and its paired environment appear (Simondon 2009, 4–5, 14 n.2): an impersonal individuating force that precedes relation, preceding but acting to gather an ecology. The new dimensions of the shadow-play event in *Re:Positioning Fear* did not exist within the initial registers of the systems (technological, psychological, social). The plane connecting one participant to another, to the lights, to the artist, composed itself as components folded, gathering force for a collective individuation and the evolution of a shared associated milieu.[288] This was interfacing as not only unimagined prior to the event, but 'unreasoned' and unthinkable in its entirety, in that it's potential might be 'impossibly enveloped in a...still undefined experience, compoundly unpreviewed' (Massumi 2002, 97): known and knowable only in its performative individuation, in its relativity to the genesis of its collective invention.[289]

Concretisation and the diagrammatic

I suggest that it was through these particular interfacings that the machine of *Re:Positioning Fear* underwent a process of concretisation: shifting systems from a limited, linear or closed functioning, towards self-regulation and sustenance, and consequently, towards a 'solidarity of openness', an increase in self-generative capacities (LaMarre in Combes 92–3).[290] This might be a critical point in the folding in of the outside at which new system-level rules begin to operate.[291]

Interfacing here might be seen to have incited a phase or register-shift through transduction, implicating the external. That is, these radical interfacings acted to create completely new milieus.[292] More than modulating transduction, a new machine was produced from the field when the system passed a 'threshold of [qualitative] intensity' (DeLanda 2005, 18–19), forcing new flows, with their attendant individuations, to begin. The interfacing of the incompossible, here 'vibrating against the conformal' (Whitehead 1978, 188), instigated a leap or jump of registers, whereby a point of 'absolute origin' (LaMarre in Combes 2013, 86) of a new event (and a new type of event) was produced.[293]

As I have hinted at in the previous section, one might term such an ongoing and provisional and essentially *co-producing* and becoming-concrete type of event 'diagrammatic': a system of 'ongoingly organized and redistributing gatherings' of its own making (Arakawa and Gins 2006, 56). Here what *Re:Positioning Fear* becomes as it moves from the linear to the concrete is a super-charged, dynamic ecology. This is not the replacement of order with chaos, but a different mode of operation that perhaps 'leaps over chaos', a 'catastrophe' (for the original artwork) that is also a 'germ of (new) order or rhythm' (Deleuze 2002a, 84, 83).[294] A diagrammatic modell*ing* (for it is never a 'model' in any fixed sense but an ongoing process of re-inquiry into its own status or dimensions – a metamodelling) moves towards an immanence of production and connection, across (and in conversation with) both actualised and potential planes, and can only be understood on a global or ecological level. Simondon argues that Euclidean notions of relation between fixed entities are inadequate to think the dynamics of over-lapping, intertwined and ongoing individuations, and describes this new and precarious mode of operation as topological (1995b, 223). Topological relationality creates a diagrammatic connectivity passing at once between such fixed points while at the same time expressing the whole event, not as a reunified object, but as the system of rhythms of contrasts or tensions or forces (Deleuze 2002a, 85–6).

In the new 'charged grounding' (LaMarre in Combes 2013, 93) between internal spacing and external contrast a larger machine ecology began to gather or self-modulate on another scale[295]. Not only the event, but also the *field itself* had changed. *Re:Positioning Fear* had changed its nature, not only by actualising a previously un-actualised potential, but also by rewriting the very field of potential available to it. This meant that the work gained a greater capacity to generate its own emergent difference – a parasitic operation – and in this the parasitic actions on relation lead to a state of greater self-regulation and sustenance.[296]

Conclusion

The shifts that occur in *Re:Positioning Fear* as a result of interfacing were both materially (ontologically) slight and processually (ontogenetically) significant. What the participants brought to the event that instigated such a shift was, in a sense, no more than a new intention, or perhaps even less distinctively, a new tonality that infected the work to produce something new. This is not to suggest necessarily that what it shifted *to* was in itself significant, but that the way that interfacings performed such a shift was of philosophical and artistic interest, in that it provides a potential tactic towards the thinking of more open-ended systems of interactivity, suggesting a potential machinic, 'minor' art event, concerned less with signification than a collective becoming (O'Sullivan 2006, 69–71). This performative interfacing perhaps acted as a 'lure' towards feeling or transduction, as a pull towards the future (Manning 2013a, 57), a pre-relational tendency towards affectual relation or as a productive diagrammatic tension.

Re:Positioning Fear was concerned not with utility in technology, but with, as LaMarre articulates, Simondon's plea for relations with machines that might instigate sustained inventive engagement (LaMarre in Combes 2013, 97). The objects, such as they were, in *Re:Positioning Fear* – lights, buildings, shadows – can then be seen to move towards what Manning has termed the 'objectile': propositions for engagement 'emphasiz[ing] the temporal and qualitative' (2013a, 148, 149). The event, one might say, answered Stern's call for interactive art to move away from privileging signs and images at the interface, and the demonstration or fetishisation of the technology in the work. Instead the event engaged, as Stern proposes, with the invention of styles or qualities or emergence, with the implicit and the potential – to construct new ways of relating through interfacing (2012, 10).

Refrain: Fuzzy interfacing

In *Momo* interfacing occurred between bodies and the sculptural forms (see Figure 8.2) through a series of light sensors embedded in the main form, and movement sensors positioned throughout the space.[297] Shadows cast by bodies on the central sculpture increased the volume of various audio tracks, providing a fluid mix of sounds.[298] This operation of interfacing was qualitative in its nature as multiple light sensors spread over the surface of the sculpture registered subtle variations in the intensity of shadows falling across its form. These variations were dependent on such factors as the distance of bodies from the sculpture, the density of materials blocking light (a thin fabric versus a limb, for example), the exact angle of a particular light sensor in the folds of fabric, or the collective volume of the shadows of bodies momentarily overlapping, alongside subtle potential changes in the overall light in the room.

Such qualitatively based sensor interfacings were perhaps a step towards a more fluid connection of components that began to move away from a focus on delineating and capturing or interpreting individual bodily actions and towards a fuzzy collective expression of the movement of the event itself. By this I do not mean to imply here any set division between analogue and digital sensors. Rather, there might be some distinction between motion *capture* systems such as those utilised in Wii or Xbox to translate body part movements onto a Cartesian grid (and that seek to address not only the participant's body to the exclusion of any other environmental changes, but also to focus rigidly on a relation between the intentional actions of the subject and the software), and the fuzziness of a qualitative sensor registering the variation in the collective sum of a particular force over time. Beyond this hardware-based interfacing of the sensors, *Momo* also proposed more ephemeral interfacings. These speculated on the resonance of the meeting of affectual tonalities between the participant and aspects of the work: the infective tonal qualities of the vocal qualities and the garish colour palette, for example.

Such partially unintentional interfaces began to capture difference on an environmental level. These were not only well outside subjective consciousness, but also outside a larger sense of a single body. This fluidity created inexact, unstable connections: a disruption of clear relation through a vagueness that might be 'due to an excess of identification', not a lack of connection, as Whitehead states (1978, 111–12). Here the contrasts between groups of actual objects that the sensors sought to hold a relation to were indistinct and appeared as 'one extensive whole' (though this whole was divisible), and the feelings prehended were therefore sensed as 'chaotic factors' (Whitehead 1978, 111–12). Given the somewhat abrasive and confrontational nature of the sounds emanating from the sculpture, and its increased vocal 'agitation' in reaction to the proximity of the participant, these sounds then might be seen to have begun to feed back into the styles of movement of bodies within the space. In this way, the event perhaps began to take on its own collective energy, a folding in the meeting of affectual tonalities of the event and the participant – a resonating of different moods and intensities – a collective shifting and gathering.

This interfacing gathered, to some extent at least, qualitative gestures within the event, rather than enforcing privileged conversations. That is, the event became sensitive to collective sums of reactions, directions, styles and speeds. These might be seen as transversal connections, as ongoing acts of the transduction of flows of forces across bodies and objects that co-implicated them in a collective, performative emergence leading towards concretisation – a shared potential or transindividuality (Simondon 2009, 9). In this, it began to gather a collective field for the event to draw on, beyond the combined individual potential of the component parts. More than simply being entities communicating across an interface, bodies, sounds, colours and lights became fluid (topological) genetic components intensively driving an event of collective expression.

Such concretisation, through a shared responsibility for the emergent event, neither subsumed the will of the work to that of the participant, nor vice versa. Though participants affected the modulation and flows of sound, as the installation contained the potential to coax certain styles of behaviour from bodies, the expressions of both added further variation and intensive movement. Connective possibilities generated and intensified, rather than collapsed, difference. For example (on the most concrete level), a gesture of one arm created subtle variations in shadows across a number of light sensors and simultaneously triggered the switching of audio samples through sensed movement. Meanwhile the counter-movements of the other arm might temporally combine with areas of shadow and send contradictory sample-swapping messages to the computer system (again an increase of resonance or held contrast in and driving the individuations of event). Interfacing here potentially directed intentional and accidental movements into multiple and overlapping chains of causality – creating multiple relations between a body part and the work – and also provided mechanisms for variation through instability of its relations.

Again, it is important to note that the event was not concerned with *representing* these interfacings to the participant, or with enforcing any one particular set of relations, style of movement or feeling of connection, but with affording a variety of potential connections. In this instance interactive interfacing at least began to move towards the consideration of the infective potential of a series of resonating or contrasting styles and tonalities. It began to consider interfacing as an intensive (and therefore parasitic) action within an event – a folding back of the event into itself to gather collective forces – with inexact edges and eddies at which difference might pool.

A thousand tiny interfacings 197

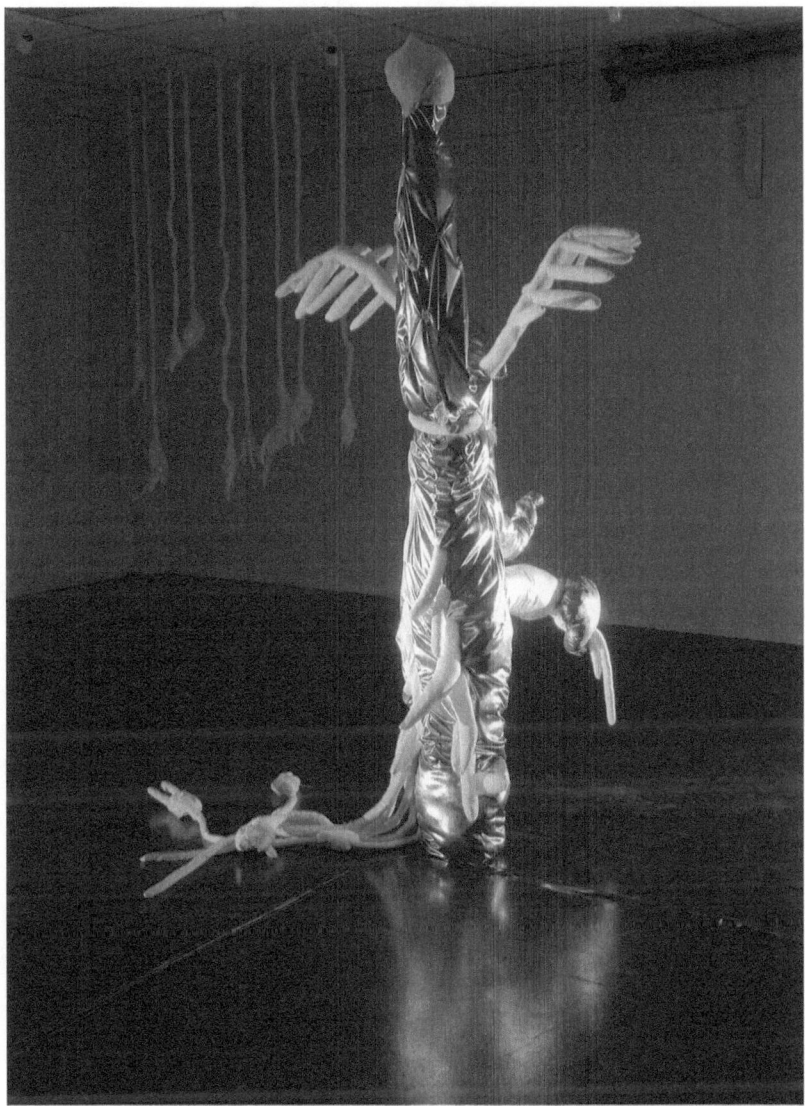

Figure 8.3 Andrew Goodman, *Momo*, (detail), 2011. Paradise Hills Gallery, Melbourne.

9

Sacrificial RAM: locating feeling and the virtual in software

> One of the questions ahead of us now is this: what are the conditions of digitization and binarization? Can we produce technologies of other kinds? Is technology inherently a simplification and reduction of the real... What might a technology of process, of intuition rather than things and practices look like?
> *Elizabeth Grosz*

> How is it possible to think through from a normative freeze-frame of representational to a more machinic or rhizomic approach to technology?
> *Andrew Murphie*

Introduction: towards a technical ontogenesis

In 1996, Rafael Lozano-Hemmer published a short article entitled 'Perverting Technological Correctness' in which he suggests a number of potential 'misuses' of technology to trouble the aura of 'technological correctness' surrounding the promotion of digital technologies within art practice (1996, 5). While the suggestions themselves are lighthearted (they include wearing a hollowed-out computer on one's head), they reveal a commonly held suspicion about the mechanical role of the computer in art, and the dangers of 'perfect replication' through the use of the digital (Lozano-Hemmer 1996, 6). How to make a computer program in itself behave in anything remotely approaching a 'relational' mode rather than simply working around such issues is important, and inherently political (Fuller 2003, 29–30; Dery 1996, 14). That is, in order to question and pursue the further molecularisation of an interactive artwork across all its registers, the speculative and non-totalising potential of algorithms must be addressed. In this we might seek to liberate digital programming from representation and productive 'purposefulness' that are its legacy in disciplinary structures. Within an expanded empiricist framework, all relations demand to be seen as real forces that must be accounted for within an ecology. Yet the actual nature of algorithmic events, as Luciana Parisi argues (2013, 10–11), is often denied adequate explanation within the schema of relations. In order to remain true to a process philosophy view of the world the becoming potential of an algorithm must be explored, alongside that of the potential of all the other components of an interactive artwork. Here we might seek a way of thinking the primacy of technical process or techno-genesis within computers.

Whitehead seeks to develop a process-based philosophy 'applicable to any kind of actual occasion' (Stenner 2008, 99). For this to be consistent, as Whitehead aims, I would argue that it is necessary that it be as applicable to the workings of a set of code as to any other occasion. Thus rethinking software interactions demands the finding of a becoming-minoritarian potential of computational processes – an ability to disrupt structuring and destabilise any 'whole' that is based on the transcendent replicability of software process. Again, as Parisi advocates, it is necessary to question the whole philosophical basis of thinking about code in order to find a new and specific way of tackling the problem at hand (2013, 3–5). Therefore, contrary to notions of code as a mechanical process incapable of further potentiality, or as immaterial representations that are transcendent of empirical dynamics,[299] an algorithm must be shown to be 'machinic'. That is, it must be capable of acting as an assemblage primed and therefore capable of shaping it's becoming as a real event, in and of itself, rather than a mechanical assemblage that produces a repeatable result. If we want to truly concern ourselves with the 'ethics of relation', that is, an attention to the event in its emergence that does not deny the potency of any of the composing forces (Manning 2013a, 213, 171), then we need to consider seriously how to afford the performativity of algorithms. This involves thinking through how the potential written into code can become temporal events of actualisation, and addressing an algorithm's ongoing potential for engagement with both actualised entities and 'eternal objects' – the infinite potential variety within these entities (Parisi 2013, 63).

In this chapter, I will attempt to think the machinic potential of an algorithm (a 'step by step procedure for calculations') (Parisi 2013, 259)[300] and a software patch (a set of sequences of algorithmic processes created within a software program). This discussion, unlike most of the preceding main chapters that have other artists' work as their primary discussion points, moves for practical reasons directly to focus on a software patch developed for *Orgasmatron* – one of the works made in conjunction with this book.[301] After a brief description of the relevant aspects of the work, I discuss the software patch in relation to some relevant common aspects of generative software design in order to discuss both these concepts' relevance to the artwork, and how the software design attempts to move beyond these paradigms.

In thinking beyond these concepts, I then discuss the work in relation to the more promising potential of algorithmic prehension in order to argue for an algorithm's acceptance as an entity in its own right, and then examine how the design utilises systems of parametrically linked multiple attractors to modulate data in non-linear ways.

Orgasmatron

In *Orgasmatron*,[302] data from pairs of sensors[303] embedded in the structure of the work was fed into the computer to be utilised by the software patch, created in the *Isadora* program.[304] Through a series of algorithmic processes this data drove ongoing variations in light, sound, sound spatialisation and vibration. The processes by which incoming data was modulated are briefly described here (see Figure 9.1).[305]

Firstly, 'Differential' actors: here the data from a pair of sensors was processed in an algorithm utilising a differential equation to calculate the rate of their difference differing over time. For example, two pressure sensors (embedded in opposite sides of the floor of the work) measured the shifts in pressure as a body moved across the surface. As an equation this can be expressed by $(x_i - x)/(y_i - y)$, where 'x' and 'y' are the initial readings of the two pressure, and 'x_i' and 'y_i' are the pressure sensor readings taken 0.1 of a second later. This provided a series of numbers that reflect the rate of change of pressure on one side of the structure relative to the rate of change of pressure on the other side. The result of this equation was then constrained within a range of 0–100.

Secondly, 'Watching' actors: Here a set of algorithmic actors watched the numbers outputted from these equations, looking for a particular range of numbers with which they interacted, and then counted the incidence of such numbers within the constraining parameters. For example, one such algorithm might look for numbers between 0.001 and 1.0, or between 10 and 20, and so on. In this sense, these algorithms acted as a 'gate', allowing the flow-on of certain data through to the rest of the system, while ignoring other data. That is, the watching actor had the capacity to be positively affected by, or interact with, certain data and had a relation of non-relation with other data, as it actively ignored data outside certain ranges, dividing data into two groups, creating a 'positive' relation with data accepted, and a 'negative' relation to rejected data. As will become important to the argument that develops below, each evolving set of differentials was 'watched' by (or was capable of interacting with) more than one of these 'watching' actors, each with gates of different parameters, so that the affectual potential of the flow of data was split in ways that might also overlap.

Thirdly, 'Triggering' actors: Once the watching actor had counted to a set number of positive interactions, this triggered the sending of data to the next series of algorithmic actors for further modulation. This next set of actors also watched for numbers within certain parameters with which they could interact, while similarly rejecting other data. These actors counted a certain number of interactions, and then sent the data flow to further algorithms that triggered a range of video projections and sound events.[306]

Fourthly, within both the watching and triggering algorithmic actors, the ranges of data looked for, and the numbers of such incidents counted, were designed with variable parameters. While each of these parameters had an initial set range or number, they were linked to both its own and each other's outputs, so that they changed over time. That is, the range of numbers being accepted at each 'gate' increased or decreased in response to the amount of stimuli received by the set of actors, while the threshold number of such events being counted before triggering the flow-on of data also changed in response to the activities of the system. In this way, the ability of an algorithm to be affected developed complexly in relation to its neighboring algorithms.[307]

Fifthly, amongst the triggering set of actors described above were actors whose outcomes triggered the activation of additional watching and triggering actors, thus potentially utilising and splitting the data flow-on in further directions. This will be discussed later in the chapter in terms of a 'bifurcation' of the system that created a new set of relations inclusive of previous relational factors within the system.

Generative software design

Any discussion of the programmatic nature of computer operations and codes, within any artwork that is attempting a generative or open-ended approach, must acknowledge some of the strategies that have been previously employed and their (at least) partial success in creating larger systems that have open-ended characteristics. In most cases, however, these strategies do not adequately address the non-linear potential of algorithmic process itself. While it is not within the scope of this chapter to provide a detailed account of the various approaches that have been taken, I want to here very briefly discuss three areas that retain relevance to the larger system utilised in the *Orgasmatron* project.[308] These (related) approaches, at their simplest, concern: firstly, attempts to 'diffuse' the linear nature of computer processes through their integration into larger and principally analogue based systems; secondly, the use of complex feedback systems interacting with software processes to create biologically imitative self-generative systems (second-order cybernetics); and thirdly, attempts to make code itself behave in a generative or evolutionary manner through the use of parametric feedback.

Diffusion

In practice, many software-generative works are in fact assemblages of software, sensors, participants' bodies, and other aesthetic elements such as larger environments of sound, light or sculpture. Many such works rely on the integration of these components with software to 'diffuse' the digital technologies. The supposedly prescriptive digital data is 'diffused' within an analogue field, as qualitative flows of data stimulate movement in the software through the transduction of analogue signals into the digital, acting parasitically on each other. The analogue qualitative flow is disrupted by its digitisation and translation into binary code, while the excess of the analogue disrupts the digital. As such, it is easy to argue that in the larger context of its place within assemblages that include other elements, and within the larger social field within which it must also be seen to operate, an algorithm or code begins to become extensively indeterminate.[309] In these tactics the injections of data might be said to be relational rather than purely chaotic. But while they may have clear creative potential in opening systems to novelty, in isolation (that is, when they are proposed as the only generative tactics rather than perhaps operating as one element on a particular scale in conjunction with other generative propositions), these approaches still rely on working around algorithmic prescriptiveness and ignore Parisi's more radical proposition that an algorithm itself might be thought of as intensively indeterminate.

Potentially implied in this approach is the problematic acceptance of an always-clear analogue/digital divide. As Anthony Wilden argues, distinctions can be made between the continuous qualities of analogue variation, and the discontinuous scales of digital differentiation that then operate through different kinds of differentiation (1980, 158). However, he also argues that discrete definitions of the two are problematic, and more concerned with the ways in which entities relate than any innate qualities. Many processes in the world involve both analogue and digital on differing scales within the one event of communication (1980, 188–9).[310] In addition, when viewed as events of relation, the digital is always saturated with the rhythms of the analogue in the form of gaps, interruptions, processing time, and signaletic noises (Wilden 1980, 158).[311] Thus, as Wilden acknowledges, the translation from analogue to digital can result in loss of ambiguity and meaning (1980, 163), implying that the digital

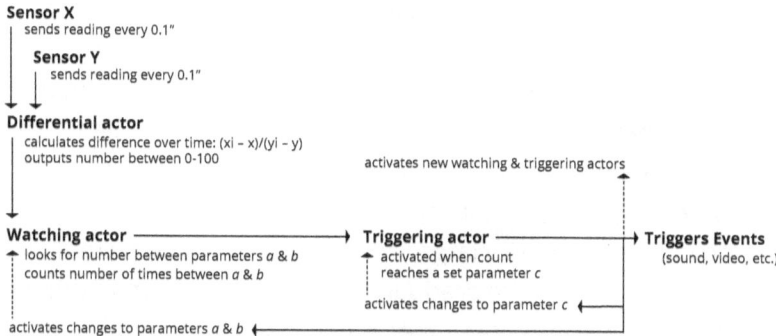

Figure 9.1 Simplified graphic representation of Actors in Orgasmatron patch.

is just a poor replica of the 'real' analogue experience. I would argue that within an expanded empiricism the digital might also be thought of as a different but potentially creative and real mode in its own right.[312]

Second-order cybernetics

A second-order cybernetics approach involves assemblages of positive feedback chains between components in order to develop complex systems of relation from the 'bottom up' (Parisi 2013, 261). Such systems, as Francisco Varela examines in his discussion of drift, create connections of 'viable coupling' with no regard for an end point (Varela, Thompson and Rosch 1992, 205).[313] Here, feedback emphasises the processual – the ways in which elements are drawn into relation and the fact that all these components play an active role in this emergent organisation (Murphie and Potts 2003, 192). In the *Orgasmatron* system, the enmeshing of data from the larger artwork assemblage created relations between the workings of the computer and the other component parts through systems of feedback. Feedback loops were established across the various inputs and outputs, for example, as shifts in pressure triggered sound events, causing vibrations to be sensed, which then triggered light events, causing light variations to be sensed, that then cause vibrations to be sent, and so on.[314] In addition, the bodies of participants' became implicated in these systems, adding their own rhythms and disruptions to the speakers' vibrations, varying the pressure applied on parts of the floor, and creating variations in light through shadows cast (as the system also worked to disrupt the bodies' rhythms). Bodies were then drawn into relation with other components of the larger assemblage, and the system was primed to afford the gradual development of such relational complexity, as various components became further implicated in each other's expressions. Without particular concern for any endpoint, the system was always in a state of reconfiguring its feedback loops. This transduction of forces within feedback systems emphasised movement or circulation over established relations and, in this, might be seen to be heading towards becoming-molecular configurations.

Parisi, however, critiques such self-organising, second-order cybernetic models as relying on the actions of biological elements directly animating algorithmic objects to build a responsive environment (Parisi 2013, 33).[315] Again, these models might tend to imply that the environment exists only outside of algorithms, rather than seeing these objects themselves as being composed of environments of relations, and thus 'discard the possibility that change could concern the formal logic of computation' (Parisi 2013 36, 11,13). Parisi argues that such systems still treat computation as a passive, non-aesthetic component and potentially infer that aesthetics can only be found within sensation and not within algorithmic processes (Parisi 2013, xv). Thus feedback systems, Parisi argues, contain computational potential by demanding that its primarily relation is to an external environment that it responds to (2013, 155). If such systems also allow only positive and enduring connections between the components then this limitation in the rules governing their relations may well, as Parisi argues, prime them towards the organisation of a stability of connection and a molar thinking, rather than a continued emergence and ongoing potential for relational movement to be expressed (2013, 35). However I am not entirely convinced by this aspect of Parisi's critique of autopoiesis and its reliance on feedback to maintain a whole, which I read as a narrow definition of the possible range of potential becoming-autopoietic systems, and possible qualifications are discussed below.

Parametric feedback

Such systems might, for a start, be extended by a 'parametric' approach within the software patch itself. Where generative software seeks to create complex forms through sets of simple rules and variations of forms, a parametric approach, as argued by Portanova, shifts the emphasis towards the programming of relations between these rules or algorithmic processes, affording another scale on which feedback operates and co-implication develops (Portanova 2013, 87). This concept of 'parametricism' might be in line with the 'ecological' approach that Jon McCormack, amongst others, has advocated. It involves the creation of a field of what McCormack terms 'conditions and resources' (that might be better termed as a series of environmental propositions) where heterogeneously distributed 'mortal organisms' draw both from the field (in some cases including the presence of viewer's bodies) and their relations to each other, and have some ability to develop their interactive parameters (McCormack 2012, 51).[316] These systems, as McCormack argues, draw components into interdependent relations through feedback on a component-to-component level, and are self-organising and dynamic in their modulations (McCormack 2012, 45), developing system-level relationality as a by-product of these interactions (McCormack 2012, 48). As described above, the *Orgasmatron* software patch linked some of the parameters of the operations of its 'watching' and 'triggering' algorithms to each other, so that they changed over time in relation to the amount of stimulation various parts of the system received. This in itself was a parasitic disruption to established relations, as it replaced stable capacities to be affected with the vagueness and fuzzy logic of contingent and evolving parameters of potential relation.

As it gathered parameters into co-implication in each other's modulation, it also created a rolling or gathering of excitation of the system. Here stimulation lead to increased potential to be stimulated – leading the system towards a 'far-from-equilibrium' state, rather than a stasis of connectivity that cancelled further potential movement. Such far-from-equilibrium systems, Manuel DeLanda states, maintain intensive differences, 'mesh[ing] difference' rather than cancelling it, and thus the potential for change remains active within the system (2005, 74–5). Accentuating this non-equilibrium state, he argues, puts systems in a condition of heightened potential, what he terms a 'zone of intensity' of operation that moves away from linearity (DeLanda 2005, 76).[317]

Here, parametric systems might begin to escape the purely positive feedback of second-order cybernetics in utilising feedback within algorithmic relations. Instead they begin to draw together and further complexify the *computational* conditions in which such relational play might occur – encouraging an intensive movement in the shifting of relations between the component algorithms.[318] In *Orgasmatron*, local algorithmic excitations infected the parameters of neighboring algorithms, creating a molecular movement, and it is only through these complex and speculative chains that effects on the system as a whole emerged. In emphasising models of interference and parts over wholes, parametricism (as an extension of feedback systems) can, as Parisi argues, begin to escape pre-emptive control, and the smoothing or flattening of novelty that is problematic in topological systems. Parametricism thus interferes with the smooth 'capitalization of change, futurity and potentiality' (Parisi 2013, 92–3). In her critique of the problematic smoothness of such topological models of self-organising systems, which she considers as a form of 'post-cybernetic control' (Parisi 2013, xvii),[319] Parisi contrasts them to 'mereotopological' systems, which she suggests, consist of this consideration of the whole as divisible space, and a concern with its interior parts and the relations between the two (Parisi 2013, 123-4). Mereotopology, as Portanova writes, emphasises 'not only wholes and parts, but the boundaries and interiors of wholes [and] the relations of contact and connectedness between wholes and parts' (2013, 79, 76-80).

Potentially still implicit in this parametric approach is the idea that the digital can only be made to behave more open-endedly by making it operate in a pseudo-biological manner. This refusal to acknowledge the potential indeterminacy at the very heart of coding processes reflects, Goodman and Parisi write, the 'anthropocentrism of interactivity, which pervades recent conceptions of digital architecture' (2009, 1).[320] Technical machines, as Pickering argues, have their own singular ways of relating (1995, 186-7) and algorithmic processes have their own specific modes of thought (Parisi 2013, 186).[321] Their processes should not be erroneously conflated with representations of the biological world, as happens in cognitive approaches.[322] Instead of constructing algorithms as 'tools for thinking' in order to enhance abilities to plan and control – a 'mechanics of possibilities' (Parisi 2013, 169) – Parisi advocates for a 'soft(ware) thought...producing computational space-time' (2013, 169). This 'software thought', which she describes as the architecture of a new, specifically digital, mode of thought (Parisi 2013, 169), can be clearly linked to the need to rethink interactivity and its use of computer technology, moving it away from systems of control and manipulation that curtail potential, and towards more open-ended and collectively creative expressions.

The *Orgasmatron* assemblage clearly utilised combinations of analogue and digital processes and feedback systems – including parametric feedback – to varying degrees in order to create multiple systems of relation, and as such it is open to the criticisms of such approaches mentioned above. However, as I will attempt to show in the following discussions, employing these tactics did not necessarily occur at the expense of ignoring the creative potential within algorithmic processes, but as a supplement to it – allowing a range of complementary tactics within various component parts of the overall system and across relations between these parts.

In the following section, I explore how it might be possible to move beyond these limited conceptions of the operations of code through a utilisation of Whitehead's concept of prehension. In the third section of the chapter I then use this concept of algorithmic prehension, and its implication of the existence of an algorithmic potential, to lay the groundwork for the exploration of generative systems that utilise parasitic disruptions to drive creativity. This is explored through the concepts of attractors and bifurcations – emphasising the parasitic potential within generative computer processes that might move towards machine ecologies.

Algorithmic feelings: a digital mode of thought

In order to establish that algorithms are more than 'simulators of material dynamics' (Parisi 2013, 1), it is necessary to demonstrate how they are actualised entities in their own right, with accompanying obligations and powers within a schema of the play of forces. To do this, Parisi draws on Whitehead's system of prehensions, as it is, she argues, an entity's prehensive capabilities that define 'what an entity is and how it relates to others' (2013, xii). A system of prehensive feeling describes 'how any actuality…grasps, includes and excludes, and transforms data' (Parisi 2013, xii).[323] As discussed in earlier chapters, Whitehead argues that in prehending an entity creates a system of relation or 'extensive connection' – including both conjunctive and disjunctive connection – that connects it to all other actual entities (1978, 41). At the same time, this is reciprocated, as any entity also acts as an 'object' to be prehended by all other entities.[324] Thus, an actualised entity must influence the individuation of entities it forms relationships with, as they must influence it, 'however trivial or faint' this influence is (Whitehead 1978). It should be noted that there is no essential distinction in this ontology between conceptual and material entities, living and non-living, or between what constitutes a subject (that prehends) and an object (that is prehended) (Shaviro 2009, 23).

Whitehead is adamant, however, that despite drawing on the datum of objects, each new entity is 'freed from those entities' histories', having its own subjective feeling that is different to the previous entity's feeling on which it draws, and that translates (transduces), rather than simply duplicating the original force (1978, 238, 236).[325] In this there is a creative but atomic advance that builds on what exists, but which is also always capable of movement and further complexity. It is also always a singular point of complex negotiations between all the entities whose forces influence it.[326] In this system, Parisi says, Whitehead manages to conceive an understanding of relations as being 'both more than effects and less than the projections of a perceiving subject' (Parisi 2013, 59). Here prehensions form the 'indissolvable atomic architecture of any occasion' that is therefore both actual while never complete or static (Parisi 2013, 60). In this sense, no entity (including an *algorithmic* entity) can be said to be purely predetermined, but selects the manner and degree to which it is influenced by other events – it gathers singular and particular relations to the world that define its existence.[327] Actual entities are therefore always individual, actualised realisations of potentialities, but never fully stable or 'whole', and process here is conceived of not as a self-modulating whole, but as a system of parts that are nevertheless all related and capable of affecting each other (Parisi 2013, 61). Process is therefore self-organising but molecular, as each component has its own subjective power to relate and ingress into other entities without regard to any overall design or configuration.

Algorithms, Parisi argues, are necessarily engaged in prehension, or selection of numbers with which to interact from a larger field or potential that contains incomputable numbers – the actual and discrete passages between and combinations of the zeros and ones that make up binary code (Parisi 2013, 64–5) and that can be endlessly arranged and extended (Portanova 2013, 127). Parisi draws on mathematician Gregory Chaitlin's theories that classify these incomputable objects as 'Omega' (Ω) (Chaitlin 2011, 126; Parisi 2013, 17–18).[328] Chaitlin's theorem draws on earlier work by Gödel and Turing that shows that, contra to common sense, most real numbers can never be entirely or definitively calculated or known. That is, they remain problematic: incomplete and uncomfortably 'ugly',[329] and resistant to axiomatisation.[330] Omega is a real number between zero and one,[331] yet it cannot be calculated through any other, smaller processes or patterns and is therefore 'algorithmically and logically irreducible' information (Chaitlin 2011, 137).[332] Thus Omega shows that calculation of particular sequences of ones and zeroes cannot fully precede the event of that code's coming into being itself – the entity and its process of actualisation are reciprocal, belonging 'to the register of creation itself' (Stengers 2010, 42). Omega proves that there remains an excess – an incalculable and problematic uncertainty lurking behind binary code (Portanova 2013, 126). The potential in Omega lies in that it represents not simply 'an empty repetition of the same' ones and zeros (a 'self-varying deformation' or topology), but rather the potential novel and 'infinite addition of one more possibility' (an infinite number of ones and/or zeros to the sequence) (Portanova 2013, 127).

As these infinite, real infinitesimals (endlessly divisible fractions between zero and one) and sequences (endless combinatory possibilities of zeros and ones) cannot be compressed into any one algorithmic operation, Parisi says, they are best thought of as an 'incomputable virtuality'. They operate as a multiplicity or 'eternal object' – that is 'patternless and random, objective and undetermined' and that cannot be contained into any smaller set of rules (Parisi 2013, 126, 65).[333] These are 'indeterminate conditions within which algorithmic objects are able to exist', they are unsynthesisable quantities that disrupt and open algorithms to a greater potential (Parisi 2013, 204). Here there is a 'strain' between limitless (both virtual and incalculable) and limited (specific algorithmic functions) (Portanova 2013, 57). Any algorithm speculatively contracts potential and determines positive and negative relations with numbers it both can and cannot contain – 'demarcating an immanent, actual space of disjunctions and conjunctions' (Parisi 2013, 240–1).[334]

In the *Orgasmatron* software patch, not only were these incomputable and disruptive transitions inherently present within each algorithmic process, each 'watching' algorithm selected, evaluated and produced data for use by other such entities, thus becoming a 'performing extensive actuality' (Parisi 2013, ix). The 'watching' actor made a selection of some data to interact with – a positive prehension – while rejecting interaction with data outside set parameters. This selection established a positive prehensive relation with some real numbers, and a negative prehensive relation to both other real numbers and incomputable numbers: it drew positively on some of the potential, but never all of it. This was an act of selecting that was an unseen but nevertheless a real moment of transition and therefore indeterminacy between actualised determined occasions. In exercising its capacities to prehend and utilise data – in order to realise potential and resolve its satisfaction as that particular temporal and spatial algorithmic process – the 'watching' actor established itself as a singular vector of actualised relations.

Given that the parameters of numbers the 'watching' actor prehended were themselves modulating, in this it performed a certain *choice* or capacity to connect or feel that was not purely prescribed or linear (that is, a simple positive connectivity). We must remember that this was an 'automated prehension' (Parisi 2013, xii), with its own particular algorithmic type of prehension, rather than a simulation of other entities' ways of feeling. Moreover, in that each 'differential' algorithm in the system was watched by multiple algorithms with differing parameters, at any particular moment in the process, a number calculated could be 'felt' and prehensively utilised to drive the various 'watching' algorithms' processes in multiple different ways. This established extensive, but speculative, immanent connections between not only a 'differential' algorithm and each watcher, but between the watchers themselves, in that a number positively or negatively prehended by one was also either positively or negatively prehended by all the others. In this, algorithmic prehensions allowed new complexity in the form of emergent contrasts to enter into the system, which then increased in differential intensity.

These causal chains were 'ordinally' specific – they had a specific order in which their operations were linked – but left open other dimensions such as time and actual processes. Ordinal numbers ('firstness', 'secondness', and so on) specify an order but not an actual number. That is, they specify one rule governing a set of numbers, but leave all other parameters open to change, as numbers can be any quantity as long as they follow in order. Ordinal distances, DeLanda states, connect entities, creating a relation between, whereas metric distances separate events (2005, 126). Ordinal numbers are 'anexact yet rigorous', having a single determined spatial quality that allows them to function – 'this' is next to or after 'that' – while never strictly metric in leaving other spatio-temporal parameters open. This leaves as many factors as possible open to further individuation, retaining enough practical specificity to allow their structuring into a software patch (DeLanda 2005, 68, 81–2). The 'gate' function of the watcher algorithms was ordinal, specifying a position ('bigger than', 'smaller than' or 'between' numbers), while leaving the specification of these numbers open to change. Furthermore, the ordinal links ran not only from differential-to parallel watching-to-triggering algorithms, but also in multiple lines across from watching-to-watching-to-watching as they sequentially influenced each other's parameters. This constructed chains of causation that no longer prescribed to simple linear chains of events.

A set of algorithm processes can be argued to have operated here within Whitehead's system of prehensive connection. Each actively determined its own actualisation by selectively drawing on data from multiple algorithms acting as objects for it, and was an object who's felt datum affected the ways other algorithms actualise. This, one might suggest, demonstrated a logic of infection that governed algorithmic operations with an open potentiality, rather than a fixed law that remained transcendent of the play of temporal forces – a process of temporal selection that makes immanent extensive connections (Whitehead 1978, 294; Portanova 2013, 10–11).

When we consider an algorithm as an actualised machinic process, and not simply an abstract set of instructions, it is possible to argue that it is a temporal processing of data, no matter how infinitesimal that timespan is (Miyazaki 2012, 1).[335] As Shintaro Miyazaki argues, algorithms and assemblages of algorithms must all have their own singular passages or rhythms of operation that are analogue noises *within* the digital process, delineating a rhythmic actuality from a field of potential (2012, 10).[336] When this temporal quality of processing is taken into account, numbers produced by algorithmic process are always singular spatiotemporal actualities, infected with a parasitic analogue: with the micro-rhythms of transition that express a temporal ordering of processing, gathering a new relationship between the actions.[337]

Intensive rhythmic differences began to arise in the *Orgasmatron* patch as multiple 'watcher' algorithms waited for, and then actualised, the processing of data selected from a 'differential' algorithm. That is, each began at its own starting time – the moment it prehended a usable number range – and then took its own specific time to process. Thus what was a single flow of data was split (parasitically) into multiple nested cyclical timespans.[338] These potential syncopations creating new rhythmic patterns of operation were evolving algorithmic refrains (patternings of temporal contrasts).[339] As a system utilising parallel processing, and given that the 'watchers' could also affect changes in each other's operation, these relative processing times were critical to how the system developed as a whole, as well as to how its parts processed data flows.[340] The syncopation in relations between algorithmic cycles could open new potential and actual configurations of relation to invent new modulations of data.

Potential rhythms of operation are one multiplicity of qualities and quantities on which an actualised algorithmic process draws upon, along with potential ordinal sequences, potential parameters, and potential sets of numbers. In line with Whitehead's system of eternal objects, it is possible to argue that an algorithm draws on the potential of various numbers and mathematical functions as concepts, expressing some – whilst never exhausting all – of their potential. Here an algorithm 'nests' 'infinite parts of infinities' (concepts of numbers and functions[341]) within itself (Parisi 2013, 63), but these eternal objects – as 'the pure potentials of the universe' (Whitehead 1978, 149)[342] – are never fully able to be contained or compressed within any one algorithm. These incomputable quantities are a non-linear 'second order' of relation, as the algorithmic entity expresses a relation to various (but not all) potentialities.[343]

In *Orgasmatron*, each actualisation of a differential algorithm produced a specific and temporal mathematical process.[344] Here actual ordinal sequences arose out of cuts in larger potentials (*this* watcher algorithm next accepted the data, rather than *that* watcher), potential ranges of numbers were expressed and prehended, and so on. The excess of ongoing relational potential to the virtual was never exhausted by any particular actualisation. An algorithm then had a 'dipolar' relationship, drawing prehensively on both relations to the actual, determined world, and conceptually prehending 'the indeterminateness of the eternal world' (Whitehead 1978, 45).[345] This potential was irreducible data – inexpressible in its entirety – that again moved algorithms beyond being merely 'systemization[s] of the possible' (Massumi 2002, 137), and demonstrated that they were always infected with an indeterminacy of the incomputable (Massumi 2002, 62). Each enaction of code was a singular and limited nexus of both physical prehensions and prehensions expressing a particular relation to larger potentials, and a material and conceptual realisation of some of its potential to interact with other material and conceptual actualities – the electrical and mechanical components of the computer and data flows, and the mathematical concepts. Here it is possible to argue that each algorithmic event was engaged in *feeling* in the Whiteheadian sense, a spacing or patterning of sets of external and internal differential relations or contrasts that constituted its very becoming as an actualised event. This applied not only within each smaller algorithmic event (a 'watcher' or 'differential' or 'triggering' algorithm), but in the relations between these events that became further entangled and intensified through their effects on each other's becoming (a *collective* individuation, producing both new relations between events and a shared field out of which such individuations emerged) (Grosz 2012, 42–3).

This was then a speculative logic of algorithmic process, acknowledging a vagueness in its operations,[346] that positions the processing of data as an open expression of the concrescence of algorithmic entities, not because the code itself necessarily altered, but because there was a level of indeterminacy in the potentials and processes that governed its operations (Parisi 2013, 144). This could never be fully positively accounted for in any iteration of the algorithm. Exploitation of prehensive potential in algorithmic processing of data enabled not a smooth modulation, subsuming all to a continuous whole (of design function) (Parisi 2013, 167), but a series of cuts that interrupted, contradicted and problematised. These cuts molecularised relations by creating further intensification or differentiation within the data-algorithm machine. In the materiality of actualisation, with its disruptions and rhythms, and in its continued non-linear relations to the further potentials, algorithms exercised particular capacities (ways of prehending), and became charged with indeterminacy. Here, algorithmic prehension was a parasitic action within the computer's operations, in that it broke with clear and absolute transference of data between algorithms, inserting difference into these relations.

Systems modulating through disruption

In order to further articulate the intensive noise within algorithmic processes, in this next section I discuss the concept of multiple attractor systems. I want to explore how accentuated intensive disruption can drive an open-ended futurity through systems of attractors. In this, I want to move further into the concept of speculative transitions between software processing events to continue to think through the software patch developed for the *Orgasmatron* project.

Attractors

To begin this thinking through of attractors, I want to consider software patches as non-metric (that is, 'projective, differential, topological') (DeLanda 2011b, 18) 'state spaces'– consisting of a system of 'attractors' that act on and organise the potential flow of force within the system.[347] States are 'meta-stable', in that they are capable of self-organisation through their interaction with forces to accommodate change. They also have a 'tipping point', at which they 'bifurcate' and move to a new, related state with a new set of organising parameters or potentialities.[348] Here it is important to remind ourselves that these state spaces are themselves only momentary cuts in ongoing processes of individuation of a system. That is, the system is involved in ongoing exploration and genesis of its potential, rather than any state representing a final or fixed organisation of forces and relations (DeLanda 2011b, 13).[349] States organise through intensive differentiation, and the 'attractors' condition or influence the system and its modulations by influencing the long-term tendencies of differential trajectories.[350] States then are the outcomes of differential processes, with attractors implicated in the genesis of the system (DeLanda 2011b, 15), in that they condition or lure the potential of forces as potential becomings, or pulls towards change (Massumi and McKim 2009, 9).[351] An attractor is a tendency towards a terminus of a trajectory, and, while real, is never reached or fully actualised (DeLanda 2005, 29).[352]

The lure of attractors explains, without resorting to concepts of essences but instead through process, why different inputs can have a tendency to result in similar trajectories. Attractors propose a particular way of thinking through the dynamics of the modulation or differential negotiations of forces in a system in a non-prescriptive manner. They suggest, rather than prescribe, outcomes and relations. They are also impersonal or non-subjective tendencies that belong to the field and are therefore directly implicated in how events begin to gather within ecologies. Systems with multiple attractors 'break the link between necessity and determinism, giving a system a "choice" between different destinies' (DeLanda 2005, 35).[353] That is, since multiple attractors might lure towards different becomings, the actualised differences or modulations in the system have complex causes that remain relational but cannot be reduced to linear causality or replication.

Attractors themselves are not fixed. They might themselves be viewed as becoming-states, with their own set of attractors that condition their genesis. While some attractors are steady (that is, a constant lure), others can be cyclical or chaotic. Thus, states can move periodically between relatively stable and far-from-equilibrium conditions. An attractor itself might also develop or modulate the way it pulls within an event. Multiple attractors here create open, problematic and never more than partially resolved states composed of the contrasts (intensity) of contradictory potentials[354] and, as such, are of use within thinking through of open-ended algorithmic processes.

Each state might then be seen as a machine, modulating flows according to the play of the intensive dynamics of its competing attractors on forces. They are also potentially capable of moving from one particular self-organising solution into another related state that is therefore not fixed. DeLanda warns, however, that in order to actively engage with the virtual – and therefore exhibit non-linear behavior – a system of attractors also needs to maintain a far-from-equilibrium state. That is, a state in which intensive difference, as a continuous flow of energy, or data 'traverses the system…acting as a constraint maintaining intensive differences alive' (DeLanda 2005, 75).[355] Such non-equilibrium causing flow 'reveals the potentialities hidden in the non-linearities, potentialities that remain dormant at or near equilibrium' (DeLanda 2005, 75). In other words, such systems depend not only on the pull of multiple attractors to move beyond the predictable, but on the high degree of intensity that makes the system sensitive to switching between the various lures of the attractors (DeLanda 2005, 76).[356] A dynamic system, as DeLanda suggests, also needs high degrees of connectivity, which, as with parametric systems, allows the potential for various component parts to mutually influence each other's relationship to attractors (DeLanda 2005, 65).

When the *Orgasmatron* system was 'activated' by the incoming differentials provided by a participant's body,[357] it moved from a state of high stability to one in which the increased flows of data from sensors became intensified (more differentialised), shifting rapidly between ranges of numbers. This data was processed by a differential algorithm, and was then subject to the 'pull' of multiple watcher algorithms. That is, the data had a potential to become through interaction with a watcher that drew it towards that watcher's particular modulation of the flow. Here the watcher algorithms were the collective potential futures of the data, multiplicities towards with which it could engage and actualise its transduction. The tension of the potential for the data to be drawn instead towards relationship with one of the other watcher algorithms, or to be split and interact with two or more simultaneously was always inherent. These watchers were constant attractors for a flow, and the data could oscillate between the potential pulls of them because it was a set of unstable or changing numbers.[358] As with the prehensive capacity of the algorithms, the lure of attractors was here automated,[359] yet it retained its dynamic potential through the unresolvable tensions of multiple attractors.

While these watcher actors were stable attractors operating throughout the *Orgasmatron's* processes, the 'triggering' algorithms could be considered to be cyclical attractors. That is, they counted interactions before triggering a further event; luring interactions with data flows until a limit point was reached. Then the cycle of attraction effectively reset and began again, creating multiple and overlapping rhythms of operation within the system.

Alongside this, the cross-links between the parameters of watching attractors' inputs and other watchers' outputs meant that a gate parameter of an algorithm, acting as an attractor for a flow of data, was itself attracted towards realising a potential in its continued development.[360] A more complex system arose here that moved towards concretisation, as potential was intertwined and co-produced. That is, it was a system of causality that was irresolvable into a linear chain, as attractors effectively nested inside each other by co-producing each other's parameters: 'A' nested in 'B' while 'B' was also nested within 'A' simultaneously. This was a parasitic mode of operation, with each attractor held together by the dynamic and potentially disruptive pull of the forces of other attractors on it. The relation between an attractor and the system or field within which it nested was 'charged', as attractor and field became implicit in each other's production.[361]

Limits and bifurcations

State systems can move further away from self-preservation by incorporating the ability to undergo phase transitions or bifurcations. Phase transitions 'are events which take place at a critical value of some parameter...switching a physical system from one state to another' (DeLanda 2005, 18). That is, these bifurcations shift a system from one particular set of attractors to another set, though this may include the attractors of the previous system as well as new attractors. As such phase transitions are another potentiality with which a system might engage. They are instigators of, and meaningful to, the emergence of new relations within systems, rather than necessarily changes to individual component parts (Prigogine and Stengers 1996, 45). Besides occurring within a system as a whole, a bifurcation might occur within an attractor, causing an evolution to its affectual capacities.[362] Thus systems might potentially bifurcate in multiple directions at once, without dissolving the assemblage.

In the *Orgasmatron* software patch, some of the triggering algorithms had the potential to trigger the activation of new sets of attractors that operated in addition to those already active. These algorithms were triggered into action when a certain limit of intensity of a particular activity was reached[363]. As there were multiple triggering algorithms counting and multiple new attractors waiting to be activated, this had multiple potential outcomes. These limits were relative thresholds of the system, 'above which [it] cease[ed] to be itself but [got] a new lease on life in a different mode' (Massumi 1992, 36). Thus, the bifurcatory potential created limits that became creative factors, drawing new potential from the field.[364]

These transitions of both the whole state and parts that made up a state were always a partial expression of its many potentials, both of the system as a whole, and the parts that exceeded this actualised state. Once again, increased excitement of the system primed it for change, through a system of potential shifts and disruptions to chains of causality as new relational factors arose in the system[365]. This was not a smooth modulation of the system, but an ongoing potential of sudden shifts, interruptions to established tendencies, and renegotiation of relational pulls. As algorithmic prehension demonstrates a way that such process engaged selectively and creatively with that which preceded it, concepts of attractors and bifurcations here indicate a creative and open engagement with a futurity.

Towards an ecology of patching

Within her concept of the 'minor gesture', Manning poses the question of how technology might be able to 'activate a field event without making the field about the technology itself' (2016a, 18). The challenges implied in a process-driven approach to software design might be seen here as twofold. Firstly, this might involve taking Whitehead's expanded empiricism seriously, and seeking to explicate how all components of a work, including any computer operations, can be viewed as entities or events emergent within a relational system, capable of exercising some of their potential to affect and be affected. Secondly, as Manning suggests, there is always a need to consider the ethics of not only what emerges, but also how it emerges. In the computer processes, this must then be concerned firstly with how the computer's operations affect the gathering of the larger artwork-ecology – its minor potential to move beyond predictive control and representation. Secondly attention must be given to how these operations are able to move towards an intensively minor state; a concretisation of a 'machine ecology' (Penny 2011, 100) that preserves potential as it draws algorithmic processes into collective individuation.

The tactics explored here begin to suggest ways in which a software patch might remain intensively problematic: always irresolvable as a whole, while also immanently offering partial solutions. For Simondon, the ontogenetic power of a system – its capacity for emergent novelty – depends on this ability to generate problems that force the actualisation of partial solutions as new sets of relations that establish a milieu (Vollrath 2013, 46). Thus the role of intensity is crucial here in gathering an emergent ecology within the software patch while still keeping the system open to the disruptive pull of multiple eternal entities that it can then draw from. The *Orgasmatron* system attempted to provide this intensity through the multiple tipping points that were always cycling: through the constant unresolvable pull of the stable attractors; through the entanglement of parameters with algorithmic actualisations; and, through the strain of the cut of negative and positive prehensions. In this, it was an assemblage of 'non-linear combinatorics' – various self-organising structural operations negotiating to produce novel structures (DeLanda 2011a, 16, 277 n.5), producing algorithmic processes through a differential or parasitic approach, or 'new ways of folding the world into itself' (O'Sullivan 2006,143).

Clearly, an ethics of computer process needs to do more than just consider ways to make complex relational webs that move beyond linear causality, and allow new software modes of thinking to arise. It also needs to avoid the trap of creating topological or autopoietic systems that, in their ability to anticipate and influence future modulations, enhance rather than curtail the predictive and controlling potential of the digital.[366] Here, again, the intensively parasitic has a role to play. The proposed tactics are a gathering, but also a splitting of data or force – a continuity of becoming, rather than a smooth modulation that can be predicted and controlled. They involve a concretisation of the assemblage of the various algorithmic and analogue data, but not necessarily a preservation of the assemblage over other relational potential. Instead, such systems have component parts and processes that remain larger than any actualised whole. Through their relation to eternal objects, and through the dynamics of bifurcation, these systems are always on the verge of exceeding their limits, and become the gathering, generative collective force that catalyses new ecologies of relation.

Once again, these tactics are, to a certain extent, about enabling drift: forgoing control over outcomes, and instead concentration on the setting of conditions for events to emerge from. If it is an automated emergence, then this is because it is an algorithmic mode of thought that needs to be given its own space, style and rhythms. Algorithms are events in themselves, co-emergent with and co-causal ecologies of relation that begin to gather. Their actualisations are digital becomings that begin to draw the collective expression beyond not only the biological, but also outside of the analogue. Perhaps here, a software patch can approach a diagrammatic meta-modelling, 'strategically return[ing] its process to the quasi-chaotic field of its own emergence, in order to regenerate itself as it generates new figures, forms and contrasts, for itself and others' (Massumi 2011, 103).

Coda: Towards a gathering ecology

In *Orgasmatron*, participants entered an intimate environment designed for one or two, where their presence within the space contributed – through disruptions and additions – to the generation of rhythmic pulses of coloured light, sounds that surrounded them, and vibrations that coursed through the base of the structure (see Figure 9.2).

Participants lay in the *Orgasmatron*, relinquishing, to some extent, the possibility of feeling in control, and accepting this new posture that emphasised the pull of gravity and what at first might have felt like 'passivity' within the event. Movement shifted in register, being restricted to small, seemingly inconsequential gestures – eye movements, breath expanding the torso, a fractional turning of the head, reflex reaction to vibration under their body, a hand raised, subtle shifts in weight: small adjustments and micro-movements in sympathy with the rhythms of sound, light and vibration affecting the participant. This was a rearrangement and testing of the potential of the body that perhaps began to challenge habitual ways of moving through an interactive work, as the spatial configuration and the shift in postural schema constricted movement, bringing to attention the way forces challenged the body's freedom of action.

Lying in the *Orgasmatron*, connection to the ecology of operations in process was slowed down. There was nothing productive to 'do': no obvious action that would activate events, with a clear or immediate pay-off or resultant change in the work. Here participants were given the time to tune in to the events building around them, allowing such minor forms of bodies to be noticed and evolve. This was less a space to command, and more one to listen with one's body, to seek new connections and open out to an awareness of the gathering rhythm of events in which participants were becoming implicated. This required a new sensitivity to the prehensive pull of the event that was activated at the surface of bodies. Textures, the pressure of the base of the structure, and the vibrations building and coursing through the base of the *Orgasmatron* brought attention to the skin and the activated shared space in between, beginning to combine body, equipment and space. This was a listening with the whole surface: the body an expanded listening machine (an ear). The experience conflated senses, as it was perhaps also a new reflexive listening to or doubling of experience, a reflexive consciousness of this disruption of habits. Micro-perceptive vibrations addressed various sensory organs; pulses of light, sound and the participants' own bodily rhythms combined and syncopated in this surface-to-surface interfacing. Thus the body itself was reconfigured in a minor form as a 'sensor' – transducing different vibrational forces from the event – testing and opening up its affectual capacities to new intensities.

The *Orgasmatron* itself was a combined 'sensor', its components tuned, not only towards the presence of the participant's body entering, and their micro-movements that reflected slight shifts in attention, but also always tuning towards the multiple expressions of its own machinations. While the *Orgasmatron* was sensitive to a participant's weight, vibrations, gestures, sounds and shadows that were a source of disruption to the systems, it also had sensors capable of interacting with its own expressions of light, sound and vibration. Here, in a complex series of feedback circuits, some sensors fed data from changing pulses of light into the development of sound events, others collected vibrational permutations that then affected lighting, while others sensed pressure changes in the floor of the pod that caused further expressions of vibrations, sound and/or lighting. This was a constantly shifting web of parasitic actions – a molecularisation of components: as pressure differentials disrupted light; light differentials disrupted sound (cutting, layering spatialising); and sound differentials altered vibration. The actions of bodies within this environment provided further parasitic disruptions to these emerging causalities: further variations in pressure, light or vibration as the *Orgasmatron* listened to and fed on (in its own way) its own constant permutations and exploratory combinations.

These sensory capacities (capacities to *feel*) of the machine (bodies and technical components) folded into one another, to begin the collective individuation of the event: a mixing and shaping of a shared potential and responsibility. Such a turn towards a collective listening and expressing might be a tending towards a 'self-tuning': the will of the event to emerge and to carry forward. This questioned the position of the participants as the focus of the gathering of forces, as the work perhaps began to trouble distinctions between the subject of the event and the field from which it drew its energies. Rather, participants shared responsibility for this gathering, adding their own attention, care and potential to the attention and sensitivities that the *Orgasmatron* was itself able to generate. The concern here was less with being, and more concerned with a communication or engagement across a vibrational plane: a collective feeling for the gathering that was distributed throughout the components of the event.

The system disrupted the representation and comprehension of causal chains – how a particular rhythm, sound or pulse of light was connected to previous actions or events – as both participants and work were immersed in the ongoing collection of sensations (relationality in its own right). The engagement with affectual forces – both the collectively engagement of the event, and individual engagement by various components with different appetites or capacities – split, folded and remixed causality. The dynamic, complex and qualitative interfacings and parasitic actions cultivated a suspension in the gathering of relation – creating a pull towards further relational iteration. In this, the parasite forced an opening to further expression, connectivity, and an ability to affect and be affected. This was a turning towards immanent construction of relation taking precedence over its stratification (that is, an opening of sense experiences – of both the participant and other components).

The 'working out' of these relational disruptions moved the system towards a concretisation. The components of the event were no longer as dependent on 'outside' intervention to facilitate communication between them – whether the participant's body providing this interfacing or the work of a computer that stood outside of the mobile parameters of the work itself. Instead, the components were able to utilise their transductive sensitivities to create their own local relational interactions and to produce affects 'that [were] independent of the design plan' (Simondon 1980, 31). But it was a concretis*ing*, in that this was never resolved to a fixed state of intertwined sub-systems, fully subsumed to the functioning of the whole (Simondon 1980, 30), but any move towards resolution continued to be challenged by the disruptions that forced a re-gathering.

There was always some further potential for agitation, for the continued parasitic disruption allowing new connections to be performed. This was an agitation that was not reliant on a human participant for its energy, but was able to activate itself, to generate the minor gestures from within the event. This further potential was the tension that drove the transduction of the system, its provisional resolution of multiple potentials, and the ongoing working out of the problem of disruption and reconnection.[367] This was the conversation between the various interferences of one force on another that formed a collective individuation located in the event as it gathered.

Orgasmatron proposed a field of potential sensitivities and potential disruptions from which provisional connections and disconnections might begin to form a relational web. Here, I term the act of the *Orgasmatron* tuning into this potential – to begin to become an event – a 'gathering ecology'. A gathering ecology implies a particular attention to the event's own ability

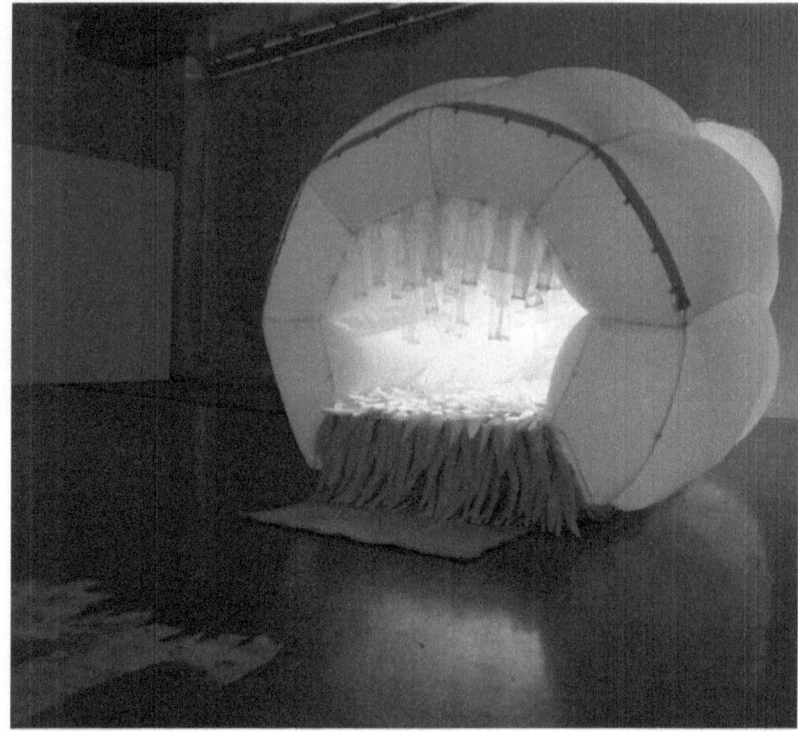

Figure 9.2 Andrew Goodman, Orgasmatron (detail), Blindside, Melbourne, 2013.

to prehend the potential of the field and gather or implicate components' individual and shared capacities for connection and disruption into a collective event, and to give attention to the 'minor gestures' that are the event's own intensive drivers of individuation. This focus on a gathering ecology shifts interaction further, from the fixed or linear sets of relations between technical objects and bodies, towards what might be thought of as an ethics of relation, in that it places a focus not just on the flexibility and complexity of relations, but squarely on the opening of conditions for the event's emergence.

A potential politics of interactive art might be an ethics that addresses not the representation of relation, but its immanent construction, enabling an opening to further expression, connectivity and an ability to affect and be affected: to affirm both the singular nature of events and openness of relational potential (Simondon cited Combes 2013, 65).[368] It might seek to encourage 'the suspension of normal co-ordinates of sensory experience' (Rancière 2009, 25), that is, an opening of sense experience towards the new – the preservation of difference (Murphie 1997, 163–5) in a gathering ecology.

Conclusion

> Now more than ever, nature cannot be separated from culture; in order to comprehend the interactions between ecosystems...we must learn to think transversally.
>
> *Felix Guattari*

Parasitic friends and enemies

The parasite disrupts and creates; it 'makes life and kills' (Serres 2007, 168). It is the instigator of the new, it is 'an expansion; it runs and grows' (Serres 2007, 253). It causes disruption to gather and multiply. It bifurcates all, driving systems towards the novelty of new connection as it makes new systems. It is the best friend of complex emergent relation.

The parasite 'invades and occupies' (Serres 2007, 253); it troubles orders, disrupts connections. It is a noise that 'destroys and horrifies' (127), pulls things apart, confuses and obscures (Serres 2007,12), lays waste to plans. It is the worst enemy of the clear and simple relation.

Parasitic procedures trouble totalities, creatively disrupting clear communications, orders, hierarchies and dichotomies. Parasites can be thought not only as a third factor in relation, shifting the already established, but also as a difference that might be original, thrusting us always in to the middle of things going on. In the interactive art event, parasites fragment the simple causal relationship of a participant's intentional action and comprehendible change in the work. They coax into existence minor interactive potentials that are situated within the major, problematising interactivity's boundaries, questioning both its definition and its mechanisms.

The parasite is a noise that, though disruptive, is far from being chaotic. Rather it is intensely and complexly relational, implicating elements of systems into each other's ongoing individuation. In this, it is potentialising – saturating the actualised with an inbuilt ability to continue to grow, modulate and add to itself.

The parasite is the friend of noise and the noise within friendships, but it is never friendless and never outside of relation.

Parasitic feelings

To feel, for Whitehead, is to be involved in processes of the becoming of novelty, and it is also to be involved in processes of ingression and entanglement. In feeling, an emergent entity grasps datum from the world as a selfish and parasitic activity (reaching into and feeding off not only the actualised world, but also ingressing into the virtual plane of the eternal objects). At the same time, and in the same action of feeling, the world 'steals in' (Jones 1998, 3)[369] or ingresses into the entity as its very core of becoming. This enfolding or nesting is problematising: entities parasite for their own selfish means, but are in turn subject to the parasitic ingressions of others.

Feeling produces a resonance that is both intensive (valuated and patterned contrasts) and extensive (a differing from what already is and a selection from the larger potential). It utilises the tensions involved not to homogenise and consolidate, but as an adventure that explores potential in novel combinations that intensify difference. In this feelings are always transductive – reaching forward, moving beyond the realised, turning many things into one new thing, again to be folded into another eruption of novelty.

The parasitic actions of feeling on the 'world-as-it-is' to individuate the 'world-as-it-will-be' suggest an interactivity of occasions and potentials that is never going to be contained in simplistic viewer-to-artwork conversations, but that is an emergent and parasitic ecology of ingressions, transgressions, interruptions and additions.

Parasitic ecologies

The gathering of an ecology is a machinic act, that is, the immanent production of a symbiotic entanglement,[370] no more a bottom-up phenomenon than it is top-down. It is a system-wide productivity (though not totalising), passing through scales and dimensions, a becoming that is a qualitative increase in intensity (Braidotti 2002, 147). It is a gathering (not resolving) of difference, and therefore a gathering of an ecology that is auto-parasitic. The generation of its minor gestures is 'in the wind', as the affectual force of the event, an evolving capacity to prehend or tune to the potential of the field (to gather on the level of the virtual). These gestures that produce and drive the ecology are the will of the event. As a gathering ecology is an 'immediatory'[371] process, it might not be known through any predetermined configuration, but only through the field's continued exercising of self-productive expressions. A gathering ecology retains this capacity to gather in its connection to the virtual. It is never 'gathered' as a final act that exhausts potential or resolves beyond the provisional differentiation of forces and relations, but is always a question of process (Stengers 2010, 33). In this sense there is never 'an' ecology, but only the transductive process of becoming-ecology or gathering.

'Ecologies' here do not submit to exterior truths but produce and are produced through continued experimentation. Thus the ecological could be described as inherently minor, as it is concerned with 'the production of new, immanent modes of existence, and not the recognition of a more powerful interest before which divergent particular interests would have to bow down' (Stengers 2010, 35). Neither is this a question of the identities of components, which cannot be reduced to, nor deduced by the role each plays in the ecology (Stengers 2010, 34–5). For interactive art this might suggest a move away from the reinforcement of identity of the experimenter and components (what are they, how have they related?). Instead interactivity might be better served to invent ways to embrace the ecological with its 'disparate causalities' and 'unintentional creations of meaning' (Stengers 2010, 34) (how could it become?). This then might move towards an interactive system that creates relation without having the nature of those relations fully prescribed, or the manner in which they might individuate. Nor need the design prescribe the scale or extent of those interactions, or the outcomes for either components parts (participants, affects, sensations, technical objects), or the system as an evolving whole. Thus it is concerned with an 'ecology of the virtual' that can 'engender conditions for the creation and development of unprecedented formations of subjectivity that have never been seen and never been felt' (Guattari 1995a, 91). For this to occur a work needs to be rich with minor gestures as lures towards novelty that 'seed' the potential for further gathering of ecological force. Here we might seek an art that operates as a field through system-level dynamics, parasitically inserting difference into such relations, and through this held intensity allows for relations to arise and gather.

Parasitic politics

One might argue that our contemporary world already offers unparalleled connectivity through the globalised economy and the collapse of time and distance through the so-called 'virtual' world of the internet (and of course the effects of this on art have been momentous and neither entirely negative or positive). It is also possible to argue that there has been a proliferation of difference and experimentation – one that can be seen in the post-millennium art world with its furious multiplication of styles, diverging trends and voices. Perhaps too there has already been an unprecedented blurring of human and non-human life and the technical, with increasing incursion of algorithms into the political, social and personal sphere, to name just one example.[372]

However a closer examination of these conditions of contemporary living shows little to be enthusiastic about. As Braidotti has so eloquently pointed out, the connectivity offered within neoliberalism is principally one of a shared precarity (2014, 40). That is, it is an ecological and political *vulnerability* that we share in across borders with other social groups, with other animals on whose lives global capitalism encroaches on and into for its own purposes, and with the greater ecology that is also commodified and exploited. This vulnerability is evident in terms of the increasing precarity of a global environment under ecological crisis that affects and connects us all in a decidedly negative manner.[373] If advanced capitalism produces difference, it is only for the sake of further commodification. If it encourages experimentation, it is to harness this potential within a subjectivity based on passivity and individualism (Braidotti 2014, 58, 61). So too, if capitalism blurs the human and non-human it is to further advance networks of control in order to exploit and profit from them (Braidotti 2014, 63). Capitalism, for all its relational flexibility, has no ethics, no care for or interest in the potential of the events that emerge beyond their vulnerability to be exploited. It is a 'steamroller' enforcing 'capitalistic subjectivity – the subjectivity of one-dimensionality, generalised equivalence, segregation, and deafness to true alterity' (Guattari 1995a, 91). The connectivity offered in this world tends towards a greater surveillance and biopolitical control of life that now grips the social/political, the personal or psychic and the ecological planes to an unprecedented extent. Ultimately such processes of connectivity collapse difference as they subjugate: they are operations of power that are restrictive and repetitious rather than productive of any larger sense of novelty. Why then would we want an interactive art experience that merely mimics this precarity, one that at once instrumentalises our bodies as it reinforces subjectivity and our separation from the field and its further collective potential?

I say all this not to make any great claims for the artworks discussed in this book, but to suggest that they all exhibit, in various and modest ways, the beginnings of different ways of operating. They point towards transversal and immanent practices or *technics* of becoming-with ecologies of relations that embrace complexity, disruption and novelty. It will be evident that none of these artworks directly address the ecological and political crises we face. These are not 'issue' based works seeking to explore the negative aspects of our situation. This is not to argue that such messages do not have a place in our thinking, but that art, and perhaps interactive or relational artworks in particular, might have a different and more *affirmative* and forward-reaching or speculative role to play.

Affirmation, as Manning articulates, is a very particular type of positivity that is propositional (2016b, 196). That is, it enables invention rather than compliance, and in this it opens up events to further evolution rather than collapsing difference in relational consensus (Manning 2016b, 196). An affirmative relational artwork might seek to move away from a capitalistic model of self-organisation to 'imagine a form of self-organization that is not exploitative' but a 'genuine novelty' (Shaviro 2009, 128 n.16). This is an affirmative ethics that extends care towards the quality of expression of a system. It seeks to nourish the potential for creative movement or exploration within an event, with attention to and care for the conditions of emergence as well as what emerges.

This is not the artwork of grand gestures and political sloganeering, but of attention to what else is going on beyond, beside and throughout events of relation. It requires that we develop capacities to listen and give care to the resolutely non-human and the more-than human: to the diffractions and conversations of sound waves with spaces, to the algorithmic appetites, to the rhythms of collaborations between bodies and spaces, bodies and bodies, bodies and technical objects, and within bodies themselves. In this it might seek to experiment with technics that move us beyond shared precarity (and the capitalisation of emergence) and begin to bring new and affirmative potential ecologies into being.

Technicity, as Manning states, is 'the associated milieu of technique'. That is, it addresses the generation or gathering of a field of potentiality as much or more than the individual technique (Manning 2013a, 34). Technicity therefore speaks to the gathering ecology in the realm of the political, a realm that permeates relational or interactive art, which always expresses a politics (whether productive or repressive). Affirmative technics addresses the construction of an ethics of immanence: an ethics of experimentation with the construction of the contrasts and differential intensities in relations that enlarges collective potential rather than reverting to individualism or negativity.[374] This must be an emergent ethics that operates transindividually, at a collective and ecological level. In this positivity one might seek to move beyond a criticism of the state of interactivity and to seek to generate new concepts of what might constitute an expanded notion of interactivity: that is, to begin to generate new potentials and futures for the genre itself.

Such ethics must remain firmly grounded in the 'how' of collective enunciation (Manning 2013a, 35), in the questions of the individuation of the field or ecology, in order not to simply replicate the neoliberal repressive responsibility of the individual towards the state or the status quo (Braidotti 2014, 116). That is, energy and attention needs to be invested in the pre-relational gathering of ecologies – into the nurturing and tentative feeling-out of the minor gestures that emerge from a complex ecology's own feeling of potential and that tend towards a feeling of events in the beginnings of formation (Manning 2013, 6–7). These gestures – as a series of differential events within a field that catalyse a collective tuning towards the field's potential concrescence into a dynamic and enmeshed ecology – are the seeds that ensure that ecologies adventure into the unknown as they individuate. That is, they are *performative* and belong to the ecology's gathering. The 'how' of this gathering must of course always be open in itself. There can be no definitive answer to this but only a series of practices that continue to explore the problem – that meta-model or 'stay with the trouble' to quote Haraway (2016, passim). In this each well-thought and constructed interactive event can contribute (in its own tentative way and within its own area of concern) to the collective thinking-through of the problem of not only how to live in this world, but how to begin minoritarian transformations of it.

Politics, or even ethics, may still seem a heavy burden for such simple relational works. But it is, I would argue, a politics of dissention, of reconfiguration and extension, of etching out further space or potential no matter how slight. I have contended that the programmatic tendencies of interactive artworks contain difference and universalise experience – a politics in itself, albeit an oppressive one. Aesthetic acts that extend and prolong contrasts can be seen instead as ethical politics, making felt novel relational connections and new collective capacities (Massumi and McKim 2009, 12). The capacity for these aesthetic acts to produce 'mutant percepts and affects' gives them an important role in the liberation from the merely possible: the cannibalistic moves of capitalism to reiterate and mutate existing relations and subjectivities (Guattari 1995a, 91, 131). Aesthetic acts are transversal, operating through 'affective contamination'. They have the potential not only to operate as the 'nuclei of differentiation', but also to operate 'between the different domains in order to accentuate their heterogeneity' (Guattari 1995a, 93–4). The 'beauty' of the aesthetic act is in its ability to sustain contrasts, to extend differentials.

Such aesthetic politics need not be conceived of as necessarily earnest. Rather, they may be better situated in play and the disruptive power of such unproductive action that proposes starting rather than endpoints of relations. Here, again, my argument seeks to arrive not at any solution, but rather to build conceptual machines with which to allow a working through both of the potential of parasitic actions, and a questioning of the limits of interactivity.

This book has intentionally examined works that cover a broad range of relational experiences, and that move somewhat away from easy classification as 'interactive', while still involving many elements of such systems. Near these edges or limits, the question must always arise: 'But is this still interactive?' This, I would suggest, is in itself productive, capable of always provoking some uncertainty as to what does or does not constitute an interactive work. It is an interactivity that by its existence challenges interactivity from within, injects tentativeness into its identity. It is a questioning that is productively disruptive to the very concept of interactivity: a parasite. As such, the thinking as a whole might perhaps be positioned as both parasitic and a minor practice; a gathering of an ecology, a rethinking of interactivity that seeds further potential disruptions, always attempting to take it beyond the re-emerging majoritarian forms.

Notes

1. For an extended discussion of the concept of immanent critique, see also Manning (2016b, Chapter One).
2. Various authors give different names to this approach, it might be termed organic, relational, performative or anti-representational, or one of radical, deep or expanded empiricism. All these terms are put to use in this research – here broadly grouped under the term 'process', with an implication that, as Ilya Prigogine says, an open-ended futurity requires understanding that the laws of nature are based on possibilities not 'certitudes' (Prigogine and Stengers 1996, 183).
3. This emphasis an on an 'additive' approach, Massumi states, as the 'key to an expanded Empiricism. There is always enough room in the world for more, more modulation, more "belonging"' (2000, 216).
4. This 'creative advance' of the universe is, as Whitehead sees it, the driving force behind process (1978, 21). See also Stengers (2011, 257–9).
5. While a sustained critique of the term new media is outside the scope of this discussion, it is, as a number of writers note, a problematic term. The 'newness' in new media, as Fuery notes, is limited to technical rather than artistic invention and creates an artificial stabilization of investigations that are ongoing processes of innovation (Fuery, 2009, 9). This, as Munster says, calls attention to the medium as the definer of artistic outcomes (2006, 154), and it might, as Murphie claims, leads to a fetishisation of the technological invention for its own sake, rather than a measured consideration of their interactive and ethical potentials (2005b, 31).
6. Relation here concerns a much broader span and range of forces than most interactive works acknowledge. It would, I believe, be possible to argue that many more 'traditional' art forms successfully exploit a wide range of relational forces in ways that are often more subtle and complex than many prescribed interactive

artworks. On painting and relation, for example, see Irwin (2011); Manning (2009, 55–63); and Massumi (2011, 127–30).

7. This ontology is 'abstracted' in that Whitehead, like James, is at pains to make it an ontology applicable to all occasions without exception. 'Becoming,' in the sense that Massumi uses it, 'open(s) up spaces and maps new virtual landscapes', it is a movement of invention, necessarily always an emergent model, in the process of being (re)invented. Therefore a 'becoming' model would be one that continually adapts to new information, heads in multiple directions: a kind of rhizomic 'anti' model (1992, 101–2).

8. This is a secondary meaning of 'parasite' adopted by Serres in *The Parasite* to explore the productive disruptions to relation.

9. Feelings, for Whitehead, are also part of a parasitic system, both in their drawing of datum from other, objectified, events, and in that each feeling is divisible into other feelings, with differences preserved.

10. In forming relations an entity 'expresses' or performs some of its capacity to affect and be affected by other entities and forces.

11. That is to say, the expressive capacities of technical components must be taken into account and enabled, but at the same time their own particular (and *non-biological*) potential must be allowed to emerge, rather than seeking to consider their operations as biological equivalents as in some cybernetic modelling. See Chapter Nine for some discussion of this issue, and Parisi.

12. Later in the same essay Simondon writes: 'transduction, as opposed to *deduction*, does not search elsewhere for a principle to resolve the problem of a domain: it extracts the resolving structure from the tensions of the domain themselves, just as a supersaturated solution crystallises using its own potentials and according to the chemical species it contains, not using some foreign form added from the outside. Nor is transduction comparable to *induction*, because although induction retains the characteristics of the terms of reality that are contained within the studied domain, extracting the structures of the analysis of these terms themselves, induction only retains that which is positive – *that which is common* to all of the terms –eliminating that which is singular to them' (2009, 12).

13. Guattari's concept relates directly to his idea of schitzoanalysis as an alternative to conventional psychoanalytic models. This is productively expanded in *Fibreculture*, vol. 12, 2008, an issue devoted to metamodelling. See also Massumi (2011, 87–104), for further extrapolation of the concept relevant to embodied experience of the world.

14. The meta-model, Manning and Massumi argue, is necessarily virtual as it remains at a point of emergence and therefore perishes in actualization (2010, 25). See: Lynn on the virtues of complexity as an escape from both identity and dialectic contradiction (1998, 161).

15. See also Shaviro (2009, 148–9). It is worth noting, I think, that Serres' own philosophical writing is one of the best examples I know of metamodelling within philosophy. In *The Parasite* he takes the problem of 'noise', and, beginning with a short fable from Boursault, dissects the story multiple times from different angles, each time bringing in new conceptual material and propositions in a way that both builds on the original concept and layers and fragments it with new and inventive potential. As Cary Wolfe writes in the introduction to the English language version, Serres' writing is 'not analytical but experimental…not linear but meandering, doubling back on itself to remind itself of stones left unturned, details too readily smoothed over, conclusions too well varnished' (Wolfe in Serres 2007, xiii). Similarly, in the writing of both Whitehead and Simondon, one can see a continued return to problems from new angles, with new examples and workings-through that complicate rather than resolve.

16. At its most simplistic, rather than reflecting genuine parallel enquiries informing and enriching one another, this results in exegetic writing by artists that seeks to veneer over the cracks in a practice, or worse still artworks that essentially illustrate theory. Practical investigations of course outstrip or spill over outside the scope of theoretical discussions in the way that art always does. Art perhaps does itself a disservice in trying to articulate theory or tie itself too directly to conceptual frameworks. Perhaps, for an artist, writing might be considered a creative act that creates texts as 'little bombs' that might be productive in their scattering of ideas and establishing of new linkages (Grosz 2001, 58; Deleuze and Guattari 1994, 66), as art might be a method of 'thinking' through embodied participation Here the speculative

and propositional nature of the theoretical discussions is, I would argue, both a philosophical choice in line with process philosophy, and a practical technique for dealing with the necessarily open-ended nature of propositional art events – bringing to attention that 'theory-making itself, [is] a messy, fleshy practice' (Loveless 2012, 95).

17. Such criticisms are also leveled by Barad at a system such as Newtonian physics that assumes the existence of objects prior to their interaction. (2007, 197 and passim)

18. Whether we even sustain such a category of art as 'interactivity', and why we would want to – when one considers the contemporary collapse of traditional boundaries – between painting and photography, sculpture and drawing, no longer seem justifiable or useful – is a debate deflected here by the adoption of a wider relational model, with its acknowledgement of the participatory aspects and the potential of any art event.

19. See also Claire Bishop's critique of the focus on participatory art's social rather than aesthetic qualities that tend to flatten all artistic social experience to the same level (2009, 240).

20. In something of a widening of the parameters of the interactive, Stern proposes a number of types, some of which imply a relational mode of thinking: navigable, reactive or responsive environments, participatory and collaborative interactions (2012, 28–9). See also Pierre Levy for a discussion of a number of types of interactivity (2001, 61, 115–s6).

21. 'Free will', as Valentine Moulard-Leonard argues when discussing the philosophies of Henri Bergson, could in itself be seen on some levels as a 'false problem', presuming a preformed, singular subjectivity from which to deliberate on the world – whereas, in reality, deliberate and spontaneously arising actions might not be so simply divisible (2008, 18–19). See also Jones on freedom as a falsely conceived force (1998, 147).

22. Lev Manovich describes the rise of interactive art as a shift from representation to manipulation (1996, 1), and Florence de Mèredieu likewise warns that 'we should not delude ourselves: interactivity can conceal programmed actions and predetermined pseudo-choices' (2003, 230).

23. Barad defines 'representationalism' as 'a system where representations mediate between independently existing entities', and 'essentialism' as 'a metaphysics that takes for granted the existence of individual entities. Each with its own roster of non-relational properties' (Barad 2007, 47, 55).

24. In a similar discussion of this dynamic, de Mèredieu gives a pertinent example of an 'Ageing Machine' that was first developed as an artistic project but whose program is now used by the FBI to help trace criminals (2003, 172).

25. We must remember that 'interactivity' has in itself become a marketing tool for a whole range of games and other electronic devices (Fuery 2009, 41–2), as it has been sold for its 'novelty' within the art world (Penny 2011, 72–109, 99), while the rise in digital arts funding could be linked to the potential future commercial applications of such artistic research, thus funding structures privilege a focus on learning, results and quantifiable changes (Manning and Massumi 2010, 2). For discussion of the links between industrial culture and interactive technologies, see Birringer (2005, 153).

26. See also Levy's critique the difference between interactivity modelled on communication systems, whether consisting of 'monologue', 'dialogue' or 'multilogue' as being in opposition to an interactivity co-producing its subjects (2001, 115–6).

27. This is certainly not to imply that less programmatically interactive works can easily escape the commodification of the art market. As the history of performance art processes has shown, over time such immaterial practices can easily be accommodated into the gallery and funding systems, and indeed may have helped to spark further areas of entanglement with government and business through the development of funding bodies, creative PhD programs and the accompanying training of generations of artists in the self-management and shaping of their careers around the carefully curated statements of intent, budget management and interactions with gallery and educational bureaucracies necessary to achieve funding and exhibition space.

28. Interactivity's representational issues tend to have, as discussed in the next section, more to do with representations of its dynamics and/or mechanics.

29. By which I mean that an interactive work might, for example, literally generate new combinations of sound and visual data out

of the participant's movements. The term 'mechanical' is not here used to infer negative connotations to such processes.

30. And, we must remember, the very production of subjectivity itself has become 'the immaterial gross product of the neoconservative state' (Massumi 1992, 201, n.66). On the broader problems of exchange value in the digital realm, see Pasquinelli (2008, 72–90 and passim).

31. My argument here is less intended as a critique of gaming and museum culture than of the limitation of interactivity within art events to such models. Anna Munster, for example, has argued for the positive aspects of the use of multi-media in interactive museum displays, which can allow for 'affective experience' that emphasises relations rather than objects (2006, 56–8).

32. See Massumi for a discussion of Deleuze and Guattari's interpretation of the shift in capitalism from use-value to exchange-value and the rise of new forms of surplus value (1992, 199–202).

33. Even generative models utilised within software programming for 'evolutionary' art, such a fractal or fitness based systems, while potentially divergent in the paths, still involve linear dynamics of cause and effect (alternative, ecological approaches are speculated on in Chapter Nine).

34. Stern describes such systems as operations of a 'passive trace', utilizing gesture and response (2012, 68).

35. For example, Lozano-Hemmer optimistically attributes these types of systems to the early developments in interactivity, stating that greater 'sophistication' developed later as artists began to consider the question of how to include more ambiguous and less productively orientated relationships (Lozano-Hemmer, Boucher and Harrop 2012, 152).

36. See also Manning's critique of linearity (2009, 62–4), and Stern's critique of representational modes within interactivity (2012, 10).

37. In Whitehead's system of perception, for example, 'causal efficacy' and 'presentational immediacy' (as the factors are named) are two intertwined components of any experience. However the emphasis in interactive art has often been on demonstration of its mechanics of relation. See Brian Massumi's discussion of these concepts (2008), and Chapter Six of this book for a discussion of these terms in detail.

38. See also: Karen Barad (2007, 46–50), *Meeting the Universe Halfway*, on the naturalisation of representationalism.

39. In a discussion of his work *Very Nervous System*, Rokeby outlines the problematics of this issue, and the need to balance emergent and potential relations with a certain level of demonstrable connection in order to encourage the participant to continue to engage. Here he explains how the complex and multiply interwoven relational parameters built into this work caused participants to feel as if they were not in fact interacting and to then lose interest in participating (NDb).

40. If we read the 'possible' as that which is already contained within the actual then it is, in a sense, tautological. The possible is defined retroactively and offering no forward movement from a position – rather it acts to contain and limit (Deleuze 1994, 211–12).

41. As Dery does points out, the concept that reuse or re-purposing of equipment is necessarily a radical act against capitalist models can be wishful thinking. Software producers often encouraging innovative 'misuse' of their technologies, and building potential for adaptation into the product as part of an extension of its modes of production and as a marketing asset (Dery 1996, 78). See also Pasquinelli's discussion of the tactical alliance between free software development and corporations as 'macroparasitic' (2008, 48).

42. Penny also notes the irony that the 'harnessing of the flesh to the machine [of the military] was clad in the rhetoric of liberation in the heyday of interactive multimedia' (2003, 268; Cf. Grau 2003, 169).

43. For example, Lozano-Hemmer's claim that his work, reliant as it is on technologies of surveillance – and potentially complicit in their construction through the use of custom software that extends the scope of their ability to productively map bodies within space – operates as a 'perversion' of these technologies (Gorschluter 2009, 103). Potentially, they both pervert and critique as they also employ power relationships, and perhaps some of his works are more successful than others in achieving his aims.

44. Though it would be incorrect to link this control simply to vision or the visible as is often implied (Jay 1988, 2–23). Contemporary surveillance and interactive technologies show us that movement,

sound, vibrations, infra-red waves, pressure, heat, and so on, can be mapped and plotted alongside the visible.

45. For example, the use of X-Box or Wii to interface between bodies and software means that movements are mapped onto a Cartesian grid in a simplified manner that not only erases the subtlety of actions but ignores the larger field within which the bodies are situated (as of course they must for the games the systems are design for to function correctly). This is not a criticism of the games themselves or gaming in general, but a concern about their easy adoption and cooption of the potentially more complex fields of interaction that artists may wish to create.

46. As Massumi notes, 'bodies that fall prey to such transcendence... [have] their corporeality...stripped from them, in favour of a supposed substrate – soul, subjectivity, personality, identity' (1992, 112.) See also Brad Epps on interactivity as 'exercises in control' (Cited in Braidotti 2002, 253).

47. On the first point, Pasquinelli notes, for example, that while the unstoppable sharing of digital music files has freed one aspect of the music industry from capitalist exchange, the real winners from this are the producers of the material support products such as mp3 players and tablets – thus the market has shifted its sphere of capitalisation rather than collapsed (Pasquinelli 2008, 176). On the second point, he argues that, seen in a wider context, the battles over the 'cognitive' work of the internet must be seen as an internalization of social systems of stratification and exploitation, which have now been 'inoculated and "securitized" into the individual' as an 'immaterial civil war [that] is the internal border (indeed biopolitical border) of a broader *immaterial class conflict*' (Pasquinelli 2008, 110, emphasis in the original).

48. Pasquinelli argues that this new form is parasitic in operating as 'rent' that extracts a surplus and further adds to the precarity of labour conditions (2008, 91–3).

49. See also Penny's advocation of a 'performative ontology' as 'exploration of embodied interaction' rather than an exploration of content (2011, 94–5). This might be described as a process of 'subjectivation', which, 'although operating within social machines, uses processes of these social machines to form lines of escape from them' – as opposed to 'subjectification', which 'implies a thoroughly stratified or captured position. One's subjectivity is

aligned with the major, one's flows contained within its antiproductive maneuvering' (Murphie 1996, 17).

50. See, for example, Whitehead's demonstration of how the problem of Zeno's arrow can be solved through a shift to organic modelling (1978, 68-79). See also Stengers (2011, 16-17) and Jones (1998, 120).

51. Similarly, Manning describes interaction as an 'encounter between two bounded entities' (2013a, 28).

52. An 'actual entity' is anything that is actualised: object, person, atom, feeling, sound, etc. Whitehead also uses the term 'occasion' as interchangeable with entity, and this perhaps expresses the eventness of things more overtly.

53. The self here still exists, but as 'a modality – a singularity on the plane of individuation' (Manning 2013a, 2-3). For Simondon relation is the 'non-identity of a being to itself', it expresses 'more than a unity and more than an identity' (1992, 312).

54. However relationality and interactivity are perhaps better not described in simple binary opposition. Rather, relation, as Manning notes, is 'active to the tendencies of interaction, but not limited to them' (2013a, 29). In this line McCormack proposes, after Di Scipio, that interactions are byproducts of smaller interdependent relations within ecological systems (McCormack & d'Inverno, editors, 2012, 48).

55. Perhaps one could go back further in artists' writings, and quote, as Manning does In *Relationscapes* (2009), from the futurist Boccioni, who calls for a 'fusion of environment and object', and a 'sculptural simultaneity', a 'form-force' that expresses a continuity of becoming, and the abolition of subject matter replaced instead by the 'reality' of experience (Boccioni 2000, 40-51).

56. See also Andrew Pickering (2010, 324).

57. See also Haque (2006, 4) and Fernadez (2009, 2).

58. For a good description of some of Pask's artistic projects see Fernandez (2009, passim).

59. Clark's work might be seen to encourage a felt experience of the forces making the body and to privilege 'relations across differing modalities' (Osthoff 1997, 286). See also Manning (2008, 12).

250 Notes

60. It could be argued that in many artists' work there remains a gap between the thinking and proposing of work as relational and the works themselves. Lozano-Hemmer's work, while it includes many interesting experiments in multi-layered relation (the ongoing *Relational Architecture* series, for example, discussed in Chapter Eight), also includes works that fall back into an object-orientated, demonstrative and fairly linear approach (such as *Tape Recorders*, 2011). In Penny's writing, despite his advocacy for relation, he fails to make the leap to a model in which force is primary, ignoring the distinction between relation preceding form and relation between the already formed, and such an issue could perhaps be seen to arise in his artwork, with a similar dependence on the demonstration of connection. This is less intended here as a criticism than a pertinent reminder of the difficulty within practice of actualising theoretical material that interrupts the 'normative' understanding and use of objects and bodies within art.

61. See: Arakawa and Gins (2002; 1997). See also Reversible Destiny (www.reversibledestiny.org/#!bioscleave-house-%e2%96%91%e2%96%91-lifespan-extending villa) for the Bioscleave House, an example of their 'procedural architecture'.

62. Dery criticises the 'cyborg' model for preaching 'transcendence through technology' (1996, 161). For a succinct discussion of Simondon's critique of cybernetics see Combes (2013, 79–83). See also Manning's distinction between the cybernetic and the prosthetic use of technology (2009, 63; Cf. Massumi 2002, Chapter Four, for an alternative reading of Stelarc's work that emphasises his 'tweak of the human body-object into a sensitivity to new forces, or neglected aspects of familiar forces') (112). Perhaps Stelarc is his own worst enemy in the transcendent language of his writing used to describe his experiments. The artworks themselves present the possibility of more nuanced and complex readings (for example, Stelarc's proposition of the 'obsolescence' of bodies (http://stelarc.org/?catID=20317).For a balanced discussion of the relational pros and cons of Stelarc's work and writing and the gap between the two, see Murphie (1997, 147–8).

63. To move relationally, Manning says, is 'to harness the preaccelerations, becomings, futureness of movements' (2009, 26).

64. 'Co-causal' is the term favoured by Manning and Massumi to describe this mutual emergence of the new through the flux of

the forces of relations (2010, 42, n.2). As Francisco Varela argues, such events of relation between the world and bodies are always events of mutual creation – neither wholly internal nor external (Varela, Thompson and Rosch 1992, 198–205). In a similar vein, Karen Barad uses 'intra-action' to describe a system where cause and effect emerges as the differential materialisation of bodies. Barad writes that 'intra-actions are non-arbitrary, nondeterministic causal enactments through which matter-in-process-of-becoming is iteratively enfolded into its ongoing differential materialization' (2007, 176, 169). This Barad terms a system of 'agential realism' (2007, 132–88 and passim). Lone Bertelsen uses the term 'trans-subjective' after Ettinger, to move beyond interactivity and describe responsibility as a shared concern between all emergent aspects of an event (2012, 31–71).

65. That is, to be further immersed in a field rather than to emerge out of the field.

66. An assemblage is a productive network of variable, contingent connections that produce something more than the individual components.

67. *Into the Midst* was a five-day collaborative research-creation workshop in the *SATosphere*, the Society for Art and Technology's interactive immersive projection environment. The workshop featured hands-on experimentation toward exploring the potential for the SAT building to host the emergence of new forms of experience. The experimentation was preceded by online philosophical explorations over the previous year aimed at fashioning a shared vocabulary and understanding of the concepts. Key issues the workshop attempted to address were: how interactive movement within the space could modulate the experience of the projected space (and vice versa) in ways that altered habitual modes of perception; how the relationship between inside and outside spaces might be modulated, using the SAT building and its immediate urban surroundings as raw material; how frustrations of expectations regarding the responsiveness of interactive systems might lead, positively, to new qualities of aesthetic experience. The results were presented performatively to the pubic in the *SATosphere* – a space constructed as a large, high ceilinged dome designed for 360-degree interactive video and still image projection, with thirty two-channel surround audio built into the walls of the room – over a two-hour period at the end of

252   Notes

the workshop. (This description is adapted from the blurb on the project on the Senselab site, available at: senselab.ca/wp2/events/into-the-midst/).

68. In addition, the gallery delineated very clear and problematic divisions between the interior presentation space and the physical and social realities of the gallery's geographical position within a politically charged area of downtown Montreal.

69. Specific tactics utilised included: creating relational play between artists and audience members with yarn that was crocheted between bodies; improvised movement procedures and generated sounds that sought to activate the perimeter of the dome; projections of images and videos that disturbed clear spatial representation; and sudden shifts between centralised, immersive images and sound and multiple smaller images; a sudden cut to projected imagery; and a soundscape that attempted to locate viewers back into their specific spatial configurations by playing words whispered softly through individual speakers in a random pattern (these consisted of movement prompts in a number of languages), and that could only be understood by walking around the perimeter of the space more subtle and directed sounds. As part of the project, a number of parallel experiments in relation were carried out around the site of the SAT and then folded back into the space. Chapter Five discusses one such experiment – an iteration of Nathaniel Stern's ongoing *Compressionism* project.

70. Beyond the physical structuring of a clear divide between the technical machinations and the viewers, perhaps the history of the use of the space for spectacle had naturalised a certain type of expectation in viewers of particular type of relationship that denied for many of them the possibility of thinking beyond these modes of interacting, preemptively modelling and limiting the potential of the event. The cost of the construction of the SAT's immersive dome has led to the need to hire it out for events of mass spectacle, and therefore to configure the technology to primarily provide this over other forms of engagement. This perhaps was not its intended primary use when first envisaged, as the SAT previously had been known for much more open and experimental uses of media technologies.

71. As Penny says: 'We appear to have advanced little in our ability to qualitatively discuss the characteristics of aesthetically rich

interaction and interactivity and the complexities of designing interaction as artistic process' (2011, 72).

72. Here it may be that the power of the 'weak' and the almost silent – that Serres identifies as the parasite – is precisely the tactic of the minor revolution, agitating change through the unseen gesture that disturbs the balance rather than the grand act that incites reaction, as it 'multiplies wildly with its smallness; it occupies space with its imperceptability' (2007, 194).

73. In taking this stance perhaps it is possible to avoid viewing the major and minor as essentially positive or negative. In this Meagan Morris is somewhat right, I think, to critique the use of the 'minor' as a default position within certain contemporary thinking (1990, 29). Certainly, as noted in the arguments about relationality, it does not seem enough to promote the so-called 'minor' as necessarily radical in itself; rather attention must always be paid to what alternatives are being created. The limitation to Morris's argument (though not necessarily her intent) is perhaps in misreading the 'minor' as a position, rather than a tactic that is all in the making. That is, the minor does not lead to a better place, the freedom it provides is only in-process, through the agitation and disruption: it is in its production of movement that is radical.

74. De Certeau's concept of the tactic can be closely aligned with Deleuze and Guattari's notion of the minor, being also concerned with performative reconfiguration of a stratified form (101–2). See Chapter Five for a discussion of the tactic of walking as a minor practice.

75. See Braidotti (2002, 147–8).

76. Despite the terms, the molecular/molar divide has nothing here to do with scale, but is defined by the way relation is controlled or opened up (Massumi 1992, 55).

77. Guattari writes: 'It is precisely this singular, minor production, this singular point of creativity, that will have a maximum impact on the production of mutation of sensibility, in all the different fields, that I call molecular revolution' (Guattari and Rolnik 2005, 161). See also Michel De Certeau on the 'swellings, shrinkings and fragmentations' of totalities that allows new spatial systems to arise (1988, 101–2).

78. As DeLanda states, 'in many respects the circulation is what matters, not the particular forms that it causes to energize' (2011, 104).
79. This might be an increased self-production (autopoiesis), and/or the production of something other than themselves (allopoiesis). See Guattari (1995a, 39) and Maturana and Varela (1980, 68).
80. See DeLanda (2011, passim), for a detailed examination of the city as a machine processing flows of energy and biomass.
81. For example a machinic body that also contains machines/ organs that process light, sound, food, etc.
82. Machines here are 'proximity grouping[s]...[of] man-tool-animal' (Murphy 1997).
83. Such machines are 'about symbolic alliances and fusion...about viral or parasitic interdependence' (Braidotti 2002, 254).
84. Similarly Whitehead shifts philosophical discussion from 'questions of essence' (what is it?) to questions of manner (how is it possible?) (Shaviro 2009, 72).
85. Here, in DeLanda's example, a piece of ground may have a slope as an intrinsic property, but this ground also has a capacity to affect the production of a style of movement of a walker in a body-ground-gravitational pull assemblage (2005, 72–3).
86. While internal differentiation moves the system away from a molar expression, this increased movement or molecularisation of the system leads not to the destruction of coherence, but is the very logic that provides coherence through emergent co-causality – the implication of components in each other's individuation. That is, it is difference as a unifying element (Deleuze 1994, 56).
87. For example, an eye and a light sensor are both affected by light modulations in a space, but express different capacities to react to this light. Light level or colour variations might also create shifts in affectual tonalities that then alter the mood and affect bodies in other ways as well. Here the machine operates not as a homogeneous processor of flows of forces, but rather its component parts produce singular modulations of forces, producing a further internal molecularisation through creating difference within both the transduction of force and the components. Difference is both actualised and maintains a virtual difference or potential to continue to produce further differentiations through ongoing

modulation and interaction and the ongoing tensions between the modulating affectual capacities of parts on the force.

88. *A Chorus of Idle Feet* was completed in 2010 and exhibited in a busy walkway outside *Allan's Walk ARI* in Bendigo as part *Metasonic II* curated by Jacques Sodell, as a satellite event of the Australia-wide 2010 *Liquid Architecture* festival. A number of analogue movement, proximity and light sensors were placed along a section of the walkway and within the adjoining gallery spaces. The walkway was chosen both for its proximity to the main gallery space, and because it was a busy corridor between a main road and the central city Mall that would then provide a richly varying flow of data for the sensor systems. These sensors used the movement of both gallery visitors and those using the passageway to go about their daily business to generate changes in a soundscape that was broadcast into the walkway. In this the work sought to harness the energy of all the people walking the space, with the potential for their different speeds, paths and intentions to generate more complex data for use in the system. The soundscape generated by this system consisted of eight layers of five simple notes that pulsed at approximately eighty pulses per minute. See www.andrewgoodman.com.au/a-chorus-of-idle-feet/.

89. The sensor's silicate material has the capacity to modulate its electrical resistance in affectual response to changes in light. this produces variation in the flow of electrons through the sensor.

90. In Whitehead's terminology, when an entity or event reaches 'satisfaction' it ceases to become, having achieved resolution of its bonds with the universe into 'one complex feeling' (1978, 44).

91. Whitehead uses the term 'prehension' to include both positive feelings (the incorporation of some data into an entity's becoming), and negative feelings (to actively not incorporate some data). 'Feelings' in the sense of prehensions, are not necessarily anything to do with conscious thought. See Chapter Three for a detailed explanation of the concept of prehension. In Whitehead's schema, while the 'satisfaction' or resolution of an event of becoming of an entity is singular and terminal in the actual plane, it is not prescribed, as the entity is a multiplicity on the virtual level, having always the potential for further actualisations.

92. These circumstances include those selected by the artist (layout, software, sounds, images, shapes), plus what the participants

bring (physical capabilities, tastes, moods), plus the worldly circumstances surrounding the art event (culture, politics, geography, art histories, weather), which all co-create the event's virtual milieu.

93. In Whitehead's schema, while entities themselves continually perish and are replaced, the things we experience as enduring actualities, such as art objects or people, are termed 'societies' (Whitehead 1978, 34–5, 89). The 'society' that is the artwork assemblage can endure because new entities emerging within the art-assemblage conform to common feelings – their emergence is shaped in part by their relation to the society – 'conditions imposed upon prehensions of other members of the nexus' that is a 'positive feeling' (Whitehead 1978, 34). See also Stengers (2011, 47).

94. As Manning writes, 'The challenge is to create the conditions for the work to work in an ecology of relation that does not privilege the interactive but seeks to open the way for the activation of the more-than the work has to offer' (2013a, 132).

95. See Varela, Thompson and Rosch for a relevant critique of neo-Darwinism (1992, 185–207). See also Glanville (2001, 660–1); and Bak (1997, 120–123). For a discussion of the difference between neo-Darwinist and co-causal models, see Lamarre (in Combes 2013, 56).

96. See also Pickering on drift as 'evolving within fields of agency in dialectics of resistance and accommodation' (1995, 247–8).

97. That is, it does not preference certain possible outcomes or types of outcomes, rather outcomes or connections arise through non-prescriptive processes. See Priogogine (1980, 189).

98. See also McCormack and d'Inverno (editors, 2012, 45); and Chapter Nine, note 308, of this book for a critique of fitness based generative programming.

99. Causing, for example, a change in the flow of electrons through the larger sensor-wiring-computer interface assemblage, and potentially affecting the MIDI code-sampler patch assemblage in the computer.

100. Such diffractive events, where two or more waves become catalysts in each other's differentiation is an example of what DeLanda terms an 'autocatalytic loop' (2011, 63). See also Chapter

Seven of this book for an extended discussion of diffraction as a generative differential force within a system.

101. It becomes evident that the entities are all connected, whether directly or in various smaller and less direct relational routes: degrees of prehension. These new prehensive potentials must enter into a conversation with other propositional pulls in order to affect individuation of an entity. See Whitehead on the relation between all actualised entities (1978, 226–9).

102. Again, the increased potential is at a system level: individual components have not necessarily increased their expressive potential, but the system as an ecology has created further expressive pontentialities.

103. Drift could imply, to some extent, that a system is 'autopoietic'. Humberto Maturana and Varela define an autopoietic machine as one capable of generating its own organisation (1980, 79) by producing a 'relationship between processes of production of components' (80). Such a relationship is the evolution of a shared potentiality, as much as any actualised co-causality, an implication of relation on a virtual plane. However as drift is less about self *preservation* than self *generation* 'autopoiesis' is a term that perhaps should be approached cautiously.

104. Though this remains possible, dynamic systems can exhibit the ability to bifurcate and shift from one system of propositional pulls to a new (if related) system – a 'phase transition' – when they move beyond a limit to which they can accommodate relational agitations. See DeLanda (2005, 70); and Chapter Eight and Nine of this book for some discussion of the creative potential of such delimiting.

105. DeLanda terms this a 'meshwork', a system with an ability to adapt to local differentiations without losing productive relation that exists because such systems are complexly interdependent but remain heterogeneous (1998, 275–85). Assemblage processes, DeLanda states elsewhere, are adaptive, giving them the 'capacity to further differentiate differences' (2005, 73).

106. 'A dynamic open whole, never fully given as it is always creating new connections and new potentials for further connection' (Massumi 1999, 52).

107. In the interactive example given, the components function not only to produce vibrations in relation to changes to light, pressure and movement, but are drawn into a system where they also function to moderate each other's individuation.

108. For Simondon concrete systems contrast with 'abstract' systems, where each component is designed to perform a 'determined function', 'has no intrinsic limits' and requires external input or organisation (Simondon 1980, 22).

109. That is, it is not that components themselves such as sensors suddenly gain greater access to the virtual, but that the larger assemblages they combine to make can access (and create) this virtual.

110. The more simplistic notions of drift concentrate excessively on the establishment of actualised feedback loops – rather than enabling the conditions for feedback loops to evolve – without an understanding that these can in themselves become rigid and programmatic. See McCormack (McCormack and d'Inverno, editors, 2012, 45) and Dery (1996, 309).

111. None of this is to necessarily promote autopoiesis as an answer to rethinking interactivity, as machinic modelling disrupts any discrete boundaries. Rather, there might be degrees to which a machine is capable of intensively becoming: of organising itself within a field of potential. The potential of transduction and feedback in systems of drift to modulate the intensive relational forces, suggests that they are important elements in thinking a system capable of generating and sustaining rich potentiality. Moreover, such modelling provides a path towards thinking differentiation as an intensively generated process, rather than one purely reliant on extensive stimuli. See Parisi for a critique of the turn towards autopoiesis in second order cybernetics as a false 'solution' to the problem of the quantitative nature of computer software (2013, 10–13); and Gordon Pask on the lack of any truly autopoietic systems other than the universe taken as a whole (1980, 272).

112. See Shaviro (2009, 128, n.16).

113. As Simondon states, relation is not primary in that it arises as 'as aspect of the internal resonance of a system of individuation', which is both the individuations of an entity, and its participation 'as an element' in greater system-wide individuations which exceeds itself (Simondon 2009, 8).

114. For a critique of the various types of posthumanism see Rosi Braidotti (2014). Braidotti identifies three strands of posthumanism: reactive (from moral philosophy), analytic (from science and technology) and critical (from Spinoza). She criticises 'reactive' posthumanism for its 'universalistic belief in individualism, fixed identities and moral ties that bind' (Braidotti 2014, 39). Braidotti finds 'analytic' posthumanism problematic, as although it acknowledges deep interconnectedness between human and non-human this is an interconnectedness based largely on 'a shared sense of vulnerability', and because the sense of global proximity promoted often breeds 'a xenophobic rejection of otherness' (Braidotti 2014, 40). The 'critical' posthumanism Braidotti advocates is 'an eco-philosophy of multiple belongings' resting on 'the ethics of becoming' (2014, 49). This third type of posthumanism is both in sympathy with the term trans-human as I use it here, and with the ethics of becoming in process philosophy. Transhumanism, in this sense, is neither the negation of human experience nor an attempt to anthropomorphise the non-human.

115. This might suggest a different slant on the issue from some other philosophical attempts to think beyond the human, such as new materialism, object orientated ontology (OOO) and actor network theory, in its stronger emphasising an *ontogenetic* approach in which relation cannot be limited to conversation between things, but must be acknowledged to be intrinsic to the becoming of any such object or event. See, for example, Steven Shaviro's pertinent critique of Graham Harman and OOO in relation to Whitehead (Shaviro 2014, 27–44). See also Tim Ingold's discussion of the limitation of relation to interactions between stable entities in actor network theory (including a discussion of the mistranslation of *acteur réseau* as actor-network and the resultant misplaced emphasis on objects (2011, 84–6, 89–94).

116. Whitehead's ontology is much more complex than the few aspects I will briefly to outline here, detailed analysis of these and other aspects can be found in Stengers (2011), Judith Jones (1998), and is discussed in much of the recent writing of Erin Manning, Andrew Murphie, Brian Massumi and Steven Shapiro.

117. 'Actuality is in its essence composition. Power is in the compulsion of composition' (Whitehead, 1968, 119).

118. In Whitehead's terminology, when an entity or event reaches 'satisfaction' it ceases to become, having achieved resolution of its bonds with the universe (Whitehead 1978, 44).
119. 'Prehension' is Whitehead's term for both positive and negative feeling (positive and negative prehensions), while he reserve 'feeling' for the positive prehensions.
120. The terms are somewhat interchangeable in Whitehead's philosophy, though perhaps in some ways event or actual occasion are better terms since they emphasise the ongoing nature and avoids any slippage back into hylomorphic thinking. It should be remembered that such 'events' include not just concrete objects and beings, but all occasions, including thoughts, emotions, ephemeral forces (wind, heat, and so on), and the atomic and subatomic.
121. It is a 'local expression' of the field (Stengers 2011, 102) – a monad perhaps, though it is not exactly a continuity of relation but the continuity of becomings that Whitehead proposes.
122. 'Every item in [an entity's] universe is involved in each concrescence' (Whitehead 1978, 22).
123. The feeling, Whitehead states, 'is an episode in self-production' of an entity (1978, 224).
124. Positioning intensity as the key brings Whitehead's work more clearly in line with Deleuze's thinking as expressions of 'differential relations and their corresponding distinctive points' (1994, 252).
125. Thus 'every realized contrast has a location, which is particular with the particularity of actual entities. It is a particular matter of fact' (Whitehead 1978, 230).
126. Here in using the term 'pattern' it must be emphasised that this is a topological rather than Euclidean patterning or spacing (Simondon 1995b, 225).
127. That is, relation of same-to-same is not a relation at all. See Jones (1998, 56), Serres (2007, 79) and Massumi on zero sum intensity as a point of no determination (1992, 70).
128. That is, the subject (or 'superject' in Whitehead's preferred term) is this satisfaction of a concrescence – the feeling and ordering of energy from the world, rather than, as Murphie notes, a Kantian notion of world energy emanating from the subject (2016, 11). Nor is there a 'mind' as a singular entity. As Jones states: 'mentality

is not linked to a singular form of experience, nor is it linked to a singular mode of organized being that performs a variety of functions' (1998, 134).

129. As Jones notes, 'much consideration of Whitehead's system seems influenced by an abiding habit of seeking subjects to which important "predicates" such as existence, agency, immediacy, and character may be attached' (11998, 01).

130. Actor network theory or new materialism at their most programmatic end, for example, or Andrew Pickering's language in *The Mangle of Practice* of 'resistance and accommodation' and the 'capturing' of agency, staged as a kind of epic battle of wills between scientist and material world (1995, 65, 92). As Karen Barad says, Pickering's concept 'takes for granted the humanist notion of agency as a property of individual entities' (2003, 807, n. 7). Pickering's work is, however, of interest for the fact that it begins to head towards a process-based understanding of physics and scientific practice, but comes to this from a different direction than most philosophically based texts on the subject. Barad's own work (2007) is perhaps a more thorough investigation of this approach.

131. Such a position 'begs the question of the nature of existence, deciding beforehand what type of entity we are looking for' (Jones 1998, 177) See also Ingold (2011, 16–17). It should be noted that some writers, such as Jane Bennett (2010), attempt to redefine 'agency' in ecological terms, and it is not these attempts that I am here critiquing.

132. See also Stengers on the importance of negative prehension (2011, 308–10).

133. Though one might perhaps less facetiously argue that complex feelings such as 'lust' may be better thought of as societies of events in themselves, composed of the concrescence of feelings drawing on multiple sensations, concepts and affects.

134. Although an entity only relates to some eternal objects, it still creates positive and negative relations in that it is only one actualised, selected possibility of hardness or redness, *not* any of the other so far undefined and inexhaustible possibilities of these qualities (Whitehead 1978, 227).

135. Again, in such a statement that clearly positions force as primary and form as secondary it becomes clear just how different process philosophy is from object orientated ontology. Despite some superficial similarities in discussing the autonomous and subjective 'life' of objects there are very real differences between Whitehead and Graham Harman, as Shaviro outlines clearly in his book *The Universe of Things*. To pick up just a few key points from Shaviro's argument, whereas for Harman all entities are ontologically equivalent because they are 'equally *withdrawn* from one another', for Whitehead their equivalence is based on the fact that entities are constituted through prehension of other entities, thus arguing against the philosophy of substances that Harman embraces (2014, 29–31; Jones 1998, 95). Here Whitehead's prehension always involves an active and subjective take on other entities that brings novelty into the world through the singular combination of these prehensions into a pattern of contrasts, whereas OOO posits a passive reception of datum and a stability of objects, and thus cannot fully account for the rise of novelty in the world (2014, 38). Further, while Harman, according to Shaviro, argues that one entity can never fully 'know' all aspects of another entity, this does not mean that one entity cannot affect all aspects of another object, and thus knowledge is not necessarily the defining aspect of the relationship (106). Shaviro sums up the difference between the two philosophies as being between 'the aesthetics of the beautiful and the aesthetics of the sublime' (2014, 42). Thus while the former describes Whitehead's view of beauty as intensive experience based on patterns of contrasts that conciliate differences without erasing them, Harman's concept of the 'allure' between objects positions difference at the point of the inaccessibility of one object for another (Shaviro 2014). Here Whitehead's world is one of a constant intermeshing and negotiation between forces and appetites for becoming, whereas Harman's world is one of strange isolation.

136. Whitehead's use of the concept of 'mediation' is specific and outside many definitions of the term. Perhaps it might be better described as 'immediation', an enrichment through enfolded differentiation whereby 'fields of relation agitate and activate to emerge into collectivities' (Brunner, Manning and Massumi 2013, 136).

137. 'Appetition is immediate matter of fact including in itself a principle of unrest, involving realization of what is not and may be...All physical experience is accompanied by an appetite for, or against, its continuance' (Whitehead 1978, 32).
138. Though, as Whitehead points out, it is a 'misconception' to think that the creative advance of the universe ever 'involves the notion of a unique seriality', which is not sustainable as an 'ultimate metaphysical principle', and truly would contradict direct experience of the world (1978, 35). As Jones states, novelty is not necessarily 'wild diversity', but a 'new perspective arrangement of the qualities proffered by the world' (1998, 69).
139. Thus what appears as the persistence of a 'thing' that is the society's continued expression of a relatively stable form is rather the continued recreation of shared patterns of intensity: shared valuations of feelings, not evidence of transcendent matter (Whitehead 1978, 107–8, 145).
140. This is, at least to some extent, counterintuitive, as what we (or for that matter the river) might experience of the rock seems to suggest that it is an enduring object, not a series of overlapping and atomic events of becoming. But each event of the becoming of each fragment of the rock (and the becoming of each atom and molecule within this fragment, and so on) is always singular: its own unique cut, its own subjective synthesis of the actual (all objective datum) and the virtual (select eternal objects). The fact that it may appear stable from our perspective (as a speck of silicate embedded in the rock, for example) does not contradict this but can be explained by the force of the patterning of the objective datum of the society within which the entity's concrescence takes place, and by the relatively small degree by which this inanimate entity is able to modify the force of this patterned objective datum through acts of conceptual prehension or 'valuation' of this datum (Jones 1998, 60). Thus the fault in assuming the stability of the rock lies in mistaking an effect or 'extensive quanta' (the seeming endurance of an object) for the categorical basis (the object as a mere fact that is necessary for an explanation of the universe) (Jones 1998, 127). This is a 'fallacy of misplaced concreteness' that mistakes 'a certain mode of abstraction about reality for the complete or definitive account of that reality or our knowledge of it' (Whitehead 1978, 7–8; Jones 1998, 7).

141. Remembering that prehensions always include the negative prehensions that enrich through the pressure of 'relevant alternatives' (Jones 1998, 68; Whitehead 1978, 249). Thus we might say that the rocks have 'a life'.

142. Amongst other subjects in this book, Darwin demonstrates the significance of the worm on the becoming of rocks through the production of carbonic acid and its erosive capacities; through the digestion of rock fragments and their abrasion in the alimentary canals of the worms; and through the burying of rocks and boulders both undermined by worm tunnels and covered (surprisingly quickly) by worm castings (Darwin 1881, 235, 246, 230-58 passim). From this evidence Darwin extrapolates the supreme important role of worms in the burying and preservation of ancient artifacts and the importance of their actions 'in the [human] history of the world' (Darwin 1881, 313). See also Ingold on the difference between a geological study of rocks as 'formless lump[s] of matter' and an anthropological or archaeologist's viewpoint 'in which stones are caught up in the lives of human beings, and given form and significance through their incorporation into the social and historical contexts of these lives' (2011, 31). Here perhaps we can see an example of the significant nesting or folding of one occasion into another across seemingly insurmountable scales, and the echoes of prehensive choices on future events. See also Eileen Crist (2004,162-4) and Bennett (2010, 55-60).

143. See Shaviro on Whitehead's theory of life as a 'theory of desire'. Shaviro states that 'an entity is alive precisely to the extent that it envisions difference and thereby strives for something other than mere continuation of what already is' (2010, 143).

144. In fact here neo-Darwinist approaches are ultimately nonsensical: were any creature to be perfectly adapted to exploit an environment it would quickly perish, as the environment itself is never static, but presents a constantly shifting set of challenges and interactive possibilities for any entity. Thus ability to change and adapt and to *make do* under a variety of conditions is what helps an entity to survive, not perfect form. Here again capacity to prehend (and thus incorporate) aspects of one's environment can be seen as key. See Varela, Thompson and Rosch (1992, 196), Shaviro (2010, passim) and Bak (1997, 120-3). On Darwin's emphasis on both the drive towards novelty of nature and its 'cruelty'

in regards to a lack of care for any particular individuation, see Adams (2000, 38–42); and Ingold (2011, 77).

145. See also Massumi (2014, 13–14).

146. Feelings are a prehensive resonance with other entities (Whitehead 1978, 220).

147. This could be seen as the worms' ability to harness an ecological intelligence, which in Darwin's time (if not today) might be seen as politically important in its emphasis on realigning our concept of creativity and power (in a Nietzschian sense) from the transcendent to the organic. See Adams (58–61).

148. 'How little of the movements of the bodies of octopuses frolicking over the reef, of guppies fluttering in the slow currents of the Amazon, of black cockatoos fluttering their acrobatics in the vines of the rain forest…of humans, are teleological!' (Lingis 2003, 168).

149. Though it should be noted that this 'augmentation' is not that of the individual but of that which is produced in supplement to the individual: further individuation. As Braidotti states, 'the Life I inhabit is not mine, it does not bear my name – it is a generative force of becoming, of individuation and differentiation: apersonal, indifferent, and generative' (2010, 224). See also Elizabeth Grosz on Simondon's definition of ethics as the inclusion of more of the pre-individual potential of an entity (2012, 50).

150. It should be noted here that Whitehead's own use of the term 'morality' is clearly in line with this definition of ethics, not morality as I define it here with its negative connotations.

151. A video demonstration of this work can be viewed at www.youtube.com/watch?v=AQRHon2eiKc.

152. Faraday's Law is expressed as: $\varepsilon = -N(\Delta\Phi/\Delta t)$ Where ε is the EMF, Φ is the sum of the field strength and the area, and t is the speed in change of flux.

153. That is, the electromagnetic field changes its strength, and/or its distance from the induction loop, and/or its area. From the position of the (presumed) stationary induction loop all these possibilities will be felt as a variation in electromagnetic strength, but such a feeling is specific to this one entity, not a universal or transcendent experience.

154. 'Every phenomenon refers to an inequality by which it is conditioned. Every diversity and every change refers to a difference which is its sufficient reason.' (Deleuze 1994, 222).
155. And, on a quantum level, each atom is a pattern of waves. See Laughlin (2005, 31).
156. Stengers notes the importance of Faraday's work in the nineteenth century for Whitehead in its thinking of the independence of the event over stable objects with fixed and reversible properties (2011, 101), as they might appear in the earlier work of Kirchoff on conservative loops. Faraday's discoveries position conservative fields as merely special cases of fields, not as the full sum of potential, as classical physics would intuit (Lewin 2002). See also Prigogine and Stengers (1996, 73), on dissipative structures and the 'arrow of time' and the importance of irreversibility for non-linear physics.
157. This is not to suggest that a work with these interests necessarily must be slow, quiet or meditative to achieve such an attention.
158. As Serres says elsewhere, 'existence is a derivation from equilibrium' (ND, unpaginated).
159. As Simondon argues, notions of form must be 'saved two times from an all too summary technical paradigmatism: first, in relation to classical culture, the notion of form must be saved from the reductive manner the notion was used in the *hylomorphic schema*; and a second time, in order to save information as signification from the *technological theory* of information in modern culture, with its experience of transmission through a channel' (2009, 12). Emphasis in the original.
160. See also Gibson on the differences between Shannon and Weaver's concept of information (1967, passim) and an ecological approach to information and perception (1979, 231–2).
161. 'Differenciation' is a virtual difference that can then actualise into individual instances of 'differentiation' (Bracken 2002, 92).
162. Exchange, Serres argues, 'does not mobilize things, it immobilizes them', whereas the parasite is always interrupting exchange and a 'derivation from equilibrium', in essence parasitism is 'taking without giving' (2007, 156, 221, 16). The parasite is, however, 'politically ambivalent', and, as Matteo Pasquinelli explores, the concept of 'rent' within the digital realm can be seen as a parasitic form of

'cognitive' capitalism exploiting immaterial labour relations, multiplying modes of exploitation and reaching across many dimensions of production (Pasquinelli 2008, 97, 91–104, passim). See also Massumi on exchange-value (1992, 199–201).

163. See also Mark Amerika on the 'hyperimprovisational' state of the digital VJ in an 'asynchronous realtime' as an 'investigation of complex *event processing* where the VJ artist becomes a multitude of flux identities nomadically circulating within the networked space of flows' that 'oftentimes produces a feeling of being both avant-garde (ahead of one's time) and time-delayed (the stutter of media consciousness losing self-awareness) while simultaneously playing the role of a nomadic net artist' (2005, 7–8).

164. As Massumi says: 'the virtual is the mode of reality implicated in the emergence of new potentials…its reality is the reality of change: the event' (1998, 16).

165. This might, as Varela proposes, create a hyper-awareness of temporality within one's body in relation to the event, making a participant hyperconscious of posture, disrupting their image of themselves. Varela argues that shifts in the affective tonality cause bodily functions, which were operating at a sub-conscious level, to suddenly rise to 'transparency' (i.e. consciousness), creating in their hyperawareness a sensation of slowed or stretched temporality (1997, 300).

166. Beyond these more concretely 'designed' aspects, it pays to remember that there is always a multitude of incidental parasitic disruptions – the way a sound bounces off a wall to diffract and interfere with other sounds for example, as discussed in Chapter Seven – and that a propositional interactive design might also consider working to enhance the potential of these other layers of parasitic action.

167. Components of these individual sounds were also constructed as micro-perceptions – not necessarily capable of being individually recognised, but layered in combinations of tones, timbres, overtones, rhythms and textures, to produce a 'society', the perceived sound, while retaining difference and their atomic nature. See Chapter Seven for an extended discussion of the parasitic potential of sound as micro-perception.

168. In an example such as this the artist proposes a multiplicity of potential sound events, in excess of possible actuality. With

causality dispersed, notions of an artist as 'agent' are replaced by a co-causal conversation between competing forces. Within such simple tactics, we begin to understand that sounds within the system become free floating events, inhabiting a virtual soundscape: sounds as societies, vibrating internally and externally with the tensions of relation – they begin to hum with difference and potential. Here it can be seen that in a system that in many ways was a relatively simple construction (utilising twenty or so basic sensors and a dozen sounds), it is possible to design the potential for a move towards greater complexity. The artist's role might be less to design the complex relations that might occur, but more to focus on setting the preconditions for these developments. And, while such a design shift certainly increases component events' implication in each other's various actualisations, this is not in any way presented as a definitive example of the scope of the parasite. Such tinkering represents both small, seemingly inconsequential moderations, and at the same time, a paradigm shift: the death of the (software) author to be replaced by the propositional event.

169. On this conception of walking Tim Ingold comments that 'the environment is a world that continually unfolds in relation to the beings that make a living there. Its reality is not *of* material objects, but *for* its inhabitants' (2011, 30, emphasis in the original).

170. In this sense, it is potentially a process of 'becoming-other', even if the outcome is ostensibly similar. The emphasis here is squarely on shifting the awareness of 'becoming' – the immersion in the emergent process – not on the 'other' (individuation not individualization). As Lygia Clark says of her own work, its function is to encourage the spectator to 'rediscover the meaning of our routine gestures' (cited in Frieling 2008, 104).

171. See also Ingold on the ability of walking to break the imposed conformity of the modern engineered environment (2011, 115).

172. 'Thus, for Lavery, the walker sees the city as 'a boundless stage where the self can be sacrificed and shattered, and where new ecstatic intensities can be experienced' (Mock 2009, 43).

173. While de Certeau names these differing concepts of an environment 'place' and 'space' respectively, confusingly many authors switch these terms around, using 'space' to denote the abstract form and 'place to denote an embodied and emergent relational

engagement between bodies and environment (de Certeau 1988, 117–18; Ingold 2011, 145–55; Gibson 1979, 35, 93).

174. See also Ingold (2011, 84–8, 92–3) for more on the concept of meshwork. Ingold, like de Certeau, considers this as a 'storied knowledge' (2011, 141–76; de Certeau 1988, 118–26).

175. I am aware of the somewhat simplistic and potentially problematic image of the walker in de Certeau's writing, who at times does come perilously close to the image of the *flâneur* with its implications of (at best) idle dandyism. De Certeau's walker remains untroubled by social constructions of the actual city (race, class, gender) that would potentially constrain 'his' actions. See Driscoll (2001) and Langer (1988) for such critiques. (Cf. Brian Morris (2004), for a measured and sympathetic debate on this issue).

176. Roland Barthe's essay 'No Address' explores such an experience in describing the attempted navigation through the streets of Tokyo, where there are no street names and directions take on a subjective, relational nature, shaped by the forces of rhythm, habits, durations and memories – position enacted through discovery that is 'intense and fragile' (1982, 36, 33–7).

177. Indeed, the saccadic micro-movements of the eyes are an essential component of the ability to perceive the world (Gibson 199–202).

178. In Whitehead's terms this is then an intensity of feeling through held contrast. Gibson, writing on the binocular quality of vision, argues that these doubled feelings are not 'resolved' in the brain into a single image, but are rather held in the body as a productive 'congruence and disparity at the same time' (1979, 203).

179. See also Steven Connor on the assymetrical nature of the body and world: 'The world is sensible because it lists, because it has orientation or laterality' (1999, 2).

180. Here, as Lingis says, 'things subsist not as givens, but as tasks to which perception finds itself devoted' (1996, 35).

181. It should be noted here that a niche, for Gibson, is not phenomenal or private, subjective world of conciousness, but belongs to the objects as much as the animal as a set of complex relations and potential relations, including the physical and social registers (1979, 121–2, 130). While Ingold asserts that Gibson's system of affordances is 'shot through with contradictions' because it assumes

that the environment exists independently and prior to engagement with inhabitants in some stable form (2011, 78), it seems clear from Gibson's own writing on the subject that his intention is ecological.

182. A shifting level underfoot, as Manning describes it, makes palpable to the walker the ground-gravity-body relationship, disrupting and reconstituting it as one stumbles: an 'active prehending' that 'reconstitut[es the ground] as novelty, intertwining with the capacities of what a gravitational body can do' (2009, 70–1). To begin to understand how gravity helps shape body-movement machines, think, for example, of the different movements that the lower gravity pull of the body in water produces.

183. 'What mindfulness disrupts is mindlessness – that is, being mindlessly involved without realizing what one is doing' (Varela, Thompson and Rosch 1992, 32). Varela's conception of the mind here is one that is resolutely constituted from enaction of body-world, and therefore, in sympathy with Manning and Arakawa and Gins' ideas, despite the terminology that might suggest a return to privileging subjectivity over embodied experience.

184. The space '*reconfigures* 'as the body *recomposes*' (Manning 2009, 15, emphasis in the original).

185. Arakawa and Gins propose three categories of landing sites: 'perceptual' that are 'specific to what presents itself; 'imaging', which cast a wider and more diffuse net; and 'dimensionalizing', which combine the previous two categories to attach more fully to an environment (Arakawa and Gins 2002, 7–8; Manning 2009, 211).

186. 'What stems from the body, by way of awareness, should be held to be of it' (Arakawa and Gins 2002).

187. Landing sites work to enrich experience with a potential further fielding of body in the world, as, for example, landing sites at their 'imaging' end (beyond the register of perceptual actuality) create the conditions (potential) for perceptual or dimensionalising sites (Manning 2009, 80). Such a moving and perceiving body is a kinesthetic body that is always dispersing and reorganizing.

188. These are the kind of spaces Arakawa and Gins have proposed and constructed, where shifting levels, varying gradients, columns of different circumferences, and so on, create a space that defers totalizing comprehension and demands considerable and

continual attention to negotiate (Arakawa and Gins 1997). The 'elastic point' at which the body 'culls from the movement's potential its becoming-form' is extended through such propositional spaces that demand a clear and ongoing shifting beyond habit (Manning 2009, 35).

189. Landing sites are always tied to styles and techniques of bodying and moving – they are specific (even in their fuzziness) and singular – for example, a baby crawling or person in a wheelchair will create different landing sites, zones of attention directly relevant to their ambulatory procedures.

190. Landing sites are constituted both within the space around and within what we think of as the discrete body and mixtures of the two, in a way that fundamentally disrupt boundaries. '(T)he body is part of the external world, continuous with it. It is as much a part of nature as anything else there...we cannot define where a body begins and where external nature ends' (Whitehead 1968, 4). This is evident with landing site operations, thought in terms not of materiality – where it is also true (shared atoms or bacteria, for example) – but the production of an immanent world-body through moving and sensing.

191. De Certeau begins his meditation on walking the city with a description of the distancing and totalising effects of sight, and vision here separates from life and works to reduce the living complexity of the city to representation – 'a projection that is a way of keeping aloof'. More recent technologies of vision (CCTV, GPS, and mobile phones with ability to immediately capture and send images from the street, and the ability they give authorities to trace users) perhaps confirm de Certeau's fears of 'the cancerous growth of vision...measuring everything by its ability to show or be shown' (1988, 92–3, xxi). Likewise the concept of occularcentrism also examines the repressive functions of vision and is especially critical of the role normally assigned to perspectival notions of vision. While it would be foolish to argue that vision cannot operate in this manner – as Foucault has shown, vision has panoptic potential as an agent of control and separation, both Arakawa and Gins and Gibson suggest a role for vision that does not so clearly separate it from the functioning of the other senses. For a discussion on the merits and limitations of occularcentrism, see Martin Jay (1988, 3–28). Cf. Massumi's discussion of vision

and perspectival painting for another way of thinking through the bodily implications of the system (2011, 127–30).
192. And, as we walk, we not only see the gravel on the road but also 'feel' its texture through sight, Massumi says, as vision becomes haptic (2002, 158).
193. Although at any one instant we can see only one side of the tree, we experience it as a three-dimensional object – this is a 'depth perception' that is, Massumi argues, a seeing of the potential to move around, through or over the object – a kind of prehension of the possibilities of movement (1998, 23). See also Gibson on occlusion and vision (1979, 78). Manning states that even before we adjust our movement to accommodate for the tree in our path, vision activates in our bodies the 'preacceleration' that is the gathering of energies, an opening up to potential (2009, 14).
194. Though, as Gibson argues, visual kinesthetics operate as more than feedback, as they also exist during passive movement (1979, 175). For example, when sitting on a stationary train while watching an adjacent train leave the station, one can experience an illusory sensation of movement provoked by this vision.
195. The version of this work discussed in this chapter was performed as part of a larger project, *Into the Midst*, by the Senselab research group in Montreal in October 2012. Of interest in this iteration is that the work was performed within the city environment as an extension of a project within the immersive dome at the Society for Art and Technology (SAT), and that the work was enacted by a number of different bodies (including the author's). Unlike some other iterations of *Compressionism* performed by Stern alone, here it was often collaboratively performed, with several people carrying connected technical components to perform a larger cooperative action. See Chapter One, 'Bridge' for further discussion of the *Into the Midst* project.
196. That is, in its intensive searching-out of the incidental and the singular, the body-scanner ignored the established networks of movement: paths, roads and doors. Gaps were also multiplied and troubled in the 'proper' space of art (in this case, the SAT Gallery), as the *Compressionist* act in the street extended and diffused the event into a larger, perhaps less passively receptive environment, requiring negotiation with a new, more complex set of parameters. The weather, hostile or friendly public, incidental

noise, available light, traffic, and so on, all became factors folded into the event by the act of walking the performance beyond the gallery, disrupting or *mutating* the event itself through chance encounters, emotional tonalities, sounds heard, time spent on detours.

197. The surface, Gibson states, is 'what touches the animal' (1979, 23).
198. 'Each time an organ – or function – is liberated from an old duty, it invents' (Serres 2008, 344).
199. This embracing of the scanning/visioning technics was perhaps a 'prosthetic gesture', opening the body up again, troubling its perceived boundaries, and creating a trans-human assemblage, a new individuation (Manning 2007, 155).
200. As Deleuze and Guattari are at pains to emphasise, the minor is not a place of refuge, but an activation that involves becoming a 'sort of stranger' within a known system (1986, 40, 26).
201. *Psychopomp* was exhibited at Kings ARI, Melbourne, November 16– December 8, 2012. The work consisted of a nearly nineteen minute performance piece in which two performers moved collaboratively in a darkened space wearing 'sound suits' that generated and responded to sound and light. It was envisaged as a 'voodoo ritual' for an imagined future – a performance situated in a liminal space between spirit world and a dystopian science fiction otherworld. The soundscape utilised samples and effects reminiscent of 1950s and 1960s science fiction films (utilising digital versions of early analogue synthesisers and sound generators such as Theremins, and featuring heavy use of effects such as reverb, distortion and chorus). The suits themselves contained a variety of sensors (tilt, bend, light, touch and proximity) that then generated analogue data in response to movements, alongside light sensors responding to the embedded LED systems in the costumes. In addition, sound sensors – placed in front of each of the four speakers that were positioned around the perimeter of the performance space – generated data in response to the changes in volume emitted by each particular speaker. The data from all the sensors was used to generate sound events – both the playing and interruption of sound samples, changes in volume, tonal qualities, and the spatialisation of each sample. Some samples were looped, so that they played until an action caused them to be replaced by another sample, while others played once

when triggered through a complex chain of relations. At certain triggers, sounds from the performance were also recorded by the computer system and then looped into increasingly complex layers and replayed into the space, and the system was configured to emphasise the potential for disturbance to any sound event.

202. 'The surface is where most of the action is' (Gibson 1979, 23).

203. Manning uses the term 'chunking' to describe the ability to filter sense information. She describes the difficulty that autistics have in efficiently controlling and ordering the flood of information, and the special attunement to the field in its emergence that this gives – in a sense, an excess of receptivity to relation, rather than a lack that creates this experience (2013a, 172–83, 275).

204. See also Manning (2013a) and Manning (2016, 48–56). Manning's recent artworks also experiment with this concept: *Stitching Time* (2012) at the Biennale of Sydney, and *Weather Patterns* (2012) at the University of Wisconsin, Milwaukee, Deakin University, Latrobe University VAC, and Bus Projects, Melbourne.

205. In Manning's usage, the 'environment' – which includes what remains of the human – is pure ecological process, a system capable of self-modulation through the accommodation of internal difference and increased relational interdependence. This is in line with Felix Guattari's concept of 'ecosophy', a generalised ecology that 'questions the whole of subjectivity and capitalistic power formations' (Guattari 2008, 34–6, 52). As Manning says: 'to feel ecologically is to directly perceive the relations out of which space-time is composed. Perceiving environmentally does not imply giving meaning to form, but forming environmentally' (Manning 2009, 73).

206. See also Whitehead (2014, unpaginated, Chapter I: section 10).

207. Presentational immediacy and causal efficacy specifically intersect in sharing elements of sense-data and locality, firstly in that the immediate that is given in sensuous perception is also always derived from the potentiality shaping it, and therefore has some relationship to causality; secondly in that the organs sensing are themselves spatially located within the environment (Whitehead 2014, unpaginated, II: 5).

208. Conscious perception of course also includes an awareness of the act of perceiving as a secondary register. Although consciousness

perception and choice is only available to select organisms, Manuel DeLanda argues that even the earliest bacteria developed internal (that is, subjective) models of their relationship to the environment through combining a primitive sensory system with a motor-driven understanding of their relationship to space – which could be viewed as a germinal version of presentational immediacy and causal efficacy, although he makes no direct mention of Whitehead's two categories of perception (2011, 80).

209. Casual efficacy is 'a direct perception of those antecedent actual occasions which are causally efficacious both for the percipient and for the relevant events' (Whitehead 1978, 169).

210. While we might baulk at Whitehead's terminology here, one could argue that his system is highly inclusive in that it resists any ontological distinction between organisms of differing capacities, particularly its resistance to placing human perception in a different classification to other animals.

211. On its own presentational immediacy is 'the perception of the contemporary world, whereas when combined with causal efficacy this is broadened to 'the present moment of experience' (Whitehead 2014, unpaginated, II: 4).

212. To give an everyday example, perhaps when standing on a beach, in the overwhelming brightness of sudden sunlight, the enveloping monochrome of the sky, and surrounded by the roar of the ocean, one might, at least for an instant, find oneself immersed in almost pure immediate experience of brightness, blueness or loudness that is a glimpse of an experience of these eternal qualities beyond their qualification into any discrete actualised event. It is thus our impression of that crystal point at which potential and actual meet: individuation in the making.

213. See also Claire Bishop's critique of the disavowal of the aesthetic in relational works, where, after Rancière, she argues that the redistribution of the sensible is as politically a charged act as the redistribution of social relations (2009, 248–9). Though here it should be noted that Whitehead, in discussing the speed in which we habitually move from presentational immediacy 'a coloured shape in front of us', to its efficious comprehension as 'a chair', argues that such quick transition from sensation to the efficacy of an object 'is a very natural one' that requires 'careful training'

- such as an artist might have – 'if we are to refrain from acting upon it' (2014, unpaginated, I: 3).
214. Without the qualification of causal efficacy presentational immediacy, Whitehead states, does not divide into truth and illusion (2014, unpaginated, I: 12).
215. See Combes (2013, 65). Ethics here, in allowing space for and giving attention to the ways in which novelty might arise, might include aesthetic acts that extend the emergent qualities of perception and thus a prehension of individuations-in-the-act.
216. That is, the event is a 'mechanics of expression rather than a signifying apparatus' (Murphie 1996, 104).
217. This, for Whitehead is an extended prehensive resonance with other entities (1978, 220).
218. This, Manning says, is the 'no-time of the decision in the present passing' (2013a, 106).
219. In the middle, Massumi says 'we become conscious of a situation always in its midst, already actively engaged in it. Our awareness is always of an already ongoing participation in an unfolding relation' (2002, 231).
220. This relates to Manning's terms 'Body-worlding', which, 'is much more than containment, much more than an envelope. It is a complex feeling-assemblage that is active between different co-constitutive milieus' (Manning 2013a, 2).
221. Deleuze's term *agencement* is usually translated as 'assemblage', however, as Manning notes, this inexact translation 'does not convey [the] force' of the act of assembling that is implied in the French term (Manning 2009, 237 note 71).
222. As Rancière also argues, an art that seeks to invest all components of an event with a shared agency is deeply political, as the 'politics of domination' rest on 'sensory division' of the world into the passive (object) and active (subject) (2009, 31).
223. 'Technicity', as Manning describes it, moves beyond 'technique' to touch again with its potential or virtual, a 'more than' of technique. In other words, it might be viewed as the way art can contract or synthesise a technique to bring new life to it (Manning 2013a, 33).

224. Perhaps here one might argue that the immersive colour fields of James Turrell and Dan Flavin's work have something to offer an expanded concept of interactivity.

225. Drawing imagery and sounds directly from the Anime film *Nausicaä, of the Valley of the Wind* (directed by Hayao Miyazaki, Topcraft studio, Japan, 1984), *Pnuema* created a windswept environment of alien forms glowing and pulsing in the dark. The work was an interactive installation that consisted of translucent sculptural forms hung in the centre of a small, darkened gallery space. A number of the sculptural pieces had internal lights, and speakers were positioned within the mass of sculptures and around the perimeter of the space. Both the rhythms of light pulses and soundscape were generated by movement in the space, as sensors captured data on the passage of participants around the space and the incidental movements of the lightweight sculptures, and light sensors fed information on the pulses of light back into the generative system triggering further changes. The work had several 'states' through which it could move, from a relatively calm and quiet state (in which 'singing' sounds emanated from the sculptures and there was a simple blue pulse in the central pieces), through to increasingly more dramatic states where more complex pulses of blue, amber and/or red lights pulsed and stormy sounds enveloped the space. This work experimented with complex layers of manipulated sounds embedded into a sample as 'unsounds' (see Chapter Seven), in order to attempt to increase the affectual force of the samples. In these hidden sounds certain very high or low frequencies were emphasised and samples other than the dominant sound were hidden just below audible volume and/or frequency range, in order to experiment with ways in which sound might operate forcefully on bodies beyond aural cognition, in another layer of relational entanglement. See http://www.andrewgoodman.com.au/pnuema/.

226. Here, in particular, one could say that the temporal and spatial anchoring of events that causal efficacy can provide was disrupted.

227. Such gestures are 'minor' in that they allow an intensive reconfiguration to occur (Manning 2016a, 48).

228. A parallel can be drawn here, I think, between the concept of the minor gesture and Simondon's expanded concept of individuation, in that for Simondon ontogenesis must be thought of as a

'becoming of the being in general [that] produces *both* the individual *and its environment'* (Simondon 2009, 14, note 2).

229. Closely related to the star fish, brittle stars have a calcite structure that focuses light directly onto bundles of nerve endings, thus its whole surface functions as a multiple 360-degree eye. It too has no 'brain' with which to perceive such sensations, yet it responds to light (Barad 2007, 369–84).

230. See also Massumi (2002, 14).

231. In this process-based understanding of the universe, affect is a force existing prior to, and bringing into existence, object and subjects and relations between such entities. This has a basis both within 'process' philosophies and within non-Newtonian (quantum) physics. See Barad (2007), for an example of a process-based approach from the perspective of quantum physics that is compatible with Whitehead's philosophical schema. Affect can be distinguished clearly, in this definition, from emotion, which might be thought of more as the qualification or cognition of the *effects* of affect on a body (Bertelsen and Murphie 2010, 148).

232. We might think of this larger and perceptible sound event as a 'superject', composed of ongoing and related smaller events and contrasts held together through a shared inheritance.

233. This concept of transduction holds not only for physical objects, Combes argues, but 'for any domain' including 'matter, life, mind, society'. Further on Combes notes that relation as an aspect of the system of individuation has 'a rank of being'. In this way it might be considered a radical empiricist approach (Combes 2013, 6–7, 16).

234. The connection to a Whiteheadian concept of contrast is made evident in Adrian Mackenzie's argument that, 'transduction is a process whereby a disparity or difference is topologically and temporally restructured across an interface' (Mackenzie 2002, 25). Becoming, for Simondon, resolves tensions of difference in that it is a 'conservation of these tensions in the form of a structure' (Simondon 2009, 6).

235. Here the individuation of the perception 'mediates between two incompatible orders, inventing ways of bringing them together' (Grosz 2012, 40).

236. The play is Artaud's 'most intensive realization of his plan to atomize and recast the entire conception of the human body' (Barber 1999, 6).
237. 'The scream is the very sublimation of speech into the body' (Weiss 1992, 288–9).
238. This, Aden Evans considers as the balance between implication and explication that allows a flow forward of sound and listening (in Massumi 2002, 179–83).
239. 'The ear is no more located in one place than the skin…the body itself is caught up in a process of hearing, which implicates skin, bone, skull, feet and muscle' (Conner 1999, 4).
240. An 'appetite' as opposed to the teleos of an 'instinct', the former suggests potential multiplicity of future creativity, rather than the linear and prescriptive nature of the latter system of thinking.
241. See also Roads (2001, 7) for more detailed explanation of the physics.
242. *Space-Shifter* was first exhibited at Conical ARI in Melbourne in 2009. Details of the work can be found on the artists' website at www.waxsm.com.au/spaceshifter.htm, and a short video demonstration can be viewed at www.youtube.com/watch?v=3c8gLZq1BQM.
243. See Manuel DeLanda (2005), for an extensive discussion of the role of attractors in modulation of forces within states; and Chapter Nine of this book for a discussion of attractors and force in a different context.
244. 'Shifters' are mythical tricksters, capable of changing appearance, who disrupt semiotic order and are invoked by the artists in their explanation of the work. David Chesworth and Sonia Leber, *Space-Shifter*.
245. The soundscape of the work uses a choir singing nonsense sounds and part-words. Kristeva proposes the 'Chora' as a depository of pre-language sounds in the body that work to disrupt significations through bodily material presence. In this category, she includes such eruptions of sound as sighs, burps, yawns, sneezes and song (Grosz 1989, 43; Kristeva 1986, 95).
246. David Chesworth & Sonia Leber, *Space-Shifter*.

247. For a detailed discussion of this approach to light and perception, see James J Gibson (1979, 41–103 and passim).

248. Pitch and rhythm, for example, as a continuum of the same wave phenomena of differing duration – 1/16" to 1/3200" for the former, and 6" to 1/16" for the later (Roads 2001, 55, 73).

249. The vibrational is felt as duration: change over time. This duration is then contracted in perception to a quality – in itself timeless.

250. See Barad (2007, 71–96) for a detailed explanation of the phenomena.

251. 'Intra-actions are non-arbitrary, non-deterministic causal enactments through which matter-in-the-process-of-becoming is iteratively enfolded into its ongoing differential materialization' (Barad 2007, 179).

252. In that each position operates as parasite on the other positions. Parasitic actions create an equivalence between positions, interrupting orders and hierarchies (Serres 2007, 55–7).

253. As Connor states in reference to Serres' work on the senses: 'Just as the ear consists in part of a skin, so the skin itself is a kind of ear, which both excludes and transmits exterior vibrations' (1999, 5). Sound, as Goodman asserts, is synesthetic, 'us[ing] the full body as ear, treating the skin as an extended eardrum membrane' (Goodman 2010, 149).

254. Anzieu theorises a 'sound envelope' as one of a series of sensorial envelopes (also including olfactory and thermal envelopes) that extend the body into the world. These construct a 'skin ego' that both supports the construction of the psyche, and provides an extended space of exchange with the world. Some parallels might be drawn with the 'landing sites' of Arakawa and Gins that extend the body. Anzieu proposes the sound envelope as an initial primary envelope, drawing an awareness of the internal space through bodily sounds and the external space through environmental sounds, but also most importantly of the exchange between the two (1989, 157–71 and passim).

255. The skin 'forms a hollow and becomes an ear…[e]verywhere else, be it ear-drum or drum, it hears more widely and less well, but still it hears, vibrating as though auricular' (Serres 2008, 52).

256. An organ here is, as Serres says, 'capacity for doing', a potential for relating (Conner 1999, 3).

257. A syncopated rhythm has two or more attractors (potential modulators of forces), while a simple beat has only one (Goodman 2010, 116).

258. Again, this is a complex ecology, each wave potentially both felt as a vibration in itself, and as a productive factor attracting modulation of forces in which it implicates itself. Here we see that diffraction through the micro-perceptible is built into the various registers of the system as an intrinsic parasitic factor within relation.

259. Perception, as Bogue argues, is a 'secondary, rational organization' of sensation. It contracts and abstracts through cognition the concrete sensation that is prehended in the immediate, physical connection of relation (2003, 116). Bogue draws on the work of Strauss, as he claims Deleuze also did in reaching this definition. Wilden, whom Bogue also cites as an influence on Deleuze's thinking, equates sensation with the analogue, and perception with the translation of this into code, when he writes that 'perception involves the transformation of analogue into digital messages to the brain' (2003, 162). On sensation versus perception and the analogue and digital, see Massumi (2012, 97–99, 133–43).

260. *Momo* was exhibited in August–September 2011 at Paradise Hills Gallery, Richmond, Melbourne. The work drew from a text by Antonin Artaud of the same name, which formed part of the initial impetus for the work. *Momo* consisted of an installation of soft sculpture pieces utilising metallic and bright pink fabrics (with the walls of the gallery painted the same fluorescent pink), and with internal pulsing lights and generative sound. The sound was made principally of loops of words and phrases from Artaud's text, reconfigured by being cut up and reconstructed through the participants' movement. The central sculpture 'conversed' with people in the space, becoming more active as approached, and other sculptural pieces echoed these words and distributed the sounds through the space. Light sensors were embedded into the main sculpture, which then had bright lights projected onto it, and shadows formed by participants in the space then triggered sound events. See Chapter Eight, 'Refrain', for a discussion of the utilising of shadows as an interfacing between bodies and sensors. See www.andrewgoodman.com.au/momo/.

261. In *Momo*, these other sounds consisted of guttural and expressive mouth sounds, and sounds taken from the movie *Alien 4* (Directed by Jean-Pierre Jeunet, Twentieth Century Fox, 1997).
262. See also Whitehead on the complexity within a single perceived sound (1978, 234–5). As Evans states, 'every sound masks an entire history of sound, a cacophony of silence. Even our bodies hum along with the noise of the universe' (in Massumi 2002, 177).
263. Thus, one hears the roar of the ocean, a sound gathered from the individual potential combinations of all the waves and drops of water, but each listener from their singular position hears an ocean composed of different combinations of variously distinct and indistinctly expressed sounds. Each act of audition expresses the whole but in its own way. The multiplicity of micro-perception remains autonomous from individual expressions of it as perception – it is not defined by singular expression, but remains always open to further expressive potential. See also Whitehead (1978, 294–301), on 'extensive connection' and Massumi (2002, 35).
264. It has no primary or ideal identity to which it refers – rather what it refers to is its virtual plane, its un-actualised potential – but can be understood only in relation to, and in the movement of, relation. (Murphie 1997, 326).
265. Here the skin is a sensual topological palette (Serres 2008, 79–80). The skin, Serres writes, is a sense organ, it 'flows like water, a variable confluence of the qualities of the senses' (2008, 52). It is synesthetic in that it enhances the more-than qualities of sound in a way that emphasises how these elements combine to provide a clearer zone of perception. More than simply demonstrating synesthesia, it opens one to the possibility of becoming a new synesthetic machine, hearing with an extended body – composed of both body parts and relations with other surfaces – it invites a fuller participation in a vibrational ecology. See Abram (1997, 59).
266. Writing about other art events in a similar context, Murphie says: 'Such performative interactivity tends to create a series of skins as planes of interaction' (2005, 34).
267. The field of micro-perception is in this way *propositional* of perception, propositions being 'not primarily for belief, but for feeling at the physical level of unconsciousness' (Whitehead 1978, 186).

268. This, Braidotti says, is an awareness of 'the roar which lives on the other side of silence' (2002, 155).
269. For a much more nuanced description of the different types and functions of the interface, see Matthew Fuller's definition of the three levels or modes of interfacing (firstly as distributed and invisible within a system, secondly as the monitoring and control of mapped but separate elements, and thirdly as an 'associative structure independent of processes and objects') (2003, 99, 103–13).
270. See Combes for a succinct discussion of Simondon's critique of cybernetics (2013, 79–83).
271. Such concepts of 'enduring substances', Whitehead argues, while expressing an at times useful abstraction, nevertheless prove themselves mistaken when taken as a 'fundamental statement about the nature of things' (Whitehead 1978, 79).
272. For Lozano-Hemmer's reflections on the significance of this event for his practice, see Barrios and MacSween (2005, 5–6).
273. This follows Deleuze's tactic of utilising infinite verbs, not nouns, to escape representation (Deleuze and Parnet 1987, 50). As Whitehead says: 'if we start with process as fundamental, then the actualities of the present [derive] their characters from the process' (Whitehead 1978, 99).
274. We might say that it has shifted *towards* the pole of concretisation (becoming-concrete), rather than conceiving of the terms abstract and concrete as absolute and exclusive.
275. As Deleuze states, 'difference, potential difference and difference in intensity [is] the reason behind qualitative diversity' (1994, 57).
276. Here the connection between the biological and technical as 'hydrid technical objects' (Salter 2012, 126) was a tactic to *generate* difference, and must be differentiated clearly from a 'cybernetic' model, which, as LaMarre argues, seek to blur distinctions between the biological and the technical, *collapsing* difference (in Combes 2013, 79–80). Thus it produced ruptures or gaps in the processes of 'dephasing' in which a stable identity was delineated from ongoing processes of becoming.
277. See www.lozano-hemmer.com/repositioning_fear.php for short video sequences of various installations of the work.

278. 'Signaletic material', as Deleuze discusses it, is one such excessive expression of interfacing, a conditioning of force-form as it transduces. This can be found in the continual unfolding of pixels on a TV screen; a temporal event that is probably not consciously perceived but which nevertheless has an energy in itself, as a 'plastic mass, an a-signifying and a-syntaxic material' – a kind of processual 'grain' (2005, 28). See also Thomsen (2011) on signaletic material.

279. See Whitehead on the place of conceptual feelings and hybrid physical feelings (1978, 239, 246–7).

280. These were individuations that were 'mobile, strangely subtle, fortuitous and endowed with fringes and margins', that were 'no less capable of dissolving and destroying individuals than constituting them' (Deleuze 1994, 257, 38).

281. Thus resonance is not simply a tension between disparate forces, but the productive structuring of this tension without erasure of difference (Grosz 2012, 41).

282. The technological event is necessarily the producer of these parasites, 'gaps and remainders' as Munster says, that mitigate 'the failure of any fully technologically connected and serially standardized world' (2006, 6).

283. Here the 'first phase' is the pre-individual, the second the individuated entity, but the pre-individual only comes into being as a phase post-individuation – that is they are co-evolving (Combes 2013, 46).

284. As Grosz points out, such collective individuations may often be 'mediated by technical objects, which elaborate and contribute to psychic cohesion' (2012, 50). These technical entities operate as 'the support and the symbol of the relation that we would call transindividual' (Simondon cited Grosz 2012, 56 n.9).

285. Here the unresolved tension between the external and internal provided impetus for changes, its incompatability becoming 'an organizational dimension in its resolution' (Simondon cited Manning 2010, 118) – forcing an evolution in the associated milieu.

286. The outside – seen as the 'incompossible' (Deleuze 1993, 60) – defined the limit of the event (Whitehead 1978, 45; Massumi 1992, 57–8) – the dimensions and rules by which it operated. *Re:Positioning Fear* had limits defining its concrescence, both in the

types of performances it produced, and the potential from which it was drawn. The introduction of a whole new outside tactic of production, alongside the introduction or infection of the event with new intentions and tonalities of play, then delimited the *Re:Positioning Fear* event. The tactic initiated new performances and fields of potential to compose with, even as it continued to drive towards its previously instigated concrecence.

287. They are a 'preconcious verging toward a coming-to-act that tunes to the relational milieu of experience' (Manning 2013a, 187).
288. It enacted both the event of the joining of milieus (a contraction/synthesis) and an expanding of potential – that is, the production of a new milieu: a 'double process of amplification and condensation' (Simondon 2009, 16 note 24). Chris Salter provides a lucid account of the process of the development of a common milieu through concretisation (2012, 117–8).
289. As Simondon states, the individual is relative not only to the field within and with which it individuates, but also to the process of individuation itself (2009, 5).
290. The system moved from a more 'abstract' configuration in Simondon's terms (requiring the external input of the artist and the 'feeding in' to the system of chaotic elements – new bodies with their random actions – to initiate change), to a self-modulating model (where 'effects are produced that are independent of the design plan') (Simondon 1980, 22, 31).
291. If the folding in of the outside moves the system to a far-from-equilibrium state, then this point at which the system shifts to one of self-organising criticality is a special 'poised' state, where the fullest range of events is potentialised, and where the organisation of the system is governed by an emergent global dynamics (Bak 1997, 48, 51 and passim). On far-from-equilibrium states see also Prigogene (1980) and Prigogene and Stengers (1996).
292. Perhaps one might propose that Lozano-Hemmer already constructed the work in a limited sense as metastable – as a kind of supersaturated solution primed for dephasing, sensitive to difference, but sensitive, on this meta-level, only to certain actions (LaMarre in Combes2013, 86).
293. Interfacing, in connecting and producing the machinic, actualises a potential – a paradox in that, prior to their co-joining, the two

systems shared no potential. Where does this potential, and the actuality of unfolding connectedness arise from? Simondon's answer, as Massumi explains it, is that it is brought from the future, from a point post-concretisation. Interfacing here is the catalyst that instigates both the actual assemblage and simultaneously creates a new potential, a new milieu created immanently with the assemblage on which it has somehow already drawn, a circularity possible only within a conception of time as non-linear (Massumi, DeBoever and Rolfe 2009, 39–40).

294. The power of the parasitic actions of the shadow play on Lozano-Hemmer's work can only be felt through some understanding of the ways in which these actions twist, complicate, complement, extend and oppose the original 'givens' of the installation, as for Deleuze it is the 'givens' of an event that are overcome by the diagrammatic 'catastrophe' (2002a, 81). In this sense, Lozano-Hemmer's future Relational Architecture work that drew on the improvised shadow play of *Re:Positioning Fear* and placed these actions at the centre of the installations machinations perhaps seems less dynamic, since there is some greater resolution of internal tensions, and the intentions of artist and public coincide in cooperative play more reminiscent of some of relational aesthetics blander gestures.

295. That is, as LaMarre describes it, internal and external grounds, being different, 'have to communicate...actively across their asymmetry, and have to stabilise that communication. The result is a self-regulating individual' (LaMarre in Combes 2013, 93).

296. To its credit, *Re:Positioning Fear* was an art machine capable of using interfacing-produced parasitic action to draw into relation a wider field of possible actions, affects and intentions, immanently rewriting its productive capabilities. Its power as an artwork was perhaps that this transformation led not to the collapse of its machinic structuring, but to its concretisation.

297. These light sensors triggered volume changes and the swapping of sound samples, while movement sensors also played a role in switching audio samples. See Chapter Seven for further description of *Momo*.

298. Exactly which sound had its volume manipulated on any particular track was dependent on a series of complex disruptions and swapping of samples, similar to the parasitic system described

in *Chorus of Idle Feet* in Chapter Two. The computer system also watched for the quantity of light variation within a set timespan that, once a tipping point was reached, could then trigger further shifts in the potential range of volume (so that louder volumes were made possible). See Chapter Nine for some discussion of limits and bifurcation within software patches.

299. No entity, Whitehead states, 'can have an abstract status in a real unity'. The neglect of this, he argues, is 'a prevalent error in metaphysical reasoning' (Whitehead 1978, 225).

300. In other words, an algorithm is a set of instructions for a computer program to perform specific mathematical operations. Some algorithms can be split into smaller sets of instructions that perform parts of the larger algorithm, as they might also be combined to perform larger such procedures. Algorithms differ essentially from an algebraic formula – which might be a component part of an algorithmic sequence – in that they are non-reversible (Miyazaki 2012, 3).

301. This is not to imply at all that other artists have not attempted such design, as clearly there has been considerable work developed in this area. Both Parisi and Stamatia Portanova discuss, in the texts that inform this argument, a number of artworks that attempt to develop open-ended usages of software. These discussions, like many theoretical examinations of algorithms, centre on the philosophical and examine only the general structure of the algorithmic processes and do not provide detailed examination of software patches. See also the writing and artwork of artists such as Jon McCormack and Andrew R Brown on their own software developments, and as two Australian examples of experimentation in this area.

302. *Orgasmatron* was exhibited in October–November 2013 at Blindside, Melbourne. This discussion concentrates on the technical details of the software patching. Orgasmatron consisted of an inflatable 'pod' that one or two participants could lie down and move around in. The work drew on iterations of the orgasmatron from the films Sleeper (directed by Woody Allen, Rollins-Joffe Productions, 1973) and Barbarella (directed by Roger Vadim, Paramount Pictures, 1968), aesthetically quoting the soft machines and inflatables of the design of Barbarella by Mario Garbuglia. Projected coloured light pulsed within the interior,

changing colour and speed as the Orgasmatron became more excited; speakers surrounding the bodies whispered and spoke; and tiny speakers and a subsonic speaker sent ripples of vibrations through the base on which participants were lying. Sensors embedded in the base captured data from the weight and movement of bodies, light sensors captured shifts in brightness caused by both the projections and shadows from bodies, and vibration sensors captured the vibrations at various points in the base of both sounds and bodies. See www.andrewgoodman.com.au/orgasmatron-spaces-to-make-love-in/.

303. Pairs of vibration, pressure, light and tilt sensors gather data on variations in force and direction of pressure, movement, volume and light from the *Orgasmatron* environment.

304. *Isadora* is a program for interactive media designed by Mark Coniglio (see troikatronix.com/isadora/about/). It is similar to the *Max* programs, in that it contains a number of prewritten 'objects' (Max) or 'actors' (Isadora) that perform certain functions or processes on incoming data (for example, mathematical equations), with various programmable parameters. Both programs also allow new objects to be constructed out of combinations of existing objects, and allow for the flexible connection between objects. In total, the *Orgasmatron* computations operated across three patches in three different programs: a *Miditron* patch (which converted data from the sensors to midi signals to be utilised by the other two patches); the *Isadora* patch (which controlled and modulated data and video output); and an Ableton Live patch (which played, rerecorded and modulated sound samples and sent these to the system of fifteen speakers). It was, however, principally within the *Isadora* patch that the parasitic potential of algorithmic prehensions and competing attractors was explored, and thus it is the only patch described in detail here.

305. Beyond the more open-ended algorithmic processes discussed here, the patch itself contained more programmatic and mundane algorithms that controlled, for example, the starting up of the system as a participant entered the environment, and the processes by which it returned to its original and relatively passive state after the participant exited.

306. In the discussion of the potentialising of software, it should be noted that the triggering of video and sound events by these

processes was in itself not a simple linear process, but also engaged with parasitic tactics. As with the example discussed in Chapter Two, these triggers interfered with and disrupted each other, replacing, for example, one sound event with another, or altering its tone, volume, and so on. As with the examples discussed in Chapter Five, within the actualised sound and light events, there were further potential processes of parasitic disruption, such as the 'unsounds' embedded in the sound samples that altered perceived sound events through diffraction, and the extended moments of transition between video projections where colours and rhythms diffractively combine.

307. This capacity to develop parameters was restricted to furthering the excitation of the system (that is, an increased capacity to be affected), in line with the concept of stages of increased excitement and responsiveness during sex. However, the design had the capacity to both increase and decrease these affective capacities, and so could be utilised in a system that potentially becomes less responsive or in a system that oscillates in both directions.

308. It should be noted that a further tactic commonly utilised in generative software-based works (though rejected here), involves injections of chaos and the use of 'fitness' criteria to generate controlled novelty. Utilising fitness criteria involves the use of algorithms to randomly generate new outcomes, and then subjecting these outcomes to a set of prescribed criteria that determine which of these novel iterations (usually a series of small modulations on existing patterns) will survive and which will perish. Whether or not the initial generation of novelty in such systems is relational (caused by some processing of existing intensive factors) or random (through injections of unrelated data), such a process is clearly not open-ended. Rather, as Jon McCormack and Philip Galanter both argue, it is a top-down or teleological approach that drives the system towards a set outcome, even if it allows some movement within the processes that lead to this (McCormack 2003, 193; Galanter 329). In this, it clearly denies a relational modelling by subordinating exploration to a single dominant form. Such systems might therefore be thought of as adaptive systems that are goal orientated, seeking new patterns or behaviors that 'benefit' the system (that is, lead to greater efficiency or growth within a set of defined parameters), whereas a truly generative system, as Oliver Bown argues,

disregards the benefits or costs to the system of its creativity (2012, 364). McCormack argues that fitness-driven evolutionary art is a contradictory term, being anything but evolutionary in nature (2013, 5). It does, however, fit neatly into goal-orientated, neo-Darwinist theories of transcendence – a working or evolving towards an ideal form, as discussed in Chapter Two in relation to drift. The secondary tactic – employed both within fitness-based systems and on its own – has been to use injections of chaos or external randomness to generate change. Such systems, whereby an unrelated set of parameters are used as raw data converted to some artistic output through computational processes (such as weather data converted to shifts in colours on a screen, for example), are, as McCormack and others argue, a poor 'proxy' for intensive complexity (McCormack et al 2014, 8). While fitness-based systems concentrate on positive, directed connectivity at the expense of exploratory room to move, random data creates systems concerned with the superficial appearance of complexity rather than its actualization. See also Per Bak's discussion of the misunderstandings of the operation of fitness within much scientific discussion (1997, 142).

309. As Anna Munster states: 'the technical element is always in a relation with elements outside itself, its form is therefore indeterminate and virtual' (2006, 14). Munster argues that bodies are 'the chaos and interruption with which the machine cannot dispense' (2006, 185). See also Murphie and Potts (2003, 31–2). It could be argued that simply through the processes of flows of data translating from software platform to software platform within a computer this data undergoes a transduction, shifting from one coded flow to another, with accompanied and somewhat unpredictable losses through the noise of translation (Newman 2012, 135–7). For example, in the movement of data through the series of patches utilised in the *Orgasmatron* system, numerical data is transduced from voltage flows (positive numbers between 0 and 5 volts), to midi in the first patch (positive integers between 0 and 127), then in the second patch to numbers between -100 and +100, then back to MIDI in the third patch. The social aspects of code provide another register in which any determinate nature of algorithms might also be disturbed. As Adrian Mackenzie charts in his discussion of Java, the software operates more as an unstable 'collection of resources with multiple potential machinic productions'

than as a fixed object (2006, 95). Here Java, with its constant upgrades, user initiated fixes and modifications, independently operating layers of code and ability to work within other coding languages across platforms, operates as an indeterminate 'virtual' that is differentially actualised in each specific operational event (Mackenzie 2006, 96–102).

310. See Wilden's discussion of the paradoxical operations of brain messages, which appear both as analogue and digital depending on the scale of the examination (1980, 175–7).
311. On signaletic creativity, see Brunner (2012, 7) and Thomsen (2011, 43–62).
312. For example, the fact that the digital can encompass both zero and negative numbers while the analogue contains only positive numbers shows that it has its own particular mode of operating, and, in this one respect at least, its own and potentially wider parameters (Wilden 1980. 167). On the loss of excess in the digital, see also Simon Penny's statement that digital technologies 'thin out' experience, (2013, 269–70) see also Massumi (2002, 133–43) and Grosz (2001, 183).
313. See also Chapter Two. Roy Ascott has argued that the use of feedback as an organizing tactic 'furnishes [a system with] its own controlling energy', allowing an intensively 'rich interplay' (2003, 128). See also Bateson (2000, 379–80).
314. This is only a partial example of the feedback loops established. In reality, data sensed from any one set of sensors affects all the other systems – pressure variation affecting sound events, spatial configurations, and light events, for example.
315. However, the model of feedback systems I have described in the *Orgasmatron* would seem to suggest that it is, at least, also possible to create feedback between the various technical entities.
316. McCormack has written and experimented extensively in this area. See, for example, his "Creative Ecosystems," (2012, 39–60). See also his artwork, *Eden* (2000–10) at jonmccormack.info/~jonmc/sa/artworks/eden/. Accessed October, 2014. Gordon Pask's early 'conversational' model might be seen to fit loosely within this parametric and ecological paradigm. Pask's early experiments with electro-chemical systems, capable of creating their own sensors out of a field of solutions of chemical

components and electrical charges, is perhaps one of the most interesting experiments in ecological 'programming', concerned with how a field of potential is able to organise its own gathering into an assemblage capable of expressing relation (see Pask 1960; Cariani 1997). This is the type of evolutionary art that Galanter advocates, one capable of creating new sensing machines (and therefore evolving its own parameters) as well as operating machinically (2010, 6).

317. See also Bak (1997, passim) and Prigogene and Stengers (1996, 42–4 and passim).

318. This, Parisi argues, is a system modifying through qualitative and local intensities (2013, 112).

319. Parisi argues that topology conflates points and singularities within the various inputs of a system into a continuous flow of infinitesimals, connectively subsuming atomic differences into a whole that, in this case, is also a modulating surface, turning 'the potential effects of the future into operative procedures within the present' (2013). Topological calculation, as Parisi states, now also allows economic factors to be calculated as parameters within architectural design, directly linking potential profit to aesthetic considerations, a tending towards creating a topology of networked capitalist control (2013, 103–5). Autopoietic systems are often referred to as topological, though they are not necessarily so. Technically speaking, topological systems, according to DeLanda, operate specifically through a system of a single attractor, which explains both their erasure of negative relation and the simplicity of their operations. Multiple attractor systems, as will be explored later in this chapter, are capable of operating through intensive difference that creates both compossible and incompossible relational pulls (DeLanda 2005, 24).

320. Parisi and Goodman continue: 'We ask instead, what if the user is any actual entity whatever among the other components of an ecology, and therefore that novelty does not necessarily involve the activity of a human participant. Specifically, we wonder about the perpetual neglect to deal with the weirdness of mathematics, the potential of nameable, yet undefinable, infinitesimal, numbers to generate prehensive novelty' (2009). Gilbert Simondon's call for a philosophy of technology, as Paul Dumouchel describes it, also advocates for a move beyond approaches that describe

technologies' inputs and outputs while ignoring their internal working structures (1992, 410).

321. Not only can second-order cybernetics assume that systems depend on the generative capacities of the biological environment to instigate change, as Parisi argues (Parisi 2013, 11), but, as Portanova writes, many configurations of generative software project biological modelling onto their design, viewing cognitive processes as the only model for algorithmic process (2013, 87).

322. In taking their models of self-generation and organisation from the biological, bottom-up learning systems and autopoietic feedback loops risk presenting digital architectures as merely representational of a 'real' world from which they are supposedly separate. For example, simulations of neural activity that conceive of computational activity as abstractions of brain activities. See Parisi on this 'neurophenominology' (2013, 169–85). At the other extreme, there have of course been attempts to reduce the biological world's operations to algorithms, the 'metadigital fallacy' as Parisi terms it (2013, 36–47); see also Dery (1996, 232), for a critique of this approach.

323. Whitehead states that an entity's relational matrix is composed of its abilities to interact with forces and to forcefully impact on other entities (1978, 220). As Parisi points out, it is the act of prehension that 'allow[s] complexity to enter into existing sets of data' (2013, 70).

324. 'Any entity, thus intervening in processes transcending itself, is said to be functioning as an "object"' (Whitehead 1978, 220). An entity, Whitehead states, 'retains the impression of what it might have been, but is not' (1978, 226–7).

325. See also Shaviro, who states that 'there is always a glitch in the course of the "vector transmission" of energy and affect from past to present' (2009, 86).

326. As Shaviro says, 'multiple prehensions are combined or coordinated by their adoption to a particular subjective aim – even though this aim does not preexist, but itself only emerges in the course of this adaption' (2009, 74).

327. That is, it autonomously acquires determination from indeterminate conditions (Parisi 2013, 59).

328. This essay of Chaitlin's is recommended as an entry-level philosophical and (relatively) lay-mathematical discussion of the topic.
329. 'Ugliness' is here opposed to 'beauty' in mathematics. That is, as Matthew Fuller points out, there is a direct and problematic link between the search for beauty and simplicity in mathematics (universal equations that express everything at some base level) and its aesthetic fetishisation in programming, and transcendental philosophies of pure abstract forms that the real world must then be ordered to conform with and which then collaborate with 'hierarchies of every kind' (2003, 15–16). Perhaps, with this in mind, the exploration of awkward mathematical and algorithmic work-arounds and deliberately incomplete and non-universal processes have an ethical role in thinking the processual, as a new and 'speculative' software.
330. That is, they resist acting as a proof that mathematics as a whole can be reduced to a universal or all-encompassing 'theory of everything' (Chaitlin 2011, 126). Turing's work, according to Chaitlin, shows that 'that there are things that no computer can calculate' (2011,127).
331. Expressed in the binary code of the computer $0 < W = 0.11011100 \ldots < 1$, where the actual 1s and 0s are dependent on the calculation at hand (Chaitlin 2011, 136).
332. Thus, as Chaitlin states, 'it looks like it is contingent' despite being a necessary truth (2011, 137). See also Portanova (2013, 126–7).
333. They are 'patternless' in the sense that the virtual contains the undifferentiated potential for all patterns.
334. These uncontainable 'infinite quantities of data…define the space of transition between algorithmic sequences' (Parisi 2013, 240).
335. There is also, as Mackenzie notes, the practical spacing of algorithmic processes within a computer that must juggle the simultaneous processing demands of multiple algorithms and software platforms (2006, 176–7).
336. See also Wilden (1980, 158) and Mackenzie on the instability of code that exists both as expression and operation (2006, 36–7).
337. Rhythm, as Manning states, is 'a passage from one milieu to another' (2008, 5).
338. There were multiple cycles that occurred, establishing a series of potentialities of temporal scales rather than a uniform

temporality, and overlapping potentialities or temporal multiplicities. See DeLanda (2005, 107–8).

339. A refrain is 'any kind of rhythmic pattern that stakes out a territory', a 'point of stability, a property and an openness to the outside' (Bogue 1991, 88). On algorithmic refrains, see Miyazaki (2012, passim) and Parisi (2013, 83–4).

340. While considered independently, the mathematical operations of an algorithm are rate-independent (1+1 = 2, no matter how slowly it is calculated). Within systems of interconnected parallel processes, where the results of one calculation have potential influence over other processes, the temporal progression of all operations is crucial to the whole system's actualisation, and these parallel temporal process allow novelty to arise in otherwise ordinally set and rate-independent procedures. See DeLanda (2005, 116–18); and Parisi (2013, 108), on overlapping temporal multiplicities.

341. A number as a concept has no causal efficacy, no definite relations that cut a determination from its pure potential, however, once it enters into the actuality of an equation, it becomes a definite (limited) event with specific relations or causal efficacy. For example, the number five has no definite meaning as a pure idea, but in its incorporation into an event – five apples, or '5' in the number '50' – comes to have specific connections delineating it from its other potential meanings – for instance, three apples, or five oranges, or the '5' in '500'. See Portanova (2013, 107) and Whitehead (1957, 1). Similarly, a mathematical function such as '+' is a pure idea that is then defined in its actual use – in conjunction with real numbers and/or other mathematical functions (Whitehead 2012, 54–66).

342. Eternal entities are 'becomings without being' (DeLanda 2005, 127).

343. Unlike other actualised entities to which it necessarily forms a relationship, it has only a relation to some eternal objects from which it selects its potential.

344. That is, the undifferentiated potentiality of 'x's and 'y's to express an infinity of equations was replaced by actual numbers that create a defined and limited relation to the larger potential. Each algorithm then might be said to have drawn prehensively on its own past and future potential iterations, other potential actions

on a flow of data, either accommodating some of their potential (but in its own way, making it a new process), or differing from it.

345. This is the 'eternal character of ideas' that are the same for all entities, though 'differently and infinitely actualized by them' (Portanova 2013, 46). The number five, for example, is an eternal object that is actualised in many ways (groups of objects, beats, age, temperature, and so on). It has a relationship to all these entities, while never being exhausted by its various ingressions into actualities. Each entity has an actual or definite relationship to 'fiveness' as a concept and so represents a definite cut in its virtual, indeterminate status – it moves from the non-precise differential of the idea to the precision of a cut (ibid. 46), drawing a concept into spatiotemporal association (Portanova 2013, 38). Eternal objects are therefore 'immanent to, and part and parcel of any actual entities' (Portanova 2013, 63).

346. On excess and vagueness see Whitehead (1978, 111–12).

347. This is based on DeLanda's work, most specifically *Intensive Science*, which draws direct links between state systems in physics and process philosophy. He draws extensively on Deleuze's thinking, whose relation to non-equilibrium physics is perhaps most evident in evident from *Difference and Repetition* and *The Fold: Leibniz and the Baroque*.

348. DeLanda calls this 'asymtomatic stability', whereby shocks to the system – new forces or modulations to forces for example – can dislodge the system's trajectory. It may also return to its defined stable state if the shock is not too great (2005, 29). A simple example of these self-organising capacities can be found in the way water moves through a series of stable states as it is heated, reorganising the molecules in a different way at each distinct stage. That is, the water will move from a frozen crystalline organisation, to conduction, then to convection, turbulence, and finally steam or a gaseous state – each state with its own particular organising parameters. The states shift at specific critical temperatures, as the system breaks a limit that defines a particular organising dynamic (DeLanda 2005, 19).

349. The state of a system is then a 'single point in the manifold', where the manifold is the 'space of [all] possible states' (DeLanda 2005, 13).

350. The trajectories chart how difference differs over time, as can be expressed in a differential equation (DeLanda 2011b, 14). Trajectories are a direct consequence of the attractors that shape the dynamics of the field, though this can be far from a linear dynamic (DeLanda 2011b, 33).
351. In this sense, an attractor might be seen as a 'will to power': an 'internal will' that is 'the differential and genetic element of a force' (Deleuze 2002b, 51).
352. In other words, it remains an ongoing potential or virtual dimension to the trajectory.
353. Systems with a single attractor are relatively stable, in that they have a tendency to move towards a single potential end point. Such linear systems, however, are the exception rather than the rule, DeLanda argues, contra to what materialist or essentialist approaches to science might have one believe (2005, Chapter Four). 'Non-linear models and their multiple attractors, as well as non-linear causes and their complex capacities to affect and be affected, define a world capable of surprising us through the emergence of unexpected novelty' (DeLanda 2005, 187).
354. As it can never reach its multiple potential and contradictory attractors, the individuation of a difference is always a 'partial and relative resolution manifested in a system that contains latent potential and harbours incompatibility with itself' (Simondon 1992, 300).
355. DeLanda acknowledges that he takes this idea from the work of Ilya Prigogine and Gregoire Nicolis. See Prigogine (1980) and Prigogine and Stengers (1996) and Simondon (2009, 6) on the exclusion of becoming in stable systems.
356. For some discussion of the role of attractors in creating differential potential or intensity, see Massumi (1992, 58–61).
357. As noted before, excitement had a 'roll-on' effect on the *Orgasmatron*, stimulating more excitement throughout the system. As such, the participant, though stimulating the initial rise in differential data flow, was only one factor among many that continued to stimulate the system.
358. Whereas when in its passive or unexcited state, the numbers were relatively constant, and thus remained attracted to the same watcher.

359. It should be emphasised that the attempt here was not to make a digital system that mirrored or represented 'real world' chemical relations between molecules and forces acting on them, but – in sympathy with Parisi's attempt to delineate a digital mode of prehension and a digital relation to the virtual – to think further into a specifically digital mode of attractor and bifurcatory operations.
360. As explained earlier, the parameters of any watcher's gate (the numbers it looked for in a data flow) were capable of being adjusted by triggers from other watchers.
361. Here, multiple attractor systems were self-organising, but not exactly autopoietic, since any stability evolved only as a result of negotiations, forces and potentials of forces, which in their virtuality remained larger than this 'whole'. In situating such a system at a far-from-equilibrium state, where it was primed to switch between attractors with variations in data flows, the *Orgasmatron* software patch exhibited a connectivity that was more like an 'open whole' that selected and accessed multiple potentialities than an autopoietic system that 'subordinate[d] all changes to the maintenance of [its] own organization' (Maturana and Varela 1980, 80).
362. Such as a shift from operating as a stable to a periodic or chaotic mode (DeLanda 2005, 19).
363. These algorithms looked for the amount of a certain activity within a specific timeframe (such as the number of triggers sent by a particular algorithm or set of algorithms), and were triggered if a specified threshold number of such activities were noted. Again the threshold itself was a mutable number.
364. On the creative role of the limit, see Manning and Massumi (2011, 32–3).
365. This might be thought of as a 'weak' causality in the system, operating 'by way of little frictions' that 'pull' on existing causal chains (Serres 1995, 71–3).
366. As Andrew Murphie notes, 'vigilance' is required to ensure artistic practices concerned with technologies enable lines of flight rather than 'align with…social axiomatics (particularly of control)' (1996, 101). See also Laura Lotti's discussion of the evils of 'algorithmic trading' on the stock exchange (Lotti 2015, 28–9 & passim).

367. This, Simondon states, is a characteristic of concretization or the intertwining of components in each other's realisation, a 'discovery of the dimensions according to which a problematic can be defined' (1992, 313).
368. Jacques Rancière describes ethics as including an 'identity between environments...[and] a principle of action', which perhaps could be seen in the concept of shared individuation, the emergent or gathering of an ecology that this research has promoted (2009, 111). See also Bennett (2010, 14).
369. 'Whitehead's metaphysics could be described as an account of how the "greater world without" any entity "steals in" upon it, how one existent manifests itself in the very fabric of another.' (Jones 1998, 3)
370. This is a symbiotic relationship where 'every protagonist is interested in the success of the other for its own reason' (Stengers 2010, 35). Here 'protagonist' must be thought to include forces, events, and events within events.
371. On the concept of immediation, see Manning, Munster and Stavning Thomsen (Forthcoming, 2018).
372. For example, the automated algorithmic expressions of the stock market and larger economy, or recent use of algorithms by the Australian Department of Social Security in 2016–17 to automatically generate speculative and often unwarranted debt notices to thousands of welfare recipients.
373. And here perhaps, as Braidotti notes, we also share a 'defeatism' or despair as to our powerlessness in the face of ecological disaster and capitalist machinery (2014, 49).
374. See Braidotti (2014, 190–1).

Bibliography

Abrahm, David. *The Spell of the Sensuous: Perception and Language in the More-Than-Human-World*. Toronto and New York: Vintage Books, 1997.

Adams, Phillips. *Darwin's Worms*. New York: Basic Books, 2000.

Anker, Katherine. "Exploring the Intelligent Art Installation as a Space for Expansion of the Conscious Mind." *Technoetics Arts*, vol. 6, no. 3, 2009, 251–8.

Amerika, Mark. "Excerpts from 'Portrait of the Vj'." *Fibreculture Journal*, no. 7 (2005).

Anzieu, Didier. *The Skin Ego*. New Haven: Yale University Press, 1989.

Arakawa and Madeline Gins. *Reversible Destiny*. New York: Guggenhein Museum, 1997.

———. *Architectural Body*. Alabama: University of Alabama Press, 2002.

———. *Making Dying Illegal*. Berkley: Roof Books, 2006.

Arsic, Branka. "Thinking Leaving." *Deleuze and Space*, edited by Ian Buchanan and Greg Lambert. Edinborough: Edinborough University Press, 2005.

Artaud, Antonin and Susan Sontag. *Selected Writings*. Translated by Helen Weaver. Los Angeles: University of California Press, 1988.

Ascott, Roy. "Editorial: Connectivity: Art and Interactive Telecomunications." *Leonardo*, vol. 24, no. 2, 1991: 115–117.

———. *Telematic Embrace: Visionary Theories of Art, Technology and Conciousness*. Berkley: University of California Press, 2003.

Assad, Maria L. "From Order to Chaos: Michel Serres's Field Models." *SubStance* vol. 20, no. 2, issue 65, 1991: 33–43.

Attali, Jacques. *Noise: The Political Economy of Music*. Translated by Brian Massumi. Minneapolis: University of Minnesota Press, 1985.

Bak, Per. *How Nature Works: The Science of Self-Organized Criticality*. New York: Oxford University Press, 1997.

Bak, Per and Maya Paczuski. "Complexity, Contingency, and Criticality (Macroevolution/Macroeconomics/Punctuated Equilibrium)." *Physics: the Opening to Complexity*, vol. 92, Irvine: Proceedings of the National Academy of Science USA, 1995: 6689–96.

Barad, Karen. "Posthumanist Performativity: Toward an Understanding of How Matter Comes to Matter." *Signs: Journal of Women in Culture and Society*, vol. 28, no. 3, 2003: 801–31.

———. *Meeting the Universe Halfway: Quantum Physics and the Entanglement of Matter and Meaning*. Durham and London: Duke University Press, 2007.

Barber, Stephen. *Artaud: The Screaming Body*. London: Creation Books, 1999.

Barker, Timothy. "Process and (Mixed) Reality: A Process Philosophy for Interaction in Mixed Reality Environments."*2009 IEEE International Symposium on Mixed and Augmented Reality – Arts, Media and Humanities*, edited by Raphaël Grasset, Carl Disalvo, Jarrell Pair and Jay Bolter, 26–29 October. Orlando: the Institute of Electrical and Electronics Engineers, 2009: 17–23.

Barrios, José Luis and Rebecca MacSween. "A Conversation between José Luis Barrios and Rafael Lozano-Hemmer." *Sala de Arte Público Siquieros (SAPS)*, edited by José Luis Barrios and Itala Schmelz. Mexico City: SAPS, 2005.

Barthes, Roland. *Empire of Signs*. London: Jonathan Cape, 1982.

Bataille, Georges, Fred Botting and Scott Wilson. *The Bataille Reader*. Oxford: Blackwell Publishers, 1997.

Bataille, Georges and Allan Stoekl. *Georges Bataille: Visions of Excess, Selected Writings 1927-1939*. Translated by Allan Stoekl, Carl Lovitt and Donald Lesli. Minneapolis: University of Minnesota Press, 1985.

Bateson, Gregory. *Steps to an Ecology of Mind*. Chicago: University of Chicago, 2000.

Bearn, Gordon C. "Effecting Affect: The Corporeal Ethos of Gins and Arakawa." *Journal of aesthetics education*, vol. 44, no. 2, Summer, 2010: 40-9.

Bender, Gretchen and Timothy Druckery, editors. *Culture on the Brink: Ideologies of Technology*. Seattle: Bay Press, 1994.

Bennett, Jane. *Vibrant Matter: A Political Ecology of Things*. Durham: Duke University Press, 2010.

Benthien, Claudia. *Skin: On the Cultural Border between Self and the World*. New York: Columbia University Press, 2002.

Bergson, Henri. *Matter and Memory*. New York: Dover Publications, 2004.

Bertelsen, Lone. "Affect and Care in 'Intimate Transactions'" *Fibreculture* vol. 21, 2012: 31-71.

Bertelsen, Lone and Andrew Murphie. "An Ethics of the Everyday Infinities and Powers: Félix Guattari on Affect and the Refrain." *The Affect Theory Reader*, edited by Melissa & and Gregory J. Seigworth Gregg, 138-160. Durham: Duke University Press, 2010.

Bird, Jon and Andy Webster. "The Blurring of Art and Alife." *CEMA*, edited by A Dorin. Melbourne: CEMA, 2001: 38-46.

Bird, Jon and Paul Layzell. "The Evolved Radio and Its Implications for Modeling the Evolution of Novel Sensors." *Evolutionary Computation*, vol. 2. Honolulu: IEEE, 2002: 1836-41.

Bird, Jon and Ezequiel Di Paolo. "Gordon Pask His Maverick Machines." *The Mechanical Mind in History*, edited by Phil Husbands, Owen Holland and Michael Wheeler: MIT Press: Cambridge, MA, 2008.

Birringer, Johannes. "Interactivity: 'User Testing' for Participatory Art Works." *International Journal of Performance Arts and Digital Media*, vol. 1, no. 2, 2005: 147–73.

Bishop, Claire. "Antagonism and Relational Aesthetics." *October*, vol. 110, no. Fall, 2004: 51–79.

-------. "The Social Turn: Collaboration and Its Discontents." *Rediscovering Aesthetics:Transdisciplinary Voices from Art History, Philosophy and Art Practice*, edited by Julia Jansen Francis Halsall, Tony O'Connor. Stanford: Stanford University Press, 2009: 238–255.

Boccioni, Umberto. "Technical Manifesto of Futurist Sculpture. Preface to the First Exhibition of Futurist Sculpture." *Modern Artists on Art*, edited by Robert L. Herbert. New York: Dover Publications, 2000: 40–51.

Bogue, Ronald. "Rhizomusicosmology." *Leonardo*, vol. 20, no. 1, 1991: 85–101.

-------. *Deleuze on Music, Painting and the Arts*. New York and London: Routledge, 2003.

Bois, Yves-Alain and Lygia Clark. "Nostalgia of the Body." *October* vol. 69, no. Summer, 1994: 85–109.

Bosma, Josephine and Joyce Hinterding, "Joyce Hinterding." *Nettime Mailing List Archive*, www.nettime.org/Lists-Archives/nettime-l-9808/msg00074.html. Accessed November 11, 2015.

Bown, Oliver. "Generative and Adaptive Creativity: A Unified Approach to Creativity in Nature, Humans and Machines." *Computers and Creativity*, edited by Jon McCormack and Mark d'Inverno. Heidleberg, New York, London, Dordrecht: Springer, 2012: 361–81.

Bracken, Joseph. "Whitehead and the Critique of Logocentrism," *Process and Difference: Between Cosmological and Poststructuralist Postmodernisms*, edited by Catherine Keller and Anne Daniell. Albany: State University of New York Press, 2002: 91–110.

Braidotti, Rosi. "Towards a New Nomadism: Feminist Deleuzian Tracks." *Gilles Deleuze and the Theater of Philosophy*, edited by Constantin V. Boundas and Dorothea Olkowski. New York: Routledge, 1994.

———. *Metamorphoses: Towards a Materialist Theory of Becoming*. Cornwall: MPG Books, 2002.

———. "Elemental Complexity and Relational Vitality: The Relevance of Nomadic Thought for Contemporary Science." *The Force of the Virtual: Deleuze, Science and Philosophy*, edited by Peter Gaffney. Minneapolis: University of Minnesota Press, 2010: 211–28.

———. *The Posthuman*. Cambridge: Polity Press, 2014.

Brennan, Teresa. *The Transmission of Affect*. Ithaca & London: Cornell University Press, 2004.

Broekmann, Andreas. "Vectorial Elevation: Public Spheres and Network Interfaces." *The Cybernetics Reader*. New York:Routledge, 2004: 378–381.

Brown, Neil C M, Timothy S Barker and Dennis Del Farero. "The Framework for a Theory of the Formation of Interactive Narratives." *Leonardo* vol. 44, no. 3, 2011: 212–19.

Brown, Steven D. "Michel Serres: Science, Translation and the Logic of the Parasite." *Theory, Culture and Society*, vol. 19, no. 3 (2002): 1–27.

Brunner, Christopher. "Immediation as Process and Practice of Signaletic Mattering." *Journal of Aesthetics and Culture*, vol. 4, no. 1, 2012: 1–3.

Brunner, Christopher, Erin Manning and Brian Massumi. "Fields of Potential: On Affective Immediation, Anxiety, and Necessities of Life." In *Ästhetik Der Existenz: Lebensformen Im Widerstreit*, edited by Elke Bippus, Jörg Huber and Roberto Nigro. Zurich: Edition Voldemeer, 2013: 135–50.

Buchanan, Ian. *Deleuzism: A Metacommentry*. Durham: Duke Universty Press, 2000.

Cariani, Peter. "Adaptive Connection to the World through Self-Organizing Sensors and Effectors." *Fifth IEEE International Symposium on Intelligent Control*, 5–7 September, 1990: 73–8.

Cariani, Peter. "To Evolve an Ear: Epistemological Implications of Gordon Pask's Electrochemical Devices." *Systems Research* vol., 10, no. 3, 1993: 19–33.

Cariani, Peter. "Emergence of New Signal-Primitives in Neural Systems." *Intellectica* vol. 2, no. 25, 1997: 95–143.

Cariani, Peter. "Emergence and Creativity." *Emoção Art.ficial 4.0 Emergência*, edited by Itaú Cultural. Sao Paolo, Brazil: 2008.

de Certeau, Gilles. *The Practice of Everyday Life*. Berkley: University of California Press, 1988.

Chaitin, Gregory. "How Real Are Real Numbers?" *Manuscrito*, vol. 34, no. 1, 2011: 115–41.

Crist, Eileen. "Concerned with Trifles? A Geophysiological Reading of Charles Darwin's Last Book." *Scientists Debate Gia: The Next Century*, edited by Stephen Schneider, James Miller, Eileen Crist and Penelope Boston. Cambridge, MA: MIT Press, 2004: 161–72.

Code, Murray. *Order and Organism: Steps Towards a Whiteheadian Philosophy of Mathematics and the Natural Sciences*. Albany: State University of New York Press, 1985.

Colebrook, Claire. *Understanding Deleuze*. Crows Nest: Allen and Unwin, 2002.

Collier, John. "Simulating Autonomous Anticipation: The Importance of Dubois' Conjecture." *Biosytems* vol. 91, no. 2, 2008: 346–54.

Combes, Muriel. *Gilbert Simondon and the Philosophy of the Transindividual*. Translated by Thomas LaMarre. Cambridge and London: MIT Press, 2013.

Conner, Steven. "Michel Serres' Five Senses." *Michel Serres Conference*. Birbeck College, London, 1999: unpaginated.

Couze, Venn. "Individuating, Relationality, Affect: Rethinking the Human in Relation to the Living." *Body and Society*, vol. 16, no. 1, 2010: 129–61.

Cytowic, Richard E, MD. *Synesthesia: A Union of the Senses*. Cambridge and London: MIT Press, 2002.

Darwin, Charles. *The Formation of Vegetable Mold through the Action of Worms with Observations on Their Habits*. London: John Murray, 1881.

Debaise, Didier. "What Is Relational Thinking." *Inflexions,* vol. 5, 2012: 1–11.

DeLanda, Manuel. "Nonorganic Life." *Incorporations*, edited by Jonathan Crary and Sanford Kwinter. New York: Zone Books, 1992: 129–67.

———. "Virtual Environments and the Concept of Synergy." *Leonardo*, vol. 28, no. 5 1995: 357–60.

———. "Immanence and Transcendence in the Genesis of Form." *The South Atlantic Quarterly*, vol. 96, no. 3, 1997: 499–514.

———. "Meshworks, Hierarchies and Interfaces." *The Virtual Dimension: Architecture, Representation and Crash Culture,* edited by John Beckmann. New york: Princeton Architectural Press, 1998: 275–85.

———. *Intensive Science and Virtual Philosophy*. New York and London: Continuum, 2005.

———. *A Thousand Years of Non-Linear History*. New York: Zone Books, 2011a.

———. *Philosophy and Simulation: The Emergence of Synthetic Reason*. New York: Continuum, 2011b.

Deleuze, Giles. *Bergonism*. Translated by Hugh Tomlinson and Barbara Habberjam. Brooklyn: Zone Books, 1988a.

Deleuze, Gilles. *Foucault*. Translated by Seán Hand. Minneapolis: University of Minnesota Press, 1988b.

———. *The Fold: Leibniz and the Baroque*. Translated by Tom Conley. Minneapolis: University of Minnesota Press, 1993.

———. *Difference and Repetition*. Translated by Paul Patton. New York: Columbia University Press, 1994.

———. *Negotiations*. New York: Columbia University Press, 1995.

———. *Francis Bacon: The Logic of Sensation*. Translated by Daniel W Smith. Cornwall: MPG Books, 2002a.

———. *Nietzsche and Philosophy*. Translated by Hugh Tomlinson. London and New York: Contimuum, 2002b.

———. *Desert Islands and Other Texts*. Translated by Michael Taormina. New York: semiotext(e), 2004.

———. *Cinema 2*. Translated by Hugh Tomlinson and Robert Galeta, 3rd ed. Chippenham, Wiltshire: Continuum, 2005.

Deleuze, Giles and Félix Guattari. *Kafka: Toward a Minor Literature*. Translated by Dana Polan. Minneapolis & London: University of Minesota Press, 1986.

———. *A Thousand Plateaus: Capitalism and Schizophrenia*. Edited and translated by Brian Massumi. Minneapolis: University of Minnesota Press, 1987.

———. *What Is Philosophy?* Translated by Hugh Tomlinson and Graham Burchell. New York: Columbia Universty Press, 1994.

Deleuze, Gilles, Félix Guattari and Michel Focault. *Anti-Oedipus: Capitalism and Schizophrenia*. Translated by Robert Hurley, Mark Seem and Helen Lane. New York: Penguin Group, 2009.

Deleuze, Gilles and Claire Parnet. *Dialogues II*. Translated by Hugh Tomlinson, Barbara Habberjam and Elliot Ross Albert. London and New York: Continuum, 1987.

Derrida, Jacques. "A Certain Impossibility of Saying the Event." *Critical Inquiry* vol. 33, no. 2, 2007: 441–61.

Dery, Mark. *Escape Velocity: Cyberculture at the End of the Century*. New York: Grove Press, 1996.

Downing, Keith and Julian F Miller. "Evolution *In Materio*: Looking Beyond the Silicon Box." *Evolvable Hardware*. IEEE, 2002: 167–76.

Driscoll, Catherine. "The Moving Ground: Locating Everyday Life." *South Atlantic Quarterly*, vol. 100, no. 2, Spring, 2001: 381–98.

Dubberly, Hugh, Paul Pangaro, Usman Haque. "On Modeling: What Is Interaction? Are There Different Types?" *Interactions*, no. January–February, 2009: 69–75.

Dumouchel, Paul. "Simondon's Plea for a Philosophy of Technology." *Inquiry: An Interdisciplinary Journal of Philosophy*, vol. 35, no. 3-4, 1992: 407–21.

Ednie-Brown, Pia. "All-Over, Over-All: Biothing and Emergent Composition." *ArchitDesign*, vol. 76, no.4, 2006: 72–81.

———. "Plastic Super Models: Aesthetics, Architecture and the Model of Emergence." *The Fibreculture Journal*, no. 12, 2008.

———. "The Ethics of the Imperative." *Architectural Design*, vol. 221, no. January–February, 2013: 18–23.

Elsenaar, Arthur and Remko Scha. "Electric Body Manipulation as Performance Art: A Historical Perspective." *Leonardo* vol. 12, no. Pleasure, 2002: 17–28.

Faber, Roland, Henry Krips and Daniel Pettus, editors. *Event and Decision:Ontology and Politics in Badiou, Deleuze and Whitehead.* Newcastle on Tyne: Cambridge Schoars Publishing, 2010.

Fernandez, Maria. "The Body Is More Than Flesh." *Art Journal*, vol. 65, no. 3, 2006.

--------. "Aesthetically Potent Environments, or How Gordon Pask Detourned Intstrumental Cybernetics." *White Heat Cold Logic: British Computer Art 1960-1980*, edited by Charlie Gere Paul Brown, Nicholas Lambert, Catherine Mason. Cambridge, MA: MIT Press, 2009.

Flores, Tatiana. "Rafael Lozano-Hemmer: The Historical (Self-) Concious." *Art Nexus*, vol.7, no. 71, 2008: 66-71.

Foucault, Michel. *The Foucault Reader.* Edited by Paul Rbinow. New York: Random House, 2010.

Frichot, Helene. "Daddy, Why Do Things Have Outlines? Constructing the Architectural Body." *Inflexions*, vol. 6, 2013: 112-24.

Frieling, Rudolf. *The Art of Participation: 1950 to Now.* San Francisco; London: San Francisco Museum of Modern Art, 2008.

Fristch, Johan. "Understanding Affective Engagement as a Resource in Interactive Design." *Nordic Design Conference.* Oslo: Nordes, 2009.

Fritsch, Jonas and Thomas Markussen. "Editorial: Exploring Affect in Interactive Design, Interaction Based Art and Digital Art." *Fibreculture*, vol. 21, 2012: 1-9.

Fuery, Kelli. *New Media: Culture and Image.* Hampshire and New York: Palgrave Macmillan, 2009.

Fuller, Matthew. *Beyond the Blip: Essays on the Culture of Software.* New York: Automedia, 2003.

Gaffney, Peter. "Science in the Gap." *The Force of the Virtual: Deleuze, Science and Philosophy*, edited by Peter Gaffney. Minneapolis: University of Minnesota Press, 2010.

Galanter, Philip. "The Problem with Evolutionary Art Is..." *EvoApplications Part II, LNCS 602*, edited by Cecilia DiChio. Berlin, Heidelberg: Springer-Verlag, 2010: 321–30.

Gibson, James J. *The Ecological Approach to Visual Perception*. Boston: Houghton Mifflin Company, 1979.

Gil, Jose. *Metamorphoses of the Body*. Translated by Stephen Mueke. Mineapolis and London: University of Minnesota Press, 1998.

Glanville, Ralph. "And He Was Magic." *Kybernetes*, vol. 30, no. 5/6, 2001: 652–73.

Golding, Johnny. "Fractal Philosophy (and the Small Matter of Learning How to Listen): Attunement as the Task of Art." *CTheory*, (2010). www.ctheory.net/articles.aspx?id=634. Accessed November 20, 2010.

Golyk, Vladyslav A. "Self-Organized Criticality." web.mit.edu/8.334/www/grades/projects/projects12/V.%20A.%20Golyk.pdf Accessed November 20, 2015.

Goodman, Andrew. "Black Magic: Fragility and Flux and the Rewilding of Art." *Immediations. Art, Media, Event*. Edited by Erin Manning, Anna Munster and Bodil-Marie Stavning Thomsen. Open Humanities Press, Forthcoming, 2018.

Goodman, Andrew and Erin Manning. "Entertaining the Environment: A Conversation." *Fibreculture* vol. 21, 2012: 24–35.

Goodman, Steve. *Sonic Warfare: Sound, Affect and the Ecology of Fear*. Cambridge and London: MIT Press, 2010.

Goodman, Steve and Luciana Parisi. "Extensive Continuum Towards a Rhythmic Anarchitecture." *Inflexions*, vol. 2, 2009.

Gorschluter, Peter. *The Fifth Floor – Ideas Taking Space*. Liverpool: Liverpool University Press, 2009.

Gould, Steven J. "The Evolution of the Life on the Earth." *Scientific American* vol. 271, no. 4, 1994: 84–91.

Grau, Oliver. *Virtual Art: From Illusion to Immersion*. Cambridge and London: MIT Press, 2003.

———. *Mediaarthistories*. Cambridge: MIT Press, 2007.

Gregg, Melissa and Gregory J Seigworth, editors. *The Affect Theory Reader*. Durham and London: Duke Universty Press, 2010.

Grosz, Elizabeth. *Sexual Subversions*. St Leonards: Allen and Unwin, 1989.

———. "A Thousand Tiny Sexes; Feminism and Rhizomatics." *Giles Deleuze and the Theatre of Philosophy*, edited by Constantin V Boundas and Dorothea Olkowski. New York: Routledge, 1994.

———. *Space, Time and Perversion: The Politics of Bodies*. St Leonards: Allen and Unwin, 1995.

———. *Architecture from the Outside: Essays on Virtual and Real Space*. Georgia: MIT Press, 2001.

———. *Chaos, Territory and Art: Deleuze and the Framing of the Earth*. New York: Columbia University Press, 2008.

———. "Identity and Individuation: Some Feminist Reflections." *Being and Technology*, edited by Arne De Boever, Alex Murray, Jon Roffe and Ashley Woodward. Edinburgh: Edinburgh University Press, 2012: 37–56.

Guattari, Félix. "Machinic Heterogenesis." *Rethinking Technologies*, edited by Verena Conley. Minneapolis: University of Minnesota Press, 1993: 13–27.

———. *Chaosmosis: An Ethico-Aesthetic Paradigm*. Translated by Paul Bains and Julian Pefanis. Bloomington: Indiana University Press, 1995a.

———. "On Machines." *Complexity* vol. 6, 1995b: 8–12. www.ntua.gr/archtech/forum/post2006interaction/on_machines.htm. Accessed January 28, 2013.

———. *Chaosophy: Soft Subversions*. New York: semiotext(e), 1996.

———. *The Machinic Unconcious: Essays in Schitzoanalysis*. Los Angeles: semiotext(e), 2007.

———. *The Three Ecologies*. Translated by Ian Pinder and Paul Sutton. London and New York: Continuum, 2008.

Guattari, Félix and Gary Genosho, editors. *The Guattari Reader*. Oxford: Blackwell Publishers, 1996.

Guattari, Félix and Suely Rolnik. *Molecular Revolution in Brazil*. Translated by Karel Clapshaw and Brian Holmes. Los Angeles: semiotext(e), 2005.

Haenaff, Marcel and Anne-Marie Feenberg. "Of Stones, Angels and Humans: Michel Serres and the Global City." *SubStance*, vol. 26, no. 2, i. 83, 1997: 59–80.

Hansen, Lone Koefoed. "The Interface at the Skin." *Interface Criticism:Aesthetics Beyond Buttons*. Edited by Christian Ulrik and Pold Andersen, Soren Bro. Aarhus Aarhus University Press, 2011: 63–90.

Haque, Usman. "Architecture, Interaction, Systems." *AU: Arquitetura & Urbanismo*, vol. 149, no. August, 2006: 1–5. www.haque.co.uk/papers/ArchInterSys.pdf. Accessed December 1, 2013.

———. "The Architectural Relevance of Gordon Pask." *Architectural Design*, vol. 77, no. 4, 2007: 54–61.

Haraway, Donna. *Modest_Witness@Second_Milleniu.Femalemanc_Meets_Oncomousetm: Feminism and Technoscience*. London: Routledge, 1997.

———. *Staying with the Trouble: Making Kin in the Chthulucene*. Durham: Duke University Press, 2016.

Harney, Stefano and Fred Moten. *The Undercommons: Fugitive Planning and Black Study*. New York: Minor Compositions, 2013.

Harris, Paul A. "The Itinerant Theorist: Nature and Knowledge/Ecology and Topology in Michel Serres." *SubStance*, vol. 26, no. 2, i. 83, 1997: 37-58.

Hauser, Jens, editor. *Sk-Interfaces*. Liverpool: Liverpool Universty Press, 2008.

Henry, Granville C. *Forms of Concrescence: Alfred North Whitehead's Philosophy and Computer Programming Structures*. Canbury and London: Associated University Presses, 1993.

Highmore, Ben. *Everyday Life and Cultural Theory*. London: Routledge, 2002.

Hill, David and Rafael Lozano-Hemmer. *Under Scan*. Italy: Graphic Thought Facility, 2007.

Hinterding, Joyce, "Artist Joyce Hinterding: Graphite is a Conductor." YouTube.

www.youtube.com/watch?v=AQRHon2eiKc. Accessed October 12, 2014.

Hurowitz, Michael and Timothy Leary, editors. *Chaos and Cyberculture*. California: Ronin Publishing, 1994.

Idhe, Don. *Listening and Voice: A Phenomonology of Sound*. Athens: Ohio University Press, 1976.

Ingold, Tim. *Being Alive: Essays on Movement, Knowledge and Description*. London and New york: Routledge, 2011.

Irwin, Robert. *Notes Towards a Conditional Art*. Los Ageles: J Paul Getty Museum, 2011.

James, William. *Essays in Radical Empiricism*. Memphis: Longmans, Green and Co., 2010.

Jay, Martin. "Scopic Regimes of Modernity." *Vision and Visuality*, edited by Hal Foster. Seattle: Bay Press, 1988: 3-23.

Jones, Amelia. *Self/Image: Technologies, Representation and the Contemporary Subject*. New York: Routledge, 2006.

Jones, Judith. *Intensity: An Essay in Whiteheadian Ontology*. Nashville: Vanderbilt University Press, 1998.

Kahn, Douglas. *Noise, Water, Meat: A History of Sound in the Arts*. Cambridge and London: MIT Press, 1999.

Kahn, Douglas. *Earth Sound Earth Signal*. Berkley and Los Angeles: University of California Press, 2013.

Keller, Catherine and Anne Daniell, editors. *Process and Difference: Between Cosmological and Poststructuralist Postmodernisms*. Albany: State University of New York Press, 2002.

Kirby, Peter. *Binary Lives: Steina and Woody Vasulka*. Grand Canal and Media Art Services, 1996.

Kosofsky Sedgwick, Eve. *Touching Feeling: Affect, Pedagogy, Performativity*. Durham and London: Duke Universty Press, 2003.

Lamant, Michelle. "Untitled." *The American Journal of Sociology*, vol. 93, no. 3, 1987: 720–1.

Lamarre, Thomas. "Humans and Machines." *Inflexions*, vol. 5, 2012: 29–67.

Langer, Beryl. "Untitled." *Contemporary Sociology*, vol. 17, no. 1, 1988: 122–4.

Latour, Bruno. "On Interobjectivity." *Mind, Culture and Activity*, vol. 3, no. 4, 1996: 228–45.

Laughlin, Robert B. *A Different Universe: Reinventing Physics from the Bottom Down*. New York: Basic Books, 2005.

Lewin, Walter and The Center for Future Civic Media. "Lecture 16: Electromagnetic Induction, Faraday's Law, Lenz Law, Complete Breakdown of Intuition, Non-Conservative Fields." *MIT 8.02 Physics II*, videolectures.net. videolectures.net/mit802s02_lewin_lec16/. Accessed November 8, 2015.

Levine, Joshua. "Experimental Visual Experience Devices." *Leonardo*, vol. 33, no. 1, 2000: 27–33.

Levy, Pierre. *Collective Intelligence: Mankind's Emerging World in Cyberspace*. Cambridge: Helix Books, 1997.

———. *Cyberculture* Electronic Mediations. Minneapolis: University of Minnesota Press, 2001.

Lingis, Alphonso. *Excesses*. Albany: State University of New York Press, 1983.

———. "The Society of Dismembered Body Parts." *Giles Deleuze and the Theatre of Philosophy*, edited by Constantin V Boundas and Dorothea Olkowski. New York: Routledge, 1994.

———. *Sensation: Intelligability in Sensibility*. New York: Humanity Books, 1996.

———. *The Imperative*. Bloomington: Indianna University Press, 1998.

———. "Animal Body, Inhuman Face." *Zoontologies: The Question of the Animal*. Minneapolis: University of Minnesota Press, 2003: 165–82.

———. *Body Transformations: Evolutions and Atavisms in Culture*. New York: Routledge, 2005.

Lorraine, Tamsin. "The Nomadic Subject in Smooth Space." *Deleuze and Space*, edited by Ian Buchanan and Greg Lambert. Edinburgh: Edinburgh University Press, 2005.

Lotti, Laura. "Making Sense of Power: Repurposing Gilbert Simondon's Philosophy of Individuation for a Mechanist Approach to Capitalism (by Way of François Laruelle)." *Platform: Journal of Media and Communication* vol. 6, 2015: 22–33.

Loveless, Natalie S. "Practice in the Flesh of Theory: Art, Research, and the Fine Arts PhD." *Canadian Journal of Communication*, vol. 37, no. 1, 2012: 93–108.

Lozano-Hemmer, Rafael. "Perverting Technological Correctness." *Leonardo*, vol. 29, no. 1, 1996: 5–15.

———. "Interview by Jose Luis Barrios." Edited by Gallery Guy Bärtschi. Genève, Switzerland: Gallery Guy Bärtschi, 2005. www.lozano-hemmer.com/publications.php?subtype=Interviews. Accessed April 11, 2013.

———. "Some Things Happen More Often Than All the Time." Edited by Venice Bienalle Mexico Pavillion. Spain: Turner, 2007.

———. *Rafael Lozano-Hemmer*. Radio Program. Broadcast June 18, 2010, 10:49 am. Melbourne: Radio National, 2010.

Lozano-Hemmer, Rafael, Marie-Pier Boucher and Patrick Harrop. "Alien Media: An Interview with Rafael Lozano-Hemmer." *Inflexions*, vol. 5, 2012: 149–60.

Lozano-Hemmer, Rafael, editor. "Vectorial Elevation: Relational Architecture No. 4." Edited by National Council for Culture and the Arts. Son Torge: Mexico National Council for Culture and the Arts, 2000.

Lucaciu, Mihai. "This Scream I've Thrown Ot Is a Dream: Corporeal Transformation through Sound, an Artaudian Experiement." *Studies in Musical Theatre*, vol. 4, no. 1, 2010: 67–74.

Lynn, Greg. *Folds, Bodies and Blobs*: Depot Legal: Bibliotheque Royale, 1998.

Mackenzie, Adrian. *Transductions: Bodies and Machines at Speed*. London: Continuum, 2002.

———. *Cutting Code: Software and Sociality*. New York: Peter Lang, 2006.

———. "Wirelessness as Experience of Transition." *Fibreculture*, vol. 13, 2008.

Manning, Erin. *Politics of Touch: Sense, Movement, Sovereinty*. Minneapolis: University of Minnesota Press, 2007.

―――――. "Creative Propositions for Thought in Motion." *Inflexions*, vol. 1, 2008.

―――――. *Relationscapes*. Cambridge: MIT Press, 2009.

―――――. "Always More Than One: The Collectivity of 'a Life'." *Body and Society*, vol. 16, no. 1, 2010: 117–27.

―――――. *Always More Than One: Individuation's Dance*. Durham: Duke University Press, 2013a.

―――――. "The Dance of Attention." *Inflexions*, vol. 6, 2013b.

―――――. "Weather Patterns, or How Minor Gestures Entertain the Environment." *Complex Ubiquity Effects: Individuating, Situating, Eventualizing*, edited by Jay David Bolter Ulrick Ekman, Lily Diaz, Morten Sondergaard, Maria Engberg. New York: Routledge, 2016a.

―――――. *The Minor Gesture*. Durham: Duke University Press, 2016b.

Manning, Erin and Brian Massumi. "Propositions for an Expanded Gallery: Generating the Impossible." Edited by participants in the *Generating the Impossible 2011 Convergence*, 2010: 1–43.

Manning, Erin, Anna Munster and Bodil Marie Stavning Thomsen, editors. *Immediations*, Open Humanities Press, Forthcoming, 2018.

Manovich, Lev. "On Totalitarian Interactivity (Notes from the Enemy of the People)." manovich.net/index.php/projects/on-totalitarian-interactivity. Accessed October 20, 2010.

―――――. *The Language of New Media*. Cambridge: MIT Press, 2001.

―――――. "Don't Call It Art: Ars Electronica 2003." *Ars Electronica 2003*, 2003. manovich.net/index.php/projects/don-t-call-it-art. Accessed October 20, 2010.

―――――. "New Media from Borges to HTML." *The New Media Reader*, edited by Noah Wardrip-Fruin and Nick Montfort: MIT Press, 2003.

Martin, S, A Ruiz and S Rolnik. "The Experimental Exercise of Freedom." Edited by Los Angelas Museum of Contemporary Art. Los Angeles Los Angeles Museum of Contemporary Art, 2000.

Massumi, Brian. *A User's Guide to Capitalism and Schizophrenia: Deviations from Deleuze and Guattari*. Cambridge, MA: MIT Press, 1992.

-------. "Interface and Active Space: Human Machine Design." *Sixth International Symposium on Electronic Art*. Montreal, Canada, 1995. www.brianmassumi.com/textes/INTERFACE%20AND%20ACTIVE%20SPACE.pdf. Accessed August 12, 2011.

-------. "Sensing the Virtual, Building the Insensible." *Hypersurface Architecture*, vol. 68, no. 5/6, 1998: 16–24. www.brianmassumi.com/textes/Sensing%20the%20Virtual.pdf. Accessed April 13, 2010.

-------. "The Interface and I." *Artbyte: The Magazine of Digital Arts*, vol. 1, no. 6, 1999: 30–7.

-------. "Too-Blue: Color Patch for an Expanded Empiricism." *Cultural Studies*, vol. 14, no. 2, 2000: 177–226.

-------. Navigating Movements. c2001. www.brianmassumi.com/interviews/NAVIGATINGMOVEMENTS.pdf. Accessed April 13, 2010.

-------. *Parables for the Virtual : Movement, Affect, Sensation* Post-Contemporary Interventions. Durham: Duke University Press, 2002.

-------. "Flash in Japan: Brian Massumi on Rafael Lozano-Hemmer's Amodal Suspension." *Artforum International*, vol. 42, no. 3, 2003a: 37–9.

-------. "Urban Appointment: A Possible Rendez-Vous with the City." *Making Art of Databases*, edited by Joke Brouwer and Arjen Mulder. Rotterdam: V2 Organisative, 2003b: 28–55.

———. "The Thinking-Feeling of What Happens." *Inflexions*, vol. 1, 2008.

———. "On Critique." *Inflexions*, vol. 4, 2010: 337–40.

———. *Semblance and Event*. Cambridge: MIT press, 2011.

———. *What Animals Teach Us About Politics*. Durham: Duke University Press, 2014.

Massumi, Brian, editor. *A Shock to Thought: Expression after Deleuze and Guattari*. London: Routledge, 2002.

Massumi, Brian, Arne De Boever, Alex Murray and Jon Rolfe. "Technical Mentality Revisited: Brian Massumi." *Parrhesia*, vol. 7, 2009: 36–45.

Massumi, Brian and Joel McKim. "Of Microperception and Micropolitics: An Interview with Brian Massumi." *Inflexions*, vol. 3, 2009.

Maturana, Humberto R. and Francesco J Varela. *Autopoiesis and Cognition: The Realization of the Living*. Dordrecht: Kluner Academic Publisher's Group, 1980.

McCormack, Jon, Oliver Bown, Jonathan McCabe, Alan Dorin and Gordon Monro and Mitchell Whitelaw. "Ten Questions Concerning Generative Computer Art." *Leonardo*, vol. 47, no. 2, 2014: 135–41.

McCormack, Jon. "Evolving Sonic Ecosystems." *Kybernetics*, vol. 32, no. 1/2, 2003: 184–202.

———. "Art, Aesthetics, Evolution." *EvoMUSART 2013*, edited by James McDermott, Adrian Carballa and Penousal Machado. Vienna, Austria: Heidelberg, 2013: 1–12

McCormack, Jon and Mark d'Inverno, editors. *Computers and Creativity*. Heidleberg, New York, London, Dordrecht: Springer, 2012.

McQuire, Scott. "Mobility, Cosmopolitanism and Public Space in the Media City." *Urban Screen Reader*, edited by Meredith Martin and Sabine Niederer Scott McQuire. Amsterdam: Institute of Network Cultures, 2009: 45–64.

de Mèredieu, Florence. *Digital and Video Art*. Edinborough: Chambers Harrop Publishers Ltd, 2003.

Michael, Mike. "These Boots Are Made for Walking...Mundane Technology, the Body and Human-Environment Relations." *Body and Society*, vol. 6, 2000: 107–26.

Mitchell, Robert. "Simondon, Bio-Art and the Milieu of Biotechnology." *Inflexions*, vol. 5, 2012: 68–110.

Miyazaki, Shintaro. "Algorhythmics: Understanding Micro-Temporality in Computational Cultures." *Computational Culture*, vol. 2, 2012: 1–16. computationalculture.net/article/algorhythmics-understanding-micro-temporality-in-computational-cultures. Accessed December 14, 2013.

Mock, Roberta. *Walking, Writing, Performance*. Bristol: Intellect Books, 2009.

Morris, Brian. "What We Talk About When We Talk About 'Walking the City'." *Cultural Studies* vol. 18, no. 5, 2004: 675–97.

Morris, Meaghan. "Banality in Cultural Studies." *Logics of Television*, edited by Patricia Mellencamp. Bloomington: Indianna University Press, 1990: 14–43

Moulard-Leonard, Valentine. *Bergson-Deleuze Encouters: Transcendental Experience and the Thought of the Virtual*. Albany: University of New York Press, 2008.

Munster, Anna. *Materializing New Media: Embodiment in Information Aesthetics*. Hanover and London: University of New England Press, 2006.

Murphie, Andrew. "Computers Are Not Theatre: The Machine in the Ghost in Giles Deleuze and Felix Guattari's Thought." *Convergence*, vol. 2, no. 2, 1996: 80–110.

---. "Becoming Interactive – Interactive Becomings: A Deleuze-Guattarian Approach to an Ethics of Interaction." PhD dissertation. Macquarie University, 1997.

---. "Differential Life, Perception and the Nervous Elements: Whitehead, Bergson and Virno on the Technics of Living." *Culture Machine*, vol. 7, 2005a: Unpaginated. www.culturemachine.net/index.php.cm/rt/printerFriendly/32/39. Accessed January 23, 2013.

---. "Vibrations in the Air: Performance and Interactive Technics." *Performance Paradigm*, vol. 1, 2005b: 31–46. www.performanceparadigm.net/journal/issue-1/articles/vibrations-in-the-air-performance-and-interactive-technics/. Issue 1. Accessed December 18, 2012.

---. "Convolving Signals: Thinking the Performance of Computational Processes." *Performance Paradigm*, vol. 9, 2013: 1–21.

---. "The World as Medium: Whitehead's Media Philosophy." *Immediations. Art, Media, Event*, edited by Erin Manning, Anna Munster and Bodil-Marie Stavning Thomsen. Open Humanities Press, Forthcoming, 2018: 1–31.

Murphie, Andrew and John Potts. *Culture and Technology*. New York: Palgrave Macmillan, 2003.

Nash, Adam. "Affect and the Medium of Digital Data." *Fibreculture*, vol. 21, 2012: 10–30.

Newman, James. "Parts and Patches: Digital Games as Unstable Objects." *Convergence*, vol. 18, 2012: 135–45.

O'Sullivan, Simon. *Art Encounters with Deleuze and Guattari: Thought Beyond Representation*. Hampshire and New York: Palgrave McMillan, 2006.

Osthoff, Simone. "Lygia Clark and Hélio Oiticica: A Legacy of Interactivity and Participation for a Telematic Future." *Leonardo*, vol. 30, no. 4, 1997: 279–89.

Parisi, Luciana. *Contagious Architecture: Computation, Aesthetics and Space*. Cambridge, MA: MIT Press, 2013.

Pask, Gordon. "Physical Analogues to the Growth of a Concept." *Symposium on the Mechanization of Thought Processes*. National Physics Laboratory, Teddington, Middlesex: HMSO, 1958: 1–40.

———. "The Natural History of Networks." *Self-Organizing Systems*, edited by Marshall C Yovitts and Scott Cameron. Oxford: Pergamon Press, 1960: 232–61.

———. *An Approach to Cybernetics*. London: Hutchinson and Co., 1961a.

———. "A Proposed Evolutionary Model." *Principles of Self-Organization*, edited by Heinz Von Foerster and George Zopf. London: Pergamon Press, 1961b: 229–53.

———. "Organizational Closure of Potentially Concious Systems." *Autopoiesis: A Theory of Living Organisms*, edited by Milan Zelany, 3. New York: North Holland Elsevier, 1980.

Pasquinelli, Matteo. *Animal Spirits: A Bestiary of the Commons*. Rotterdam: NAi Publishers, 2008.

Peacock, Alan, "Towards an Aesthetic of the Interactive." *Soundtoys*. 2010. www.soundtoys.net/journals/towards-an-aesthetic-of. Accessed August 25, 2010.

Penny, Simon. "Desire for Virtual Space: The Technological Imaginary in 1990's Media Art". 2009. simonpenny.net/texts/Resources/desireforvirtualspace.pdf. Accessed August 10, 2010.

———. "Towards a Performative Aesthetics of Interactivity." *Fibreculture*, vol. 19, 2011: 72–109.

———. "Trying to Be Calm: Ubiquity, Cognitivism, and Embodiment." *Throughout: Art and Culture Emerging with Ubiquitous Computing*, edited by Ulrik Ekman: Cambridge, MA: MIT Press, 2013: 263–78.

Pickering, Andrew. *The Mangel of Practice: Time, Agency and Science*. Chicago and London: University of Chicago Press, 1995.

--------. "Beyond Design: Cybernetics, Biological Computers and Hylozoism." *Synthese*, vol. 168, no. 3, 2009: 469-91.

--------. "Cybernetics and the Mangle: Ashby, Beer and Pask." 1-16. Paris: Centre Koyré, 2000.

--------. "Gordon Pask: From Chemical Computers to Adaptive Architecture." *The Cybernetic Brain: Sketches of Another Future*. University of Chicago Press, 2010: 309-77.

Poissant, Louise. "The Passage from Material to Interface." *Mediaarthistories*, edited by Oliver Grau. Cambridge, MA: MIT Press, 2007.

Pold, Søren. "Interface Realisms: The Interface as Aesthetic Form." *Postmodern Culture*, vol. 15, no. 2, 2005: unpaginated.

Portanova, Stamatia. "Infinity in a Step: On the Compression and Complexity of a Movement of Thought." *Inflexions*, vol. 1, 2008: 1-15.

--------. "Introduction: The Complexity of Collabor(El)Ation." *Inflexions*, vol. 2, 2008: 1-17.

--------. "Digital Strain." *Angelaki: Journal of the Theoretical Humanities*, vol. 15, no. 2, 2010: 149-69. dx.doi.org/10.1080/0969725X.2010.521410. Accessed January 1, 2014.

--------. *Moving Without a Body: Digital Philosophy and Choreographic Thoughts*. Cambridge, Massachusetts, London: MIT Press, 2013.

Prigogine, Ilya. *From Being to Becoming: Time and Complexity in the Physical Sciences*. San Francisco: Freeman and Co., 1980.

Prigogine, Ilya and Isabelle Stengers. *The End of Certainty: Time, Chaos and the New Laws of Nature*. New York, London, Toronto. Sydney and Singapore: The Free Press, 1996.

Puig de la Bellacasa, Maria. "Touching Technologies, Touching Visions: The Reclaiming of Sensorial Eperience and the Politics of Speculative Thinking." *Subjectivity*, vol. 28, 2009: 297–315.

Rancière, Jacques. *Aesthetics and Its Discontents*. Cambridge, MA: Polity Press, 2009.

Roads, Curtis. *Microsound*. Cambridge and London: MIT Press, 2001.

Robinson, Jeffery C. *The Walk: Notes on a Romantic Image*. Norman: University of Oklahoma Press, 1989.

Rocha, Luis Mateus. "Adaptive Recommendation and Open-Ended Semiosis." *Kybernetes*, vol. 30, no. 5/6, 2001: 821–54.

Rokeby, David. "Transforming Mirrors". David Rokeby. NDawww.davidrokeby.com/mirrorsconclusion.html. Accessed May 28, 2013.

Rokeby, David. "The Construction of Experience: Interface as Content". David Rokeby. NDb. www.davidrokeby.com/experience.html. Accessed May 28, 2013.

Salter, Chris. "Just Noticable Difference: Ontogenisis, Performativity and the Perceptual Gap." *Inflexions*, vol. 5, 2012: 111–30.

Saper, Craig "Electronic Media Studies: From Video Art to Artificial Invention." *Leonardo*, vol. 20, no. 3, 1991: 114–34.

Sarkis, Mona. "Interactivity Means Interpassivity." *Art and cyberculture*, vol. 69, no. August, 1993: 13–16.

Sauvagnargues, Anne. "Crystals and Membranes: Individuation and Temporality." *Being and Technology*, edited by Arne De Boever, Alex Murray, Jon Roffe and Ashley Woodward. Edinburgh: Edinburgh University Press, 2012: 57–72.

Scholder, Amy and Jordan Crandall, editors. *Interaction: Artistic Practice in the Network*. New York: DAP, 2001.

Semetsky, Inna. "The Complexity of Individuation." *International Journal of Applied Psychoanaltic Studies*, vol. 1, no. 4, 2004: 324–46.

Serres, Michel. *Genesis*. Michegan: University of Michigan Press, 1995.

———. *The Parasite*. Minneapolis: University of Minnesota Press, 2007.

———. *The Five Senses: A Philosophy of Mingled Sense (I)*. London and New York: Continuum, 2008.

———. "Variations on the Body." ND. www.michelserres.com. Accessed April 2, 2011.

Serres, Michel and Bruno Latour. *Conversations on Science, Culture and Time*. Ann Abor: University of Michigan Press, 2011.

Shanken, Edward, editor. *Art and Electronic Media*. London: Phaidon, 2009.

Shannon, Claude E. and Warren Weaver. *The Mathematical Theory of Communication*. Urbana: University of Illinois Press, 1967.

Shaviro, Steven. *Without Criteria: Kant, Whitehead, Deleuze and Aesthetics*. Cambridge, London: MIT Press, 2009.

———. "Interstitial Life: Remarks on Causality and Purpose in Biology." *The Force of the Virtual: Deleuze, Science and Philosophy*, edited by Peter Gaffney. Minneapolis: University of Minnesota Press, 2010: 133–46.

———. *The Universe of Things: On Speculative Realism*. Minneapolis: University of Minnesota Press, 2014.

Simondon, Gilbert. *On the Mode of Existence of Technical Objects*, 1980. aaaaarg.org/text/3070/mode-existence-technical-objects. Accessed February 2, 2012.

———. "The Genesis of the Individual." *Incorporations*. Edited by Jonathan Crary and Sanford Kwinter. New York: Zone Books, 1992: 297–319.

———. "Topology, Chronology, and Order of Magnitude of Physical Individuation." *L'individu Et Sa Genèse Physico-Biologique*. Grenoble: Millon, 1995a: 146–51.

———. "Topology and Ontogenesis." *L'individu Et Sa Genése Physico-Biologique*. Grenoble: Millon, 1995b: 222–7.

———. "Form and Matter." *The Individual and Its Physical-Biological Genesis*. 2007. Translated by Taylor Atkins. Fractal Ontology. www.fractal ontology.wordpress.com/2007/10/13/translation-simondon-and-the-physico-biological-genesis-of-the-individual. Accessed December 12, 2016.

———. "The Position of the Problem of Ontogenesis." *Parrhesia*, vol. 7, 2009: 4-16.

———. "Technical Mentality." *Being and Technology*, edited by Arne De Boever, Alex Murray, Jon Roffe and Ashley Woodward. Edingburgh: Edinburgh University Press, 2012: 1–18.

Smith, Marquard and Julie Clarke. *Stelarc: The Monograph*. Cambridge, MA: MIT Press, 2005.

Solnit, Rebecca. *Wanderlust: A History of Walking*. Ringwood: Penguin Books, 2000.

Stelarc. "Prosthetics, Robotics and Remote Existence: Postevolutionary Strategies." *Leonardo*, vol. 24, no. 5, 1991: 591–5.

Stengers, Isabelle. *Power and Invention*. Minneapolis: University of Minnesta Press, 1997.

———. "The Challenge of Complexity: Unfolding the Ethics of Science in Memorium Ilya Prigogine." *E:CO*, vol. 6, no. 1–2, 2004: 92–9.

———. "Whitehead's Account of the Sixth Day." *Configurations*, vol. 13, 2005: 35–55.

———. "Experimenting with Refrains: Subjectivity and the Challenge of Escaping Modern Dualism." *Subjectivity*, vol. 22, 2008: 38–59.

———. *Cosmopolitics I*. Translated by Robert Bononno. Minneapolis: University of Minesota Press, 2010

———. *Thinking with Whitehead: A Free and Wild Creation of Concepts*. Cambridge, MA: Harvard University Press, 2011.

Stenner, Paul. "AN Whitehead and Subjectivity." *Subjectivity*, vol. 22, 2008: 90–109.

Stern, Nathaniel. "The Implicit Body as Performative: Analysing Interactive Art." *Leonardo*, vol. 44, no. 3, 2011: 233–8.

———. "Interactive Art and Embodiment: The Implicit Body as Performance." Prepublished manuscript, 2012.

———. "'Compressionism' – Scanner Performance Art and Printmaking".Online video. 2013a. www.youtube.com/watch?v=ws2ymIITvdI. Accessed February 20, 2013.

———. "Compressionism Documentation." Nathaniel Stern. 2013b. nathanielstern.com/artwork/compressionism/. Accessed February 20, 2013.

Suchan, Jaroslaw. "Katarzyna Kobro / Lygia Clark / [Curated by] Jaroslaw Suchan." Edited by Muzeum Sztuki. Lodz: Muzeum Sztuki, 2008.

Thomsen, Bodil-Maree. "The Haptic Interface: On Signal Transmissions and Events." *Interface Criticism:Aesthetics Beyond Buttons*. Edited by Christian Ulrik and Pold Andersen, Søren Bro. Aarhus: Aarhus University Press, 2011.

Tucker, Ian. "Sense and the Limits of Knowledge: Bodily Connections in the Work of Serres." *Theory, Culture and Society*, vol. 28, no. 1, 2011: 149–60.

Varela, Francisco J. "The Specious Present: A Neurophenomenology of Time Consciousness." *Naturalizing Phenomenology: Issues in Contemporary Phenomenology and Cognitive Science*. Edited by FJ Varela, J Petitot, JM Roy, B Pachoud. Stanford: Stanford University Press, 1997: 266–314.

Varela, Francisco J, Evan Thompson and Eleanor Rosch. *The Embodied Mind*. Cambridge, MA: MIT Press, 1992.

Voegelin, Salomé. *Listening to Noise and Silence:Towards a Philosophy of Sound Art*. London, New York: Continuum, 2011.

Vollrath, Chad. "Becoming Analogical." *Reviews in Cultural Theory*, vol. 4, no. 1, 2013: 42–8.

Wall-Smith, Matt. "Toward an Ontology of Mutual Recursion: Models, Mind and Media." *Fibreculture*, vol. 12, no. Metamodels, 2008: 1–24.

Watson, Janell. "Schitzoanalysis as Metamodeling." *Fibreculture, vol.* 12, no. Metamodels, 2008: 1–18.

Weiss, Allen. "Radio, Death and the Devil: Artaud's Pour En Finer Avec Le Jugement De Dieu." *Wireless Imagination: Sound, Radio and the Avante-Garde*, edited by Douglas Kahn and Gregory Whitehead. Cambridge, MA and London: MIT Press, 1992.

Whitehead, Alfred North. "Mathematics as an Element in the History of Thought." *The World of Mathematics*, edited by James R Newman. Redmond: Tempus, 1957: 402–17.

———. *Adventures of Ideas*. New York: Free Press, 1967.

———. *Modes of Thought*. New York: Free Press, 1968.

———. *Process and Reality*. New York: Free Press, 1978.

———. *An Introduction to Mathematics*: Project Gutenberg, 2012. www.gutenberg.org/files/41568/41568-pdf. Accessed December 27, 2013.

———. *Symbolism: Its Meaning and Effect*. Business and Leadership Publishing. Kindle Edition, 2014.

Wilden, Anthony. *Systems and Structures: Essays in Communication and Exchange*. New York: Tavistock Publications, 1980.

Wood, Aylish. *Digital Encounters*. New York: Routledge, 2007.

Yates, Julian. "Towards a Theory of Agentive Drift; or, a Particular Fondness for Oranges Circa 1597." *Parallax*, vol. 8, no. 1, 2002: 47–58. dx.doi.org/10.1080/13534640110119614. Accessed March 20, 2012.

Zylinska, Joanna, editor. *The Cyborg Experiments*. Cornwall: Continuum, 2002.

Index

Aesthetics 13, 34, 206, 262 note 135.
   and politics 231, 275 note 213, 276 note 222.

Affect 12, 18-20, 47, 50, 61-63, 66, 74, 90-91, 98.

Affect theory 91, 157, 278 note 231.

Affectual tonality 104, 154, 169, 190, 193, 267 note 165.

Affirmation 16-17, 237.

Affordance 111, 118-122, 132, 139, 162, 269 note 181.

Agency 14, 59, 69-72, 81-82, 96, 102, 135, 141, 147, 152, 156, 256 note 96, 261 notes 129-131, 276 note 222.

Algorithm 15, 153, 199-225, 236, 238, 287 notes 300-301, 288 note 305, 290 note 309, 293 notes 321-322, 294 note 329, 294 note 335, 295 note 340, 295 note 344, 298 note 366, 299 note 372.

Generative algorithm 28, 103, 203-210, 246 note 33, 277 note 225, 289 note 308, 293 note 321.

Analogue 203, 215,
   and digital 181, 194, 203-5, 209, 215, 225, 255 note 88, 273 note 201, 281 note 259, 291 note 310, 291 note 312.

Arakawa and Madeline Gins 47, 112-113, 120-122, 128, 133-134, 145, 149-150, 191, 250 note 61, 270-271 notes 185-188, 280 note 254.

Ascott, Roy 32, 37, 38, 46, 291 note 313.

Associated milieu 72, 141, 148, 181, 190, 238, 284 note 285.

Artaud 159-160, 279 note 236, 281 note 260.

Attractor 167, 210, 218-224, 279 note 243, 281 note 257, 288 note 304, 292 note 319, 297 note 350-351, 297 notes 353-354, 297 note 356, 298 note 359, 298 note 361.

Autopoiesis 65-66, 207, 254 note 79, 257 note 103, 258 note 111.

Bak, Per 70, 256 note 95, 264 note 144, 285 note 291, 289-290 note 308.

Index 331

Barad, Karen 42, 44, 61, 161, 164, 168, 244 note 17, 245 note 23, 250 note64, 261 note 130, 278 note 231 280 note 151.

Bennett, Jane 59, 67, 96-97, 141, 146, 174, 261 note 131.

Bertelsen, Lone 23, 91, 151, 157, 161, 250 note 64, 278 note 231.

Binary code 204, 212, 294 note 331.

Bogue, Ronald 69, 281 note 259, 295 note 339.

Braidotti, Rosi 19, 40, 60, 90, 176, 181, 234, 236, 239, 254 note 83, 259 note 114, 265 note 149, 283 note 268, 299 note 373.

Capacities 14, 19-20, 23, 47, 55, 57, 61-65, 72, 87-91, 95-96, 113, 129-131, 145, 156, 160-165, 170, 208, 213, 222, 227-228, 230, 238-239, 242 note 11, 254 note 87, 270 note 182, 275 note 210, 289 note 307, 293 note 321, 296 note 348.

Cariani, Peter 292 note 316.

Casual efficacy 135-140, 143, 145, 150-151, 154, 246 note 37, 274 note 207, 275 notes 208, 209, 211 & 213, 276 note 214, 277 note 226, 295 note 341.
see also presentational immediacy

Causal chain 73, 100, 137, 196, 205, 214-215, 222, 223, 228, 273 note 201, 298 note 365.

Chaitlin, Gregory 212, 294 note 328, 294 notes 330-332.
see also Omega

Chesworth, David and Sonia Leber 162, 166, 279 note 244.

Clark, Lygia 32, 46, 47, 140, 142, 149, 249 note 59, 268 note 170.

Collective individuation 70, 72, 122, 136, 142, 150, 174, 183, 189-190, 217, 224, 228-229, 284 note 284.

Combes, Muriel 23, 98, 158, 164, 174, 183, 189, 250 note 62, 278 note 233, 284 note 283.

Communication theory 101-102.

Complex feeling 21, 79-80, 255 note 90, 261 note 133, 276 note 220.

Conceptual feeling 78, 83-6, 88, 95, 217, 263 note 140, 284 note 279.

Concrescence 12, 21, 45, 68, 78, 79-84, 85-86, 93, 95, 108, 137, 141, 146, 158-159, 174-175, 188, 217, 239, 260 note 122, 260 note 128, 263 note 140, 184 note 286.

Concretisation 61, 64, 65-66, 72, 181, 191-192, 195-196, 222, 224, 225, 229, 283 note 274, 285 note 288, 286 note 293, 286 note 296.

332 Index

Contrast 75, 78, 80-84, 85-86, 90, 93-96, 99, 116, 124, 136, 157-158, 160, 164, 169, 173, 188, 192, 195, 196, 214, 216, 217, 220, 225, 133, 238, 239-240, 258 note 108, 260 note 125, 262 note 135, 269 note 178, 278 note 232, 278 note 234.

Conversation theory 47.

Creativity 12, 69-71, 82, 89, 97, 100, 108, 115, 157, 177, 210, 253 note 77, 265 note 147, 279 note 240, 289 note 308.

Cybernetics 250 note 62, 258 note 111, 283 note 270.
   see also second-order cybernetics

Cyborg 250 note 62.

Darwin, Charles 76-77, 87-88, 264 note 142, 264 note 144, 265 note 147.

Datum 21, 79-83, 93, 95, 105, 137, 142-143, 146, 158, 211, 215, 233, 242 note 9, 262 note 135, 263 note 140.

DeLanda, Manuel 59, 61, 67, 84, 114, 191, 208, 214-215, 219-221, 222, 224, 254 note 78, 254 note 85, 257 note 105, 274 note 208, 292 note 319, 295 note 342, 296 notes 347-349, 297 note 350, 297 note 353.

De Certeau, Gilles 25, 110-115, 130, 253 note 74, 253 note 77, 268 note 173, 269 note 175, 271 note 191.

Deleuze 43, 92, 97, 126, 141, 148, 149, 151, 159, 160, 168, 189-190, 283 note 273, 284 note 278, 284 note 280.
   and diagram 188, 192, 286 note 294,
   and difference 84, 85, 99, 101, 107, 116, 156, 158, 188, 254 note 86, 260 note 124, 266 note 154, 283 note 275, 297 note 351.
   and Guattari 25, 56, 57-59, 63, 90, 111, 116, 127, 129, 149, 273 note 200,
   and the virtual 150, 169, 172-173.

Dery, Mark 40, 41, 48, 199, 247 note 41, 250 note 62, 293 note 322.

Didacticism 27, 37, 68.

Difference 22-23, 59, 61-65, 71, 78-80, 88, 91, 93-94, 99-104, 107-109, 156, 157, 163-164, 169, 174, 183, 187-188, 196, 208, 216, 220, 233, 236, 254 note 87, 266 note 154, 278 note234, 283 note 275, 297 note 354.

Differential 15, 22, 60, 75-76, 80, 92, 96, 100, 113, 116, 134, 153, 157, 162, 172, 173-175, 183, 214, 217, 219, 221, 238, 239, 240, 266 note 161, 297 note 351.

Diffraction 156, 162-168, 175, 238256 note 100, 281 note 258.

Diagram 104, 134, 150, 188, 191-193, 225, 286 note 294.

Drift 65-66, 69-74, 99, 101, 107, 205, 225, 256 note 96, 257 note 103, 258 note 110, 258 note 111.

Ecology 20-21, 49, 74, 79, 82-83, 87-88, 97, 106, 114, 122, 134, 147-149, 151-152, 154, 156, 164-166, 174-176, 191, 207, 223-224, 235, 236-237, 274 note 205, 282 note 265.
and intelligence 89, 93, 265 note 147.
and responsibility 23, 91, 140, 146, 237-239, 256 note 94.
see also gathering ecology, meshwork

Embodiment 35, 41, 48, 113, 122, 163, 243 note 16, 248 note 49, 268 note 173.

Entertainment 135-136, 146.

Entity 18, 21-22, 24, 45, 66, 68, 75, 77-83, 86, 95, 99, 141-142, 158-159, 181-182, 210-212, 233, 242 note 10, 249 note 52, 255 notes 90-91, 258 note 113, 260 note 118, 260 note 122, 261 note 134, 262 note 135, 263 note 140, 264 note 143, 284 note 283, 287 note 299, 293 notes 323-324, 296 note 345.

Entrainment 135-136, 146.

Eternal object 83, 86, 213, 216-217, 233 261 note 134, 263 note 140, 295 note 343, 296 note 234.

Ethics 24, 76, 90-91, 94, 98, 174, 224, 225, 259 note 114, 265 note 149, 276 note 215.
and morality 90, 265 note 150, 299 note 368.
and relation 74, 84, 97, 140, 200, 230, 237-238.
see also politics

Evans, Aden 163-164, 174, 279 note 238, 282 note 262.

Event 16-18, 23, 37, 43-46, 49-50, 63-65, 67-71, 76, 79-86, 89, 95, 99, 106-109, 117, 129, 133, 137-138, 145, 146-148, 151, 154, 164, 174, 189-191, 195-196, 200, 212, 217, 224-225, 228, 230, 239, 250 note 64, 255 note 90, 260 note 120, 267 note 164, 276 note 216, 284 note286.

Evolution 50, 101, 141, 174, 186, 188, 190, 203, 222, 246 note 33, 257 note103, 284 note 285, 289 note 308, 292 note 316.
see also neo-Darwinism

Excess 37, 71, 100, 147, 156, 157, 160, 165, 168-170, 186, 204, 212, 217, 274 note 203, 284 note 278, 291 note 312.

Extensive 22, 23, 79-80, 129, 195, 204, 213-215, 233 263 note 140, 282 note 263.
see also intensive

334 Index

Far from equilibrium 208, 220, 285 note 291, 298 note 361.

Faraday's law 93, 265 note 152, 266 note 156.
see also induction

Feeling 21-22, 66, 69, 75-97, 118-119, 136, 142, 146-147, 174, 175, 193, 195, 210-211, 217, 228, 233-234, 239, 242 note 9, 255 note 91, 256 note 93, 260 note 119, 260 note 123, 263 note 139, 265 note 146, 269 note 178, 276 note 220, 284 note 279.
see also conceptual feeling, complex feeling, negative feeling, prehension, physical feeling

Field, the 21, 25, 45, 48, 49, 61, 72-73, 76, 79, 84, 91, 92-96, 114, 120, 132-133, 136, 141, 146, 147-149, 153-154, 165, 173, 176, 182, 189, 191-192, 212, 217, 219, 222-223, 230, 234, 238-239, 260 note 121, 270 note 187, 274 note 203, 282 note 267, 297 note 350.

Fitness criteria 69, 246 note 33, 289 note 308.

Flâneur 115, 120, 269 note 175.

Fold 49, 112, 147, 174, 187-191, 195, 224, 250 note 64, 264 note 142, 285 note 291, 287 note 293.

Force 12, 18-23, 48, 50, 62-65, 68, 69, 71-72, 84-87, 96, 98, 100, 108, 111, 140, 141-143, 145-147, 148, 151-152, 156, 157-158, 160-166, 170-172, 181-183, 186, 188, 189-192, 211, 218-220, 228, 250 note 60, 251 note 64, 262 note 135, 293 note 323, 296 note 348, 297 note 351.

Foucault, Michel 37, 271 note 191.

Fuller, Matthew 187, 179, 199, 283 note 269, 294 note 329.

Gathering ecology 21, 143, 190, 192, 219, 226-231, 234, 238-239, 299 note 368

Genesis 189, 191, 199, 219-220, 277 note 228.

Generative software 203-210, 289 note 308, 293 note 322.

Gibson, James J 114, 118-119, 122-123, 132, 266 note 160, 269 notes 177-178, 269 note 181, 271 note 191, 272 note 194, 273 note 197, 274 note 202.

Goodman, Steve 156, 161, 166-167, 209, 280 not 253, 292 note 320.

Grau, Oliver 177, 181, 247 note 42.

Grosz, Elizabeth 19, 189, 198, 217, 243 note 16, 265 note149, 278 note 235, 284 note 281, 284 note 284.

Guattari, Felix 15, 18, 26-27, 35, 58, 78, 123, 151, 236, 239-240, 243 note 13, 253 note 77.

and machinic 58, 60-63,
and the three ecologies 232, 235, 274 note 205.

Harney and Moten 24, 29.

Hapticality 122, 124, 272 note 192.

Hinterding, Joyce 91-97.

Hylomorphism 18, 179, 260 note 120, 266 note 159.

Interface 15, 34, 35, 177-183, 186-188, 193, 194-195, 248 note 45, 278 note 234, 283 note 269.

Incompossible 67, 187-191, 284 note 286, 292 note 319.

Individuation 19, 45, 62, 73, 78, 89, 99, 100, 107, 115, 117, 141-143, 146-148, 149-152, 164, 174, 181-183, 190-191, 211, 219, 230, 249 note 53, 257 note 101, 258 note 113, 276 note 215, 277 note 228, 285 note 289.
see also collective individuation

Ingold, Tim 102, 113-115, 126, 127, 148, 259 note 115, 264 note 142, 268 note 169, 268 note 171, 269 note 174.
and affordance 269 note 181.
and sound 162-163.

Induction 92-97, 242 note 12, 265 note 153.
see also Faraday's law

Intensity 16, 44, 67, 69, 75-76, 80, 85-86, 93-94, 102, 108, 116-117, 127, 136, 143, 188-189, 191, 208, 220, 223, 224, 260 note 124, 260 note 127, 263 note139, 283 note 275.

Intensive 21-23, 59, 62, 70-71, 80-82, 93, 107, 112, 116, 152, 157, 164, 173, 196, 208, 218-220, 224, 233, 258 note 111, 262 note 135, 277 note 227.
see also extensive

Interactivity 20-21, 27, 30-32, 44, 53-54, 55, 56-58, 62, 96, 103, 129-130, 139, 151, 209, 232-233, 244 note 20, 244, 245 notes 25 & 26, 253 note 71.
and control 14, 33-37, 40-41, 49, 178-179, 209, note 22, 248 note 46.
and didacticism 37, 39-40, 139.
and ethics 73-74, 98-99, 230-231, 235.
and generative 63-65, 68, 69, 109, 193.
and instrumentality 33-34, 38.

336 Index

and politics 35, 230-231, 236-240.

Interface, interfacing 34-35, 177-196, 227, 229, 278 note 45, 278 note 234, 283 note 269, 284 note 278, 285 note 293, 286 note 296.

James, William 18, 77, 186.
see also radical empiricism

Jones, Judith 77, 80-84, 90-91, 99, 136, 146, 233, 260 note 128, 261 note 129, 261 note 131, 263 note 138, 263 note140, 299 note 369.

LaMarre, Thomas 181-182, 191-193, 256 note 95, 283 note 276, 285 note 292, 286 note 294.

Landing sites 112, 117-122, 128, 132, 150, 270 note 185, 270 note 187, 271 note 189, 271 note 190, 280 note 254.

Leber, Sonia, and David Chesworth 162, 166-167, 279 note 244.

Linearity 36, 37-40, 57, 67, 72, 101, 105, 152, 186, 199-200, 203, 208, 215-216, 220, 222, 230, 246 note 33, 286 note 293, 297 note 353.

Limit 26, 117, 120, 174, 176, 213, 221, 222-223, 257 note 104, 258 note 108, 284 note 286, 296 note 348, 298 note 364.

Lines of flight 43, 67, 114, 148, 151, 298 note 366.

Lingis, Aphonso 89, 110, 155, 165, 265 note 148, 269 note 180.

Listening 81, 91, 96, 156, 159, 170, 176, 227, 228.

Lozano-Hemmer, Rafael 32, 38, 46, 179-180, 184, 198-199, 246 note 35, 247 note 43, 250 note 60, 285 note 292, 286 note 294.

Machine, machinic 48, 58, 60-65, 71-73, 98-99, 101, 116, 118, 124, 142, 162, 164-165, 167-170, 174, 181, 182-183, 186, 188, 191-193, 199-200, 215, 220, 224, 227, 234, 254 notes 80-83, 254 note 87, 258 note 111, 270 note 182, 291 note 316.

MacKenzie, Adrian 157, 174-175, 182, 188, 278 note 234, 290 note 309, 294 note 335.

Manning, Erin 24, 26-29, 31, 33, 40, 45-46, 49, 74, 90, 111, 116-120, 122-123, 133-134, 135-136, 145-146, 153-154, 171, 193, 223-224, 237-239, 249 note 51, 249 note 53, 250 note 63, 256 note 94, 270 note 182, 270 note 184, 270 note 188, 272 note 193, 273 note 199, 274 note 203, 274 note 205, 276 note 218, 276 note 220, 276 note 223, 285 note 287, 294 note 337.
see also minor gesture

Manovich, Lev 36, 244 note 22.

Maturana, Humberto R 60, 254 note 79, 257 note 103, 298 note 361.

Massumi, Brian 14, 16-19, 26-27, 31, 33, 36-37, 44-46, 57-58, 65, 71-72, 90-91, 103, 106, 118, 12-130, 139, 141, 150-151, 156, 160, 177-179, 190-191, 217, 223, 225, 239, 241 note 3, 242 note 7, 243 note 14, 246 note 30, 248 note 46, 257 note 106, 267 note 164, 272 note 192, 272 note 193, 276 note 219, 285 note 293.

Meshwork 105, 114, 126, 208, 257 note 105, 269 note 174.

Mereotopology 209.

Metamodelling 26-29, 109, 192, 225, 239, 243 notes 13, 14 & 15.

Metastability 188, 218, 285 note 292.

Microsound 163, 176.

Micro-perception 156-176, 227, 267 note 167, 281 note 258, 282 note 263, 282 note 267.

Minor, the 55, 56-57, 58, 72-73, 98-99, 110-113, 121-122, 127, 129-130, 140, 193, 199, 227, 233, 235, 240, 253 notes 72-74, 253 note 77, 273 note 200, 277 note 227.
see also molar, minor flight

Minor flight 117.

Minor gesture 152-154, 171-172, 175, 223, 229-230, 234, 235, 239, 277 note 228.

Miyazaki, Shintaro 215, 287 note 300, 295 note 339.

Molar 57-58, 64, 69, 74, 100, 147, 206, 253 note 76, 254 note 86.

Molecular 57-65, 69, 99, 108, 110, 113, 116, 122, 128, 170, 206, 208, 211-212, 227, 253 note 76, 253 note 77, 254 note 86, 254 note 87.

Monad 260 note 121.

Morris, Meaghan 253 note 73.

Movement 15, 25, 38, 56, 58-59, 62-67, 71, 94, 100, 101, 111-130, 131-134, 142-143, 152-153, 182, 188, 194, 196, 206, 226, 247 note 44, 248 note 45, 250 note 63, 253 note 73, 254 note 85, 269 note 177, 270 note 182, 271 note 188, 272 note 193.

Multiplicity 80, 147-150, 160, 162167, 172-174, 176, 213, 255 note 91, 282 note 263.

Munster, Anna 178, 182, 183, 241 note 5, 246 note 31, 284 note 282, 290 note 309.

Murphie, Andrew 39, 41, 55, 60-61, 75-76, 81, 98-99, 115-116, 157, 161, 175, 182, 187, 198, 241 note 5, 248 note 49, 260 note 128, 276 note 216, 278 note 231, 282 note 264, 282 note 266, 298 note 366.

Negative feeling 80, 83, 89, 96, 99, 105, 202, 213, 213, 214, 224, 255 note 91, 260 note 119, 261 note 134, 264 note 141.

Neo-Darwinism 69, 88, 256 note 95, 264 note 144, 289 note 308.

Neoliberalism 14, 15-16, 42, 236, 239.

Nested 63, 65, 84, 95, 118, 216, 222.

Nexus 49, 79, 86, 89, 105, 142, 256 note 93.

Noise 22, 55, 100-103, 103, 106-107, 116-117, 156, 164-168, 172-174, 184-187, 204-205, 232-233, 282 note 262, 290 note 309.

Nomadic music 176.

Non-linear 40, 45, 67, 266 note 156.
    and algorithms 200, 216, 218, 220, 224.
    and relation 285 note 293, 297 note 353.
    see also linearity

Novelty 16, 25, 65-66, 77-79, 88, 90, 98, 102, 107, 143, 164, 204, 224, 232, 233-234, 237, 262 note 135, 263 note 138, 264 note 144, 276 note 215, 292 note 320, 295 note 340, 297 note 353.

Objects 18-20, 24, 32, 35, 44-46, 49, 72, 77, 82-84, 86, 93, 95, 102, 121-122, 127-128, 133, 141, 144-145, 147, 154, 158, 174, 179, 192, 193, 211-212, 215, 244 note 17, 259 note 115, 262 note 135, 263 note 140, 269 note 181, 276 note 222, 293 note 324.

Omega 212-213.

Ontogenesis 18, 24, 61, 151, 192, 223-224, 259 note 115, 277 note 228.

O'Sullivan, Simon 50, 56, 140, 151, 186, 193, 224.

Parisi, Luciana 26, 199-200, 204-207, 208-214, 216, 218, 258 note 111, 292 notes 318-320, 293 notes 321-323, 294 note 334.

Pask, Gordon 46-47, 258 note 111, 291 note 316.

Pasquinelli, Matteo 42, 246 note 30, 247 note 41, 248 notes 47-48, 266 note 162.

Parametric 207-210 220, 291 note 316.

Index 339

Pattern, patterning 21, 79-81, 83, 85-87, 89, 93, 94, 105, 136-137, 153, 167, 173, 213, 216-217, 260 note 126263 note 139, 263 note 140.

Penny, Simon 31, 34-35, 38-41, 47-48, 54, 224, 245 note 25, 247 note 42, 248 note 49, 250 note 60, 252 note 71, 291 note 312.

Perception 14, 39, 50, 120, 127, 132-133, 135-154, 156-157, 159, 165, 168, 172-175, 176.

Prehension 66, 78-80, 82-83, 85-96, 99, 105, 118, 135, 137, 141, 158, 169, 210-214, 217, 218, 223, 255 note 91, 256 note 93, 260 note 119, 262 note 135, 293 note 323, 293 note 326, 298 note 359.

Physical feeling 78, 81, 84, 106, 217.

Physics 163-164,
    and Newtonian physics 244 note 17.
    and non-linear physics 261 note 130, 266 notes 155 & 156, 296 note 347.
    and quantum physics 278 note 231.

Pickering, Andrew 209, 256 note 96, 261 note 130.

Politics 14, 24, 49, 90, 150-151, 230-231, 235-240, 276 note 222.
    see also ethics

Portanovo, Stamatia 207, 209, 212-213, 215, 287 note 301, 293 note 321, 296 note 345.

Posthuman 76, 135, 259 note 114.
    see also transhuman

Potential 12, 15-16, 18, 19, 20-22, 36, 39, 40, 45-46, 49-50, 56-61, 64-68, 72-74, 78-79, 81-82, 85-87, 89, 94-95, 100-109, 111-112, 116 -122, 127-129, 133, 136, 142-143, 145, 147-149, 153-154, 156, 157, 163, 172, 181-183, 188-189, 192, 195, 199, 206-207, 212-213, 215-218, 219-221, 234, 238-239, 242 note 11, 254 note 87, 257 note 101, 257 note 103, 265note 149, 267 note 164, 270 note 187, 275 note 212, 276 note 223, 285 note 288, 285 note 293, 294 note 338, 295 note 344, 297 notes 353 & 354.

Precarity 15, 136-238, 248 note 48.

Presentational immediacy 135-139, 143, 150, 274 note 207, 275 note 208, 275 note 211, 275 note 213, 276 note 214.
    see also casual efficacy

Prigogine, Ilya 222, 241 note 2, 266 note 156.

Problematisation 22, 29, 55, 57, 67, 80, 94, 101, 102, 112, 130, 134, 143, 175-176, 182, 212, 220, 233.

Productivity 34-37, 39, 50, 57, 71, 115, 199, 234, 246 note 35.

Proposition 25, 49, 66-69, 101, 103-105, 107-109, 140, 162-163, 237, 257 note 104, 267 note 168, 282 267.
    and spatial propositions 118, 193, 207, 270 note 188.

Proprioception 122-123.

Radical empiricism 18-19, 77, 205, 223, 241 note 2, 241 note 3.

Rancière, Jacques 231, 275 note 213, 276 note 222, 299 note 368.

Refrain 216.
    and algorithm 215-218, 295 note 339.

Relation 11-12, 18-19, 22, 59-62, 70, 71-73, 75-83, 94, 99-106, 113-114, 137, 148, 157, 164, 182, 204, 211, 249 note 53, 250 note 63, 257 note 103, 258 note 113, 259 note 115, 260 note 127, 278 note 233, 293 note 323.
    and art 18, 20, 43-49, 66-67, 73-74, 108, 126-127, 139, 146, 167, 173-174, 186-187, 207.
    and codification 14, 23, 36-43, 55-56, 178, 179, 192.
    and interactivity 30-31, 35, 49-54, 56-58, 65, 205-206, 235, 237, 241 note 6, 246 note 37, 249 note 54.
    and politics, ethics 15, 23-24, 33, 90, 98, 174, 200, 224-225, 230-231, 237-240.
    see also relational aesthetics

Relational aesthetics 16, 42, 48, 286 note 294.

Research-creation 24, 28-29.

Resonance 19, 89, 92, 94, 95-97, 136, 140, 156, 157, 158-159, 163-166, 173, 175, 180, 182, 188, 189, 133, 258 note 113, 265 note 146, 276 note 217, 284 note 281.

Rhythm 50, 63, 104, 106, 127, 155, 157, 163-164, 166-167, 192, 20, 215-218, 221, 225, 280 note 248, 281 note 257, 294 note 337, 295 note 339.

Roads, Curtis 161, 163-164, 166, 280 note 248.

Satisfaction 66-69, 78-79, 95, 83-84, 108, 117, 159, 213, 255 note 90, 255 note 91, 260 note 118, 260 note 128.

Second-order cybernetics 205-207, 208, 293 note 321.

Self-organisation 21, 60, 69-74, 180, 219, 237.
    see also autopoiesis

Index   341

Sensation 50, 115, 122, 123, 124, 131-133, 138-139, 144, 151-152, 153, 156, 165, 168, 174, 228, 267 note 165, 272 note 194, 275 note 213, 281 note 259.

Sensor 20, 29, 62-63, 66-67, 70-71, 73, 104-106, 129, 152-153, 193-196, 221, 227, 254 note 87, 255 note 89, 291 note 316.

Shaviro, Steven 211, 237, 254 note 84, 259 note 115, 262 note 135, 264 note 143, 293 notes 325-326.

Signaletic material 204, 284 note 278, 291 note 311.

Simondon, Gilbert 19, 64, 72-73, 98, 149, 158, 178, 182, 192, 224, 230-231, 249 note53, 258 note 108 ,266 note 159, 285 note 288, 286 note 293, 299 note 367.

    and individuation 45, 174, 189-190, 195, 258 note 113, 277 note 228, 285 note 289, 297 note 354.

    and resonance 158-159, 188, 284 note 285.

    and transduction 22-23, 26, 62, 141, 148, 174-175, 182-183, 229, 242 note 12, 278 note 234.

    and technical objects 23, 193.

Singularity 15, 25, 27, 36, 49, 79, 96, 111, 115, 187, 215, 249 note 53, 253 note 77, 292 note 319.

Skin-as-ear 165, 280 note 253.

Societies 68, 86, 256 note 93, 261 note 133, 263 note 139, 263 note 140, 267 note 167, 267 note 168.

Sound 62-64, 70-71, 92, 95, 104-107, 127, 138, 155-176, 195, 227, 238, 267 note 166, 267 note 168, 278 note 232, 280 note 253, 280 note 254, 282 262, 282 note 263, 282 note 265.

State space 218-219.

Stern, Nathaniel 31, 33, 36, 48, 123, 126193, 244 note 20, 246 note 34, 246 note 36.

Stengers, Isabelle 35, 94, 134, 137, 179, 187, 212, 222, 235, 260 note 121, 266 note 156, 299 note 370.

    see also Prigogine, Ilya

Style 63, 89, 95, 121, 193, 195-196, 254 note 85, 271 note 189.

Study 24, 29.

Subject 15-16, 18-19, 40-41, 43, 44-45, 48, 54, 59, 60, 79, 81, 90, 110-111, 136, 140-141, 147-148, 150, 151-152, 157, 178, 194, 211, 236-237, 240, 244 note 21, 246 note 30, 248 note 46, 248 note 49, 276 note 222.

Symbiosis 155-156.

342 Index

Symbolic reference 136, 143.

System 19, 22, 23, 36, 37, 40-41, 56-58, 64, 67, 69-74, 92-93, 99-101, 102, 106-108, 122, 123, 132, 134, 141, 147-149, 167, 181, 188, 205-209, 218-220, 222-225, 229, 254 note 86, 257 note 105, 258 note 108, 285 note 291, 292 note 319296 note 347, 296 notes 348 & 349, 297 note 353.

System-level 191-192, 207-208, 234-235, 257 note 102, 258 note 113.

Tactic 24-26, 56-57, 109, 113-114, 127, 134, 149-150, 164, 180, 204, 224-225, 253 note 72, 253 note 74, 284 note 286, 291 note 313.

Technical object 60-61, 112, 178, 183, 230, 235, 283 note 276, 284 note 284.

Technology 34, 46, 55, 61, 129-130, 187, 193, 198-199, 223, 247 note 41, 250 note 62, 284 note 282, 292 note 320.
  Of control 35, 53, 184, 187, 209, 247 note 43, 247 note 44, 271 note 191, 298 note 366.
  and fetishisation 40, 193, 241 note 5.

Topology 133, 149, 188, 192, 208-209, 212, 218, 225, 260 note 126, 278 note 234, 282 note 265, 292 note 319.

Transduction 22, 62-65, 84, 140-143, 145-146, 149, 157-159, 166, 174-175, 181-183, 186, 191, 195, 204, 206, 229, 233, 234, 242 note 12, 258 note 111, 278 note 233, 278 note 234, 290 note 309.

Transhuman 91, 259 note 114.
  see also post-human

Trans-individual 158, 174, 183, 189, 195, 238, 284 note 284.

Unsound 161-164, 169-170.

Varela, Francesco J. 49-50, 60, 69-70, 205, 250 note 64, 257 note 103, 267 note 165, 270 note 183, 298 note 361.
  see also autopoiesis, drift

Vibration 15, 66, 70, 73, 95, 104-105, 111, 146, 155-156, 159-176, 187, 191, 227-228, 280 note 249, 280 note 253, 280 note 255, 282 note 265.

Vitality 96, 141, 174, 190.

Walking 11-12, 110-113, 254 note 85, 268 note 169, 269 note 175, 270 note 182, 272 note 192.
  and the city 113-130, 268 notes 171 & 172, 271 note 191, 272 note 196.

Whitehead, Alfred North 16, 18-20, 44-45, 66, 77-86, 90, 94-95, 99-100, 118, 135-139, 143, 158-159, 191, 195, 210-211, 215, 216-217, 233, 241 note 4, 246 note 37, 249 note 52, 254 note 84, 255 note 91, 256 note 93, 260 note 124, 260 note 125, 262 note 135, 263 notes 137-139, 266 note 156, 271 note 190, 275 note 211, 275 note 213, 282 note 267, 283 note 271, 287 note 299.

    and ontology 21, 75, 77, 80, 199, 211, 242 note 7, 259 note 116, 275 note 210.

    see also concrescence, datum, entity, entrainment, event, feeling, prehension, proposition, satisfaction, societies, symbolic reference

Wilden, Anthony 204, 281 note 259 291 note 310, 291 note 312, 294 note 336.

Will to power 154, 170, 196, 228, 234, 297 note 351.

Worlding 117-123, 134, 165, 276 note 220.

www.ingramcontent.com/pod-product-compliance
Lightning Source LLC
Chambersburg PA
CBHW031607210526
45464CB00004B/1469